Challenging the Professionalization of Adult Education

Challenging the Professionalization of Adult Education

John Ohliger and Contradictions in Modern Practice

André P. Grace
Tonette S. Rocco
and Associates

Foreword by Michael R. Welton

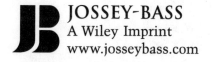

JOSSEY-BASS
A Wiley Imprint
www.josseybass.com

Published by Jossey-Bass
A Wiley Imprint
989 Market Street, San Francisco, CA 94103-1741—www.josseybass.com

The lines from "you shall above all things be glad and young," © Copyright 1938, 1966, 1991 by the Trustees for the E. E. Cummings Trust, from *Complete Poems: 1904-1962* by E. E. Cummings, edited by George J. Firmage. Used by permission of Liveright Publishing Corporation.

"Adult Education: 1984" by John Ohliger originally appeared in 1971 in *Adult Leadership*, a publication of the Learning Resources Network (LERN), and is reprinted here with permission from LERN. For further information, see www.lern.org or info@lern.org.

"September 1, 1939," copyright 1940 & renewed 1968 by W.H. Auden from *Collected Poems* by W.H. Auden. Used by permission of Random House, Inc.

Readers should be aware that Internet Web sites offered as citations and/or sources for further information may have changed or disappeared between the time this was written and when it is read.

Jossey-Bass books and products are available through most bookstores. To contact Jossey-Bass directly call our Customer Care Department within the U.S. at 800-956-7739, outside the U.S. at 317-572-3986, or fax 317-572-4002.

Jossey-Bass also publishes its books in a variety of electronic formats. Some content that appears in print may not be available in electronic books.

Library of Congress Cataloging-in-Publication Data
Grace, André P.
  Challenging the professionalization of adult education : John Ohliger and contradictions in modern practice / André P. Grace, Tonette S. Rocco, and associates ; foreword by Michael R. Welton.—1st ed.
     p. cm.
  Includes bibliographical references and index.
  ISBN 978-0-7879-7827-3 (cloth)
  1. Adult education—United States. 2. Ohliger, John—Influence. I. Rocco, Tonette S. II. Title.
  LC5251.G67 2009
  374.973—dc22

                                                                          2009008876

Printed in the United States of America
FIRST EDITION
HB Printing   10 9 8 7 6 5 4 3 2 1

The Jossey-Bass
Higher and Adult Education Series

Contents

Part Four: Narrations on the Life of a Radical Social Educator: Legacies and Critiques

For John Funnell Ohliger, our pilgrim of the obvious.
—André P. Grace and Tonette S. Rocco

For my first and most important teachers:
my mother, Joan Marie Walsh-Grace;
my aunt, Mary Susan Grace-Russell; and my grandmothers,
Mary Ellen Hogan-Grace and Margaret Ellen Power-Walsh.
I am pieces of each of you.
—André P. Grace

For my daughter, Sunny Lynne Munn, a member of a new
generation of scholars who will challenge the parameters of adult
education and social policy, continuing John Ohliger's legacy.
—Tonette S. Rocco

Foreword

I cleave to no system.
    —Mikhail Bakunin

André P. Grace and Tonette S. Rocco have assembled a variety of texts remembering, honoring, and critically examining the life and work of John Ohliger. The field of adult education ought to remember those who have labored so hard and so long in its gardens. We ought to make certain that we call them into being and reflect on their contributions to our field of study and practice when we engage in our time's search for justice and minimal decency for all.

When remembering John Ohliger, academics and graduate students, in particular, discover that he was not a systematic thinker in any conventional sense. In this light, his body of work should certainly provide us pause to reflect on how we might challenge designs and directions in adult education in contemporary times. Like many of the contributors to this book, I too have my own box full of Ohliger's bibliographies and assorted news and notes. He left the academy rather early on and lived the life of an outsider. He paid for this choice, I think, and wondered often about his impact on the world. But perhaps Ohliger's main texts were inscribed in his practice of connecting people and ideas with each other. He lived out, perhaps better than anyone, the maxim of *friends educating friends*.

Ohliger's traveling companions were other outsiders and icono-
clasts. He adored Ivan Illich, that intellectual gadfly who scorned
the establishment and whose idea of deschooling society captured
the imagination of those who wanted to choose their own learning
pathways. I bet Ohliger had tracked the origins of this idea to some
Russian revolutionary thinker in the early twentieth century. Certainly Ohliger is well known as a proponent of deschooling society
and a relentless foe of mandatory continuing education for adults.
From his doctoral dissertation on listening groups to his last breath,
he focused our attention on the resources of civil society—media,
books, radio, listening groups, film, and personal correspondence—
available to those wanting to strengthen public discourse and grassroots ownership of social matters. Ohliger's formidable energies as
an agitator who questioned, challenged, and worked for social
change in the world often remained invisible. Still, there is one important lesson that those who wish to invoke and provoke social
change can learn from Ohliger. Without the kind of vital, config-
ured networks of ideas and resources that he created, nothing gets
changed in any realm, be it politics, education, or culture. John believed deeply that people have the capacity, ability, and energy to
find and make use of these resources.

John L. Elias and Sharan B. Merriam labeled John Ohliger an
anarchist in *Philosophical Foundations of Adult Education*, their well-
known book published in 1980. Indeed John could be considered a
radical who loved making connections. I offer this one so that he
can laugh at us from wherever he may now be located. In 1871, on
the eve of the Paris Commune, the Russian anarchist Mikhail
Bakunin wrote, "No theory, no ready-made system will save the
world. I cleave to no system, I am a true seeker" (cited in Noble,
2005, p. 150). John would likely agree with Bakunin, finding him
to be a kindred spirit. No doubt, John would also have agreed with
Bakunin that human beings have "two precious faculties—the
power to think and the desire to rebel" (p. 150). The masses could
"take into their own hands the direction of their destinies" (p. 150).

Ohliger's was a life-affirming spirit, and he would have found another fellow philosophical traveler in Friedrich Wilhelm Nietzsche, who wrote in *The Twilight of the Idols*, "I mistrust all systematizers and I avoid them" (cited in Noble, 2005, p. 157).

John believed so deeply that people have the power to think that he railed against those who tried to tell us what to think, who would indoctrinate us in some ideology or other. John also believed, with good humor, that we also have the capacity to rebel and raise some hell before we lay down our bibliographies. John, we salute you!

March 2009   Michael R. Welton
Professor emeritus, Mount Saint Vincent University
Adjunct professor, Centre for Policy Studies in
Higher Education, University of British Columbia

References

Elias, J. L., & Merriam, S. B. (1980). *Philosophical foundations of adult education*. Huntington, NY: Krieger.

Noble, D. F. (2005). *Beyond the promised land: The movement and the myth*. Toronto: Between the Lines.

Preface

Since the early 1990s, the Organization for Economic Cooperation and Development (OECD) has spearheaded educational policy initiatives focused on lifelong and life-wide learning. These initiatives emphasize a new instrumentality and vocationalism, both tied to advancing the knowledge and global economies that have emerged in recent decades under neoliberalism. In this milieu, the space and place of adult education appear even more tenuous. Indeed, in a global learning culture that has become preoccupied with the OECD's buzz phrase *lifelong learning for all* (Field, 2006), adult education faces the challenge of clarifying and fortifying its parameters at a time when the enterprise seeks new direction amid the educational new wave of interest in lifelong learning.

In attending sessions and following trends at postmillennial national and international conferences on adult education and lifelong learning in Australia, Canada, the United Kingdom, and the United States, we have found academic colleagues and field practitioners more intensively scrutinizing adult education as a field of study and practice. In deliberations and exchanges at these conferences, they have challenged adult education's parameters and critically questioned its possibilities. For example, at the 2001 Standing Conference on University Teaching and Research in the Education of Adults, which was held at the University of East London in the United Kingdom, U.S. academic adult educators Arthur Wilson and

Ron Cervero raised a question that was much deliberated at that conference: "If lifelong learning is emerging as both an alternative route and destination for what used to be thought of as adult education, then what does the landscape through which we now journey look like and how shall we find our way?" (p. 435).

As these and other adult educators continue to deliberate this question across the domains of theory, research, policy, and practice, other critical questions need to be raised as we scrutinize the politics and practices of contemporary lifelong learning and consider how to revitalize and reconstitute adult education as a democratic and just field of study and practice. For example, in considering the value of adult education in institutional and community settings in contemporary times, and its import as a medium for lifelong learning, we ought to ask: In a learning-and-work world driven by economic and instrumental concerns, how might adult educators address social and cultural concerns to provide more holistic and inclusive education for adults? A turn to the scholarship and grassroots educational, social, and cultural work of John Ohliger is useful as we attempt to answer this question.

As a radical liberal who valued social democracy, John was ignored and marginalized by many of his academic peers. Indeed many of his contemporaries found his radical liberal approach to adult education to be problematic and peripheral to what professionalization of modern practice required. It was perhaps his positionality as an outsider in an emerging professional field that drove his work and his desire to create opportunities for learners to make social democracy more spacious and encompassing. With governments and employers demanding that adult learners engage in forms of continuing education to replenish an evolving information-and-skills base, Ohliger's life scholarship and work can help us to interrogate the provision of such learning. By investigating how Ohliger theorized and engaged in ethical, informal, and community-based learning and practice, we can gain insights to help us attend to the just needs of today's adult learners who may be feeling frustrated, inadequate, and never in synch with contemporary forms of learning and work. In a world marked by a swirling mixture of crisis and progress, Ohliger's social philosophy, pedagogy, and practice provide insights to help us think critically about how educators and learners as citizens and workers can mediate the intersection of instrumental, social, and cultural concerns. As the contributors to this book collectively demonstrate, examination of Ohliger's social knowledge, insights, and challenges to the field continues to have meaning and value.

Since ignoring John Ohliger has perhaps been an impediment to the social and cultural development of modern practice, this book aims to make his educational, social, and cultural work better known in adult education as a field of study and practice. Having worked as an adult educator, social activist, and cultural worker for more than five decades, Ohliger has much to offer academic educators, policymakers, practitioners, and graduate students interested in engaging in social learning to strengthen social democracy. The book is not structured as a biography, although it naturally incorporates many elements of Ohliger's life history that help to situate him as a radical social educator. Rather, it is predominantly structured as a wide-ranging, multiperspective analysis that uses Ohliger's theorizing and practice as lenses to gauge issues, concerns, and trends in contemporary adult education and lifelong learning. Thus, this book includes foci on critical perspectives, social education, lifelong learning, community building, democratic and ethical practices, and other parameters of practice. It also engages the social, cultural, and political contexts of education; alternative educational practices; mediation of interests in practice contexts; and social theories that have had an impact on the modern practice of adult education.

This book can be used as a text in university and college courses that are an introduction to adult education as a field of study and practice, or that are foundational in nature, such as the history or sociology of North American adult education. It can also be used as a text in community-based education courses and in courses focused on theorizing and learning in social movements. It would be a useful text to provide sociohistorical and political contexts in a field trends-and-issues course. This book contributes to the knowledge base in adult education by using Ohliger's eclectic writings and work in a broad-based analysis of themes and topics pervasive in the social philosophy, pedagogy, and the ethical and democratic practice of adult education. It provides new perspectives and understanding to those with interests in instrumental, social, and cultural forms of lifelong learning.

The chapters in this eclectic collection that follow the selected contributions of Ohliger reflect an array of writing styles from the academic to the popular. In this regard, the book parallels the eclecticism of John's own writing as an educator, social activist, and cultural worker who challenged his peers as he problematized professionalization and reflected critically on contradictions in the modern practice of adult education. Indeed John's work is a sweeping collage of social pedagogy and commentaries that take readers in many directions that emanate from a single focus or goal: to assist adult educators to become more socially conscious facilitators who remember the historical emphases on voluntary learning and learning for citizenship in North American adult education. Making an effort to live this out in our theorizing and everyday practice is perhaps John's great challenge in his legacy to us.

March 2009   André P. Grace
                McCalla Professor, Department of
                Educational Policy Studies,
                University of Alberta, Edmonton, Canada

                Tonette S. Rocco
                Associate Professor, Department of
                Educational Leadership and Policy Studies,
                Florida International University, Miami, Florida

References

Field, J. (2006). *Lifelong learning and the new educational order* (2nd rev. ed.). Stoke on Trent, UK: Trentham Books.

Wilson, A. L., & Cervero, R. M. (2001). Walkabout: On the nature of practice in a lifelong learning world. In L. West, N. Miller, D. O'Reilly, & R. Allen (Eds.), *Proceedings of the 31st Annual Conference of SCUTREA: The Standing Conference on University Teaching and Research in the Education of Adults, University of East London* (pp. 435–438). Nottingham, UK: University of Nottingham.

Acknowledgments

L ike John Ohliger, we know the value of networking with colleagues as a way to both "loosen," as John would say, and deepen
our thinking about adult education as social education. We thank
the contributors to this book and the reviewers who offered advice
and feedback. It was in these collective contributions that we
gained deeper insights into John the man and the social educator.
We also thank David Brightman for his guidance in this project,
which was driven by a passion to have contemporary adult educators in our field of study and practice know John better.

Including key pieces from John's eclectic body of work was important in this process. In this regard, we thank John's wife, Chris,
for permission to reproduce "You Shall Know the Truth and the
Truth Shall Make You Laugh" and "Is Lifelong Adult Education a
Guarantee of Permanent Inadequacy?" (previously published in
1974 in *Convergence*, 7(2)). We thank Tom Nesbit, editor, and the
Canadian Journal for the Study of Adult Education for permission to
use John's editorial and perspective piece, "A Cautious Welcome
to the New Millennium." As well, we thank William A. Draves,
president of Learning Resources Network, for permission to reprint
"Adult Education: 1984." A license was obtained from Sage to
reprint "The Social Uses of Theorizing in Adult Education."

The Authors

Stephen Brookfield began his teaching career in 1970. Since then he has worked in England, Canada, Australia, and the United States, teaching in a variety of adult educational, community educational, and college settings. He has written and edited twelve books on adult learning, teaching, leadership, and critical thinking, four of which have won the World Award for Literature in Adult Education (in 1986, 1989, 1996, and 2005). His work has been translated into German, Finnish, Korean, and Chinese. He has been awarded two honorary Doctor of Letters degrees from the University System of New Hampshire (1991) and Concordia University, St. Paul (2003), for his contributions to understanding adult learning and shaping adult education. In 2001 he received the Leadership Award from the Association for Continuing Higher Education, and during 2002 he was visiting professor of education at Harvard University. He is currently Distinguished University Professor of the University of St. Thomas in Minneapolis-St. Paul where, in 2008, he won the university's Diversity in Teaching and Research Award and the John Ireland Teaching and Scholarship Award. In 2008 he was also awarded the Morris T. Keeton Award from the Council on Adult and Experiential Learning.

Michael Collins is professor emeritus in adult and continuing education at the University of Saskatchewan. He has extensive experience as an adult educator and schoolteacher in Canada, England, and the United States. His major publications, spanning his academic career, include *Competence in Adult Education: A New Perspective* (University Press of America, 1987), which outlined a relevant alternative approach to competency-based education; *Adult Education as Vocation: A Critical Role for the Adult Educator* (Routledge, 1991, 1995); and *Critical Crosscurrents in Education* (Krieger, 1998). His critical pedagogy is theoretically informed by the work of Jürgen Habermas and Paulo Freire, as well as by the wider Marxian legacy. Off-campus, Collins has engaged in community-based activism and adult education in provincial and federal prisons. As an outspoken public critic of the corporate university and the marketization of higher education, he is a founding member and organizer of the People's Free University in Saskatoon. Collins is now involved in environmental issues at the local level with an interest in the transformative potential of activist engagement as a learning experience.

Phyllis M. Cunningham is professor emeritus in the Department of Counseling, Adult and Higher Education, Northern Illinois University (NIU), where she was professor in graduate studies in adult education. She earned her Ph.D. from the University of Chicago in 1973, and in 1994 she was NIU's Presidential Distinguished Teaching Professor. She has published widely in adult education and, like her kindred spirit and dear friend John Ohliger, was a visible and vocal critic of the professionalized modern practice of adult education in the United States. During her career, Cunningham's research and practice have focused on marginalized learner populations, community development, participatory research, and critical pedagogy. She was inducted into the International Adult and Continuing Education Hall of Fame in 1996. In honor of her tremendous contributions to adult education as a field of study and practice, the Adult Education Research Conference established the Phyllis M. Cunningham Annual Award for Research for Social Justice in 1996. This award recognizes academic efforts to intersect research and advocacy in adult education to benefit historically disenfranchised populations.

André P. Grace is McCalla Research Professor of Teacher Education and director of the Institute for Sexual Minority Studies and Services in the Faculty of Education, University of Alberta. He is past president of the Canadian Association for the Study of Adult Education and also a past chair of the steering committee for the U.S. Adult Education Research Conference. His work in educational policy studies focuses on comparative studies of policies, pedagogies, and practices shaping lifelong learning as critical action, especially in the contexts of member countries of the Organization for Economic Cooperation and Development. Within this research, Grace includes a major focus on sexual minorities and their issues and concerns regarding social inclusion, cohesion, and justice in education and culture. In a series of national research projects funded by the Social Sciences and Humanities Research Council of Canada, he has used qualitative methodology focused on explorations of the self, others, and culture to examine the positions and needs of sexual-minority students and teachers. He has also studied educational interest groups in political analyses of their impacts on sexual-minority inclusion and accommodation in education and culture. Grace keeps his research and service in dynamic equilibrium. He is cofounder of Camp fYrefly, Canada's largest sexual-minority youth leadership camp, and he sits on the sexual orientation and gender identity subcommittee of the Alberta Teachers' Association's Diversity, Equity, and Human Rights Committee.

Lee Karlovic has been an educational, cultural, and media worker in the United States, the Republic of Korea, and Costa Rica. During the writing of this chapter, Lee rediscovered the value of the power of community radio and is a volunteer at a local station. In her attempts to "get a life" after brain tumor surgery, Lee takes comfort from an "Ohligerism"—"I can't go on. I go on"—which she has posted along with a picture of Ohliger riding his bike in the snow. She most recently presented a workshop entitled "Eco-Theatre: Exploring Spaces Between," at the 2005 Pedagogy of the Theatre of the Oppressed Conference.

Tonette S. Rocco is associate professor and program leader of adult education and human resource development at Florida International University (FIU). Her recent publications include "Sexual Minority Issues in HRD: Raising Awareness" (a special journal issue with Julie Gedro and Martin Kormanik of *Advances in Developing Human Resources*, 2009); *Older Workers, New Directions: Employment and Development in an Ageing Labor Market* (an e-book with Jo Thijssen, 2006); and *Demystifying the Writing and Publishing Process: A Guide for Emerging Scholars* (with Tim Hatcher, Jossey-Bass, forthcoming). Rocco is coeditor of *New Horizons in Adult Education and Human Resource Development*, an electronic journal. She is a Houle Scholar, a 2008 Kauffman Entrepreneurship Professor, and a research fellow with the FIU Center for Urban Education and Innovation. Her research interests include continuing professional education; equity and privilege, specifically in terms of race/critical race theory, sexual minorities/LGBT, age, disability, and teaching for social justice; and employability/career development, entrepreneurship, and fostering student research and professional writing. While working on her Ph.D. from The Ohio State University, she began corresponding with John Ohliger, with whom she built a friendship as she explored his contributions to adult education.

Elizabeth J. Tisdell joined the faculty at Penn State—Harrisburg as associate professor of adult education in August 2002. She received her Ed.D. in adult education from the University of Georgia in 1992, an M.A. in religion from Fordham University in 1979, and a B.A. in mathematics from the University of Maine in 1977. Tisdell's research interests include spirituality and culture in adult development and adult learning, critical and feminist pedagogy, multicultural issues, and critical media literacy in teaching for diversity in adult education. Her scholarly work has appeared in numerous journals and edited books. Tisdell is the author of *Exploring Spirituality and Culture in Adult and Higher Education*, which is based on a research study of a diverse group of adult educators. She is the coeditor and contributing chapter author of two edited volumes that are part of the *New Directions for Adult and Continuing Education* series, one entitled *Team Teaching and Learning* (2000) and the other *Popular Culture, Entertainment Media, and Adult Education* (2007). Tisdell is also currently the coeditor of the journal *Adult Education Quarterly*.

Christina (Chris) Wagner met John Ohliger on April 1, 1977, when she reviewed a book for "The Madison Review of Books" on WORT, the local community radio show John helped to start. Though separated by many years in age, they soon realized they were soulmates. Chris's need to conform to conventional society and the fact that they were both stubborn delayed their marriage. However, John and Chris were wed on May 6, 1989. Although Chris often quips that she was "just a footnote" in John's very full life, she feels blessed for the wonderful years that they shared together. Wagner has been a public librarian for twenty years.

David Yamada is a professor of law and founding director of the New Workplace Institute at Suffolk University Law School in Boston, where he is an internationally recognized authority on the legal and policy implications of workplace bullying and abusive work environments. In addition, he has a long-standing interest in adult education and lifelong learning. He became friends with John Ohliger and Chris Wagner during the later years of John's life, and he served as an officer of Basic Choices and collaborated with John on several short projects. David's eclectic educational background includes degrees from Valparaiso University (B.A.), Empire State College (M.A.), and New York University School of Law (J.D.), as well as doctoral studies at the Western Institute for Social Research in Berkeley, California.

Jeff Zacharakis is an assistant professor in the Department of Educational Leadership and a faculty associate of the Institute for Civic Discourse and Democracy at Kansas State University. He has been an adult educator since the mid-1980s, working mostly with communities, local governments, and nonprofit organizations. His research areas include community, organizational, and leadership development and the history and theory of adult education. Zacharakis's friendship with Ohliger began in 1986. As with many of John's other friends, they communicated mostly through letters, e-mail, and phone calls, from which John freely quoted in his newsletters and other communications. Zacharakis considers John to be one of the most important historical figures in adult education, serving as the social conscience of the profession.

Part One

Introduction

John Funnell Ohliger

A Brief Biography of His Life and Vocations

André P. Grace and Tonette S. Rocco

John Ohliger was visible and vocal on the adult education land-scape for over fifty years. He was a radical liberal scholar, a social instigator, and a communicator extraordinaire, and his roles in-cluded union educator, a facilitator for the Great Books Foundation, proponent of media and community education, and academic adult educator. His active relationship with the field of study and prac-tice ended with his passing on January 25, 2004, but his influence remains.

Ohliger is best known for "battl[ing] self-serving professionalism and the mandatory education of adults" (Cunningham, 1991, p. 361). As William S. Griffith (1991) puts it in a backhanded compliment, "With his dedication to adult learning as a vehicle for improving the quality of life, Ohliger has served as the self-appointed con-science of the field, stimulating serious examinations of the com-monly accepted popular notions of the appropriate use of adult education" (p. 113). However, John was not haughty. Indeed, he was a humble soul who could connect with people in deep and meaningful ways and learn from his mistakes. While many of his contemporaries might have disagreed with this assessment of a man whom they usually saw as a feisty radical and field dissenter, there is much more to John than the excesses of his personality. In his heart, he was always a social democrat who valued liberal ideals as they related to learner freedom and the learner's capacity to be and develop as a person. His ambition was to have every adult learner belong as a citizen in caring communities that made social inclusion, cohesion, and justice the centerpieces of their development.

John was often an angry American. He called himself a radical liberal, a self-characterization that underscored his commitment to a social democracy where citizens as learners, workers, and community members could learn about civics, participation, ethics, and the political ideals of modernity: democracy, freedom, and social justice. John believed in the power of community and in education and activism as vehicles to advance social and cultural learning in formal and informal contexts. He placed value on media as sites to engender social conversations and on arts-based education using the power of poetry and song. He saw both media and the arts as dynamic vehicles for reflexive engagement that promoted dialogue.

Much of John's work from the 1970s onward focused on saving the best of embedded liberalism (associated with entrenching the welfare state and advancing the social; see the description in Harvey, 2005). In doing so, John challenged what is now entrenched as the ideology of neoliberalism that has found expression in the professionalization, individualization, instrumentalization, and institutionalization of adult education. In his quest to defy the systematization of adult education and revitalize social democracy, John was inspired by a lineage of social educators including Eduard Lindeman. Quoting Lindeman in a 1991 reflection on the history of the social philosophy of adult education, Ohliger suggested that these words from a speech that Lindeman gave to the New York City Adult Education Association "were sadly prophetic": "There is ultimate danger that the professional leadership in this movement might get itself in the same box as has the professional leadership in our conventional education" (p. 16). Here John singled out Malcolm Knowles for blame, noting that Knowles, during his tenure as executive director of the Adult Education Association, had sought to have adult education firmly positioned as "the fourth level of our national educational system" (p. 18). Indeed Ohliger (1975) had long seen Knowles as part of a large and successful professionalizing contingent in the field who had nevertheless naively overestimated the cultural importance of adult education amid political and economic determinants that had greater power to change culture and society. Judging their quest to professionalize adult education, Ohliger felt this contingent had contributed to controlling adult learners to fit into "a rigid, standardized, calcified, ossified, vocationalized world" where no links are made to "energy, environment, economic, population, and resource crises" (p. 39). Moreover, Ohliger (1975) believed these "professional" adult educators had incarcerated adult learners in "a [learning] society where instruction is the dominant overriding mode of learning for supposedly mature adults" (p. 38). Within this instrumentalizing milieu, Ohliger described adult learning as detached from its social history as "mutual learning, free discussion, and the raising of basic questions in educational contexts" (p. 38). Here he blamed academic adult educators for what he considered to be the social demise of the field of study and practice, stating that "too many people have become academics in adult education without any real commitment to it or any sense of responsibility to the development of the discipline" (p. 38). This left Ohliger (1975) questioning whether the notion of the learning society could be salvaged to advance equality and social justice for independent learners.

A Chronology of Ohliger's Life and His Half-Century in Adult Education

John Funnell Ohliger worked in adult education for over fifty years. He declared, "From the 1950s on I defined myself as an 'adult educator.' But that term has become encrusted with corporate sales junk about the wonders of training and engulfed with bureaucratic oppression forcing most adults to go back to school" (Ohliger, 1997, part 1, p. 4). Despite this assertion, and probably because of it, Ohliger, as a social educator, journalist, consultant, researcher, editor, writer, radio host, peace activist, and public speaker, made adult education more than his line of work. It was his heartfelt vocation, and the focal point for his commitment to and passion for radical social education and social justice that focused on the freedom of citizens as learners and workers. Ohliger's social philosophy and his radical approach to practice are variously described among more than two hundred manuscripts, from book reviews to extensive bibliographies that comprise his intellectual legacy. Of course, in his humility, Ohliger felt any sober treatment of his work in this book might give "the impression of intense, almost insane grimness" since "much of my so-called 'work' is flippant and almost all of it is superficial" (e-mail communication, March 9, 2003).

Still, such self-deprecation mixed with humility and a little humor cannot belie this fact: John Ohliger had a deep knowledge of the overall field of study and practice, which he criticized as much as he loved it. Whether colleagues were liberal or conservative, criticalist or instrumentalist, on the fringes of the field or in the mainstream, they could all feel the sting of his words when their ideas clashed. Ohliger's perception of radical social education situated adult education as proactive, voluntary, adventurous, freewheeling, and dedicated to making the lot of citizens better. Many people and many things bewildered Ohliger, not the least of which was the perplexing nature of adult education. In his Christmas 2003 *Basic Choices Newsletter*, Ohliger expressed his puzzlement: "I am still confused by the fact that, though there are more dollars and personnel devoted to adult education than all other portions of education combined, the field itself is still practically invisible" (excerpt from the newsletter, in e-mail communication, December 16, 2003).

In our early stages of researching and writing this book, John was still with us. After we shared the book proposal with him, John, being the bibliographer, journalist, and scribe that he was, commented:

> These are offhand comments and, if used, will need more complete or correct bibliographic references. First, it has just occurred to me that I'm more of a journalist than an

adult educator, or maybe a journalist on/in adult education. If a journalist writes "a first draft of history," then that's more where I am than a scholar. I've been writing journalism since high school, as well as in the army and elsewhere, and have put out a number of journalistic newsletters over the years.

I identify more with journalists in adult education (who, as I have, wrote in other fields as well) such as Sam Brightman, Ron Gross, and Bob Blakeley (an editorial writer who was VP of the Fund for Adult Education), C. Hartley Grattan (who wrote for *Atlantic Monthly* and other magazines, and author of the only history of adult education I like), and Lyman Bryson (more of a radio journalist). . . . Of course, journalists don't have a very good name these days (see *Sneer when you say journalist* by Michael D'Antonio in the *Los Angeles Times*, August 24, 2003), but perhaps citing some of the great ones from the past will help rehabilitate the label [e-mail communication, August 28, 2003].

Many of John's characteristics come through in this e-mail: his lifetime puzzlement over his space and place in the world, his fastidiousness as a journalist, his voracious appetite for reading, and his desire to acknowledge peers whom he admired. And, of course, there was his humility. In a later e-mail (August 29, 2003), he reflected, "I should have made it clear that I regard myself in the same category ('journalist') as the great and unheralded Sam Brightman . . . and others, but not the same class." John always second-guessed himself, and one could sense a pervasive insecurity about the man. Contributors to this book provide various reasons for this, not the least of which is the degradation he experienced at the hands of certain field colleagues after he left his position at Ohio State University.

What follows is a brief chronology of some highlights from John's life and career (Hiemstra & Goldstein, 1990; Nathans, 2004; Ohliger, n.d.). A more extensive chronology is found in Hiemstra and Goldstein's (1990) *John Ohliger: Personal Vita*, which is posted on a Web site that has been updated over time:

1926   Born in Cleveland, Ohio, to Louis and Aura (Funnell) Ohliger on November 11

1944   Graduated from Northern High School in Detroit, Michigan, where he grew up

1948   Completed his three-year stint as an information specialist, newspaper reporter, and writer in the U.S. Army in the former West Germany, where he had his first experience as an adult educator teaching radio Morse code to other soldiers

1951   Completed a bachelor of arts, majoring in social sciences and speech, from Wayne State University, which had taken less than three years due to special considerations given for prior learning to World War II veterans under the 1944 GI Bill

1956   Began his second adult educational venture: two years of work with the Extension Program, University of California, Los Angeles

1957   With a one-year leadership grant from the Ford Foundation's Fund for Adult Education, completed a master's in adult education from the University of California, Los Angeles

1960   Having completed advanced studies in adult education with Cyril O. Houle at the University of Chicago in the late 1950s, and following what he describes as an abortive attempt to start doctoral work with him, returned to California to work in alternative adult educational broadcasting

1966   Graduated with an educational doctorate from the University of California, Los Angeles, where he completed his dissertation, "The Listening Group in Adult Education"

1967 Completed a one-year stint in Canada as the director of continuing education at Selkirk College in Castlegar, British Columbia's first regional community college

1971 Received the Ivan D. Illich Dystopia Award, which he described as the greatest honor he had ever received, for his critical writing on lifelong schooling, notably his 1971 article, "Adult Education: 1984" (published in *Adult and Continuing Education Today* and included as Chapter Three in this book) ["My memoir mentions the party in Cuernavaca where the award was presented, where Ivan supplied a case of tequila. I still have one of the empty bottles and the powdered worm" (e-mail communication, August 28, 2003).]

1973 Having worked for several years as an assistant and then associate professor in the graduate adult education program, left Ohio State University, offering this reason: disenchantment with what he saw as the decline of social education and voluntary participation in academe and the commodification of adult education to bolster economic advancement

That same year moved to Madison, Wisconsin, and cofounded WORT-FM, an alternative, public access radio station

1976 Having consulted and freelanced as a visiting lecturer at several universities in Canada and the United States after leaving Ohio State University, founded Basic Choices in Madison, Wisconsin, as a center for exploring and clarifying social and political ideas and actions in radical education for adults

1993   Received a Certificate of Recognition from the
        Adult Education Graduate Program, Syracuse
        University, for outstanding contributions to the
        field, which Malcolm S. Knowles acknowledged
        by saying, "Just keep up the good work"

2002   Inducted into the International Adult and Con-
        tinuing Education Hall of Fame

2004   Died January 25 at age seventy-seven in Madison,
        Wisconsin

Another Pilgrim of the Obvious: Getting to Know John Ohliger

We end this brief biography with stories of how we came to know
John Ohliger. These stories help explain why we wanted to complete this edited book as a tribute to John and a testament to his influence as a radical social educator.

We both were drawn to John Ohliger's intellectual and cultural
work as graduate students, although we found him following different paths. Like Ivan Illich, who labeled himself a "pilgrim of the obvious" (Ohliger, 1997), we see John as another important pilgrim,
as a wayfarer exposing the conventional and the cliché in adult education. In the vignettes that follow, each of us describes how we
became intrigued with this man as a radical social educator and an
oppositional voice in our field of study and practice.

Tonette's Vignette: Joining the Club

William D. Dowling and John Ohliger both came to work in the
adult education program at Ohio State University in 1967. They
were colleagues until John resigned in 1973. Dowling retired in
1992, but returned frequently to visit. As a new graduate student in
the adult education program in 1992, I found Dowling's lunchtime
stories about John Ohliger fascinating and funny. However, I would

learn that these stories often misrepresented John and his intentions. For example, as a required reading, I read Phyllis Cunningham's (1992) chapter on ethics in adult education in which she presented a very different story of Ohliger. She took OSU to task for its "unethical" treatment of him, asserting, "When John Ohliger spoke out on mandatory continuing education and, on principle, resigned his tenured full professorship [sic] at Ohio State University, he was punished by many, if not most, in the professorate, who either ignored him or acted directly against him" (pp. 111–112). This piqued my curiosity, and I set out to discover, or uncover, the "truth" about John Ohliger.

Around the fall of 1993, I began corresponding with John. I presented my first paper on him in the fall of 1995. The paper made him very angry: I had promised him space in it to present his views, but this did not happen, and he demanded that I withdraw it. I went ahead with the presentation, believing that withdrawing it would be unethical too. I began by describing his anger with me and why he was angry. Various members of the audience spoke to me, welcoming me into the club of people with whom John had been variously angry over time. They assured me that it would pass and told me not to worry. Scared to death, I felt an obligation to tell John how the presentation went. We were pretty much okay after that. In 1999, when the Adult Education Research Conference was held at the University of Northern Illinois in DeKalb, John drove to meet me for the first time. I was ecstatic. My fascination—with both his views and his life—persists.

As this book was evolving, John asked me to correct the misperception that he had been a full professor when he left OSU (Cunningham, 1992). Ohliger was at Ohio State from 1967 to 1973. When he left OSU, he was an associate professor in adult education. He had become disillusioned with higher education. In his account of an interview with John for an adult education history project on leaders in the field, Andrew Goldstein related, "When I asked him what followed, he stated that he 'left' Ohio State in 1973 to 'pursue other options' [after some disagreement with Ohio State administrators]. . . . The 'social change,' as fostered by the university, served, apparently, to stifle him" (Hiemstra & Goldstein, 1990, p. 1). Ohliger did not like institutional change translated as moves toward increased professionalization and more formalized adult learning. He never served as a tenure-track faculty member again. Instead, in addition to his work with Basic Choices, his Madison, Wisconsin, center devoted to the study and practice of radical liberal education for adults, he included visiting professor or guest speaker at numerous universities among his many roles.

Throughout his life, John abhorred what he saw as an increasing use of education to correct behavior that society found deficient. He worried about the increasing gap between people with access to knowledge and those who do not have the same access. He wrote, "No conceivable society can exist without a minimum of required learning, but the requirements should arise from the necessities of the human scale situation, not from rigidly imposed laws, regulations, or social pressures. . . . Don't get me wrong. I live and breathe education most of my days, but I see it as a sacred and delicate delight only subtly approachable. It is certainly not a sledgehammer solution to our personal and social crises" (Ohliger, 1985, p. 1). For me, these words capture John's social philosophy of education.

André's Vignette: Tasting Each Situation with Gusto

My interest in John Ohliger and his work began during my doctoral studies at Dalhousie University in Halifax, Nova Scotia. Somehow on my arrival there, I was lucky enough to be assigned to Edgar Friedenberg's old office, which proved to be an intellectual gold mine. Friedenberg came to prominence as a radical educator in the 1960s. In his book *Coming of Age in America: Growth and Acquiescence* (1965), he interrogated U.S. high school education, claiming it provided youth with an undemocratic experience as it trained them to be compliant citizens who maintained the status quo. Professor Friedenberg had left many books and articles behind when he retired to live in rural Nova Scotia. As I rummaged around his bookshelves, I found, sitting alongside works by Carl Rogers, Erich Fromm, and others, writings by Ivan Illich. I was personally disillusioned with the strangulation of education by conservative forces since the 1980s, and I voraciously read these variously liberal, critical, and radical intellectuals. In particular, the transgressive nature of Illich's writings energized me. Later Michael R. Welton, my supervisor, and Michael Collins, the external examiner of my doctoral dissertation, introduced me to the work of John Ohliger, a radical social educator. I soon discovered that Ohliger knew Illich and had been deeply influenced by him, perhaps particularly in relation to his critique of mandatory continuing education (Ohliger, 1971). I was hooked, and I began to explore the abundant transgressive work of the very prolific Ohliger. I feel that he has been a conscience for our field that all too often gets caught up in clichés and bandwagons designed to ensure its instrumental survival.

When Tonette invited me to work with her on this book, I gained a new opportunity to learn about Ohliger, who was very active in the field of study and practice during the post–World War II period and beyond into the new millennium. The emergence of academic adult education in North America had been the focus of my doctoral dissertation and has remained a focus in my subsequent research (Grace, 1997, 1999, 2000a, 2000b, 2005).

When Tonette told John that she and I would be working together on the book about him, he did what John always did: he read. First, he read my doctoral dissertation, which began with a lengthy discussion of social theory and its relevance to framing historical studies of adult education. In an e-mail to Tonette, he said that he had worried at first that I was just another critical adult educator prone to write in a language that he had always found difficult and gloomy. However, after he read more of my work, especially pieces focused on the history of the modern practice of adult education, he said that he liked what I had done. I must admit that I was a little nervous approaching someone whom I considered to be a field icon. I truly admired John's work, and I wanted him to feel that I could do justice to a writing project about him. I spent quite some time drafting my first e-mail to him. He replied quickly, and his response was reassuring. I was getting to know a knowledgeable and generous man with whom I shared a love of field history. I never met John face to face, but I got to know him a little better through our e-mail correspondence. He also put me on his mailing list, which I took as a sign that he had welcomed me into his world.

One day as I worked on this book, I read one of John's pieces in which he memorialized his good friend Sam Brightman. Ohliger (1992) described this pioneer adult education journalist as "unique, incorrigible, invaluable, embarrassing, [a] person of hope, . . . [a] political agnostic, radical, . . . liberal, . . . curmudgeon, funny man, stands up for what he says, totally outrageous, . . . [a] grouchy resister of progress, . . . shrewd, constantly challenging others" (p. 21). He added that Brightman "didn't form his opinions by following some recipe. Instead, he tasted each situation with gusto; then brewed his own trenchant conclusions and mixed in [a] twist of wry, humor that is" (p. 23). I paused and thought that this eclectic characterization could be autobiographical. Indeed John had captured the person he was as much as he had captured his kindred spirit, Sam Brightman.

In the chapters that follow, you will first engage with John's own writing. Then you will engage with contributors to this book who, collectively, will take you through a varied and vivid encounter with the man, the adult educator, the social activist, and the cultural worker. Perhaps at the end of the book, you will agree with me that the above characterization is indeed autobiographical.

References

Cunningham, P. (1991). International influences on the development of knowledge. In J. M. Peters, P. Jarvis, & Associates (Eds.), *Adult education: Evolution and achievements in a developing field of study* (pp. 347–383). San Francisco: Jossey-Bass.

Cunningham, P. (1992). Adult and continuing education does not need a code of ethics. In M. W. Galbraith & B. R. Sisco (Eds.), *Confronting controversies in challenging times: A call for action* (pp. 107–114). New Directions for Adult and Continuing Education, no. 54. San Francisco: Jossey-Bass.

D'Antonio, M. (2003, August 24). Sneer when you say journalist. *Los Angeles Times*.

Friedenberg, E. Z. (1965). *Coming of age in America: Growth and acquiescence*. New York: Random House.

Grace, A. P. (1997). *Identity quest: The emergence of North American adult education (1945–70)*. Unpublished doctoral dissertation, Dalhousie University, Halifax, Nova Scotia, Canada.

Grace, A. P. (1999). Building a knowledge base in US academic adult education (1945–1970). *Studies in the Education of Adults, 31*(2), 220–236.

Grace, A. P. (2000a). Academic adult education in Canada and the United States (1917–1970): A chronology of their emergence and a conspectus of their development. *PAACE Journal of Lifelong Learning, 9*, 65–78.

Grace, A. P. (2000b). Canadian and US adult learning (1945–1970) and the cultural politics and place of lifelong learning. *International Journal of Lifelong Education, 19*(2), 141–158.

Grace, A. P. (2005). Lifelong learning chic in the modern practice of adult education: Historical and contemporary perspectives. *Journal of Adult and Continuing Education, 11*(1), 62–79.

Griffith, W. S. (1991). The impact of intellectual leadership. In J. M. Peters, P. Jarvis, & Associates (Eds.), *Adult education: Evolution and achievements in a developing field of study* (pp. 97–120). San Francisco: Jossey-Bass.

Harvey, D. (2005). *A brief history of neoliberalism*. New York: Oxford University Press.

Hiemstra, R., & Goldstein, A. (1990). *John Ohliger: Personal vita*. Retrieved October 15, 2006, from http://www-distance.syr.edu/pvitajfo.html.

Nathans, A. (2004, January 30). Ohliger dies; guided WORT: educator co-founded station. *Capital (Madison, Wisconsin) Times*, p. 3B.

Ohliger, J. (1971). *Lifelong learning or lifelong schooling? A tentative view on the ideas of Ivan Illich with a quotational bibliography*. Syracuse, NY: Syracuse University Publications in Continuing Education and ERIC Clearinghouse on Adult Education.

Ohliger, J. (1975). Prospects for a learning society. *Adult Leadership, 24*(1), 37–39.

Ohliger, J. (1985, Summer). The final solution to learning opportunities. *Tranet*, 1.

Ohliger, J. (1991). Social philosophy: Its past, present, and future. *Adult Learning, 2*(8), 16–18.

Ohliger, J. (1992, April 6). Celebrating Sam Brightman. *Adult and Continuing Education Today, 22*(13), 4.

Ohliger, J. (1997). [My search for freedom's song: Some notes for a memoir]. Third draft. Unpublished raw data.

Ohliger, J. (n. d.). *Abbreviated curriculum vitae*. Madison, WI: Basic Choices.

2

Mediating Challenges in Adult Education and Culture
John Ohliger's Radical Social Project

André P. Grace and Tonette S. Rocco

We live in times when neoliberal governments meld the social and the economic, and place fiscal responsibility before public responsibility (Grace, 2005). The neoliberal belief is that social progress is tied to economic expansion: if the economy does well, then the social will somehow advance as a domino effect. As consequences of this blind faith, privatization of learning is ascendant, and corporations have tremendous power in dictating lifelong-learning agendas tied to competition and the demands of the global economy (Grace, 2004, 2005). Indeed, governments and corporations have positioned lifelong learning as a necessity for all across the life span.

In this milieu, adult educators need lenses to help them determine what constitutes lifelong learning as a holistic, useful, just, and ethical practice that addresses instrumental, social, *and* cultural concerns. The scholarship, social activism, and educational and cultural work of John Ohliger provide one set of lenses to develop a probing social project to gauge the constitution of lifelong learning, problematize its formation, and develop worthwhile pedagogy for contemporary times. Ohliger wrote extensively about the social context of adult learning and about adult education as a field of study and practice for much of his career, and his political and pedagogical

project has always been about challenging adult educators and learners to clarify social and political options in relation to life, learning,
and work. Indeed his radical liberal project has been to assist adult
learners to make basic choices in the face of systemic and institutional forces that aid and abet dominant political and economic
interests. This project is shaped by a social philosophy in which
Ohliger (1980) calls on adult educators to exercise humility: "We
must search for a balance between our yearning for order and our desire for liberty. As adult educators we [ought to] believe that whatever minimal but essential place learning has in everyone's life, it
would be better if it were more voluntary than compulsory" (p. 23).

Ohliger expanded this social philosophy in a statement of beliefs that he developed with some colleagues in Basic Choices, an
adult learning forum that he established in Madison, Wisconsin, in
1976 to enable his work as a freelance adult educator and independent researcher (Basic Choices, 1982; Ohliger, 1997). In this quoted
statement of beliefs, positioned as guidelines for daily practice, the
group included:

- The primacy of voluntary learning.
- The basic value of free and open discussion intimately
  integrating thoughts and feelings, reflection and
  action.
- Working together toward a just society with more
  democratic control and mutual self-reliance, and
  less hierarchy, bureaucracy, and external authority.
- Working together toward a world with the best possible balance between maximum free learning and
  minimum instruction, with a significant place for
  activities not publicly defined as job-related *or* as
  learning [Basic Choices, 1982, p. 273].

Ohliger's social philosophy emphasized the learner's freedom to
choose using the vehicle of adult education as social education. He

detested anything that inhibited this freedom, and he always worried about the tendency toward the commodification of adult education so the field could align with a free enterprise society. Ohliger was often angry at mainstream adult educators who responded to change by assuming chameleonic entrepreneurial roles and conditioning citizens as learners and workers to succumb to lifelong-learning treatment, certification mania, and a mind-set that cast adult education as a compulsory venture (Ohliger & McCarthy, 1971). In a dialogue with himself (1970), he summarized his resistance to compulsory forms of adult education: "When we impose ideas on people, we train them. When we create an atmosphere in which people are free to explore ideas in dialogue and through interactions with other people, we educate them" (p. 250).

Throughout his career, Ohliger (1968, 1999) bemoaned not only what he saw as a turn toward compulsory adult education, but also what he construed as the loss of the voluntary nature of learning to the annals of history. Although Ohliger understood "the continuous pressure adult educators have created for the concept of 'lifelong learning'" as a key factor influencing this turn (Ohliger, 1968, p. 124), he felt that lifelong learning had gone off track. It had become a competency treadmill in which "professional assessment of the worth of a vocation . . . [gave] way to the measurement of competence by courses taken and examinations passed" (Lisman & Ohliger, 1978, p. 36). As he saw it, the reductionistic emphasis was on upgrades in occupational and professional skills. With Lisman, Ohliger (1978) problematized the notion of competence, arguing that "true competence is not merely *technical* competence. It [also] includes some concept of political and economic morality" (p. 37). Ohliger felt that ethics and morality had been sidelined in the commodification of adult education. He believed that the rationalization of field practices for economistic purposes served only to entrench the notion that lifelong learning had become a permanent necessity.

Always a Driven Man with a Social Mission

John Ohliger was a man who played diverse roles as an educator, an activist, and a cultural worker in order to achieve his social mission to help citizens as learners and workers attain the freedom to make basic choices in life, learning, and work. To understand this man, we might begin with certain critical incidents from his youth that shaped Ohliger as an eclectic educator deeply connected to what Freire (1998) calls the word and the world. For example, Ohliger's love of knowledge building, exchange, and distribution began at age thirteen when he had his first library job as an errand boy in the Dufferin Branch of the Detroit Public Library. Remembering this time, Ohliger (1987) reflected, "I do remember how important the books in the library were to me. I often left the public library after completing work with literally arms full of books. I believed that people were staring at me because of the huge stack I carried as I staggered home under their weight" (p. 7).

His concern with citizens as learners and workers and their dislocation due to class and other issues is also grounded in his individual history. In a reflection on his personal learning, Ohliger (1987) remembered the "strange feeling of shame" that he had felt during the Great Depression when, in the mid-1930s, he encountered his father checking books at the door of Detroit's main public library. His father did this work to receive welfare. Recounting their mutual humiliation, Ohliger related, "He seemed embarrassed also when he saw me and we never talked about it" (p. 7). Interestingly, Ohliger also related that this experience tarnished his love of libraries and may be why he did not choose to be a librarian as his initial career. On further reflection, though, he also conveyed that the sexist and heterosexist culture of the times had played a part in his career decision: "As an early teenager I considered myself and was looked on, I believe, as a 'sissy.' . . . In the United States then (and now) 'sissy' means not being interested in so-called normal boyish pursuits, being 'girlish,' or even homosexual. Library work seemed 'women's work' then and would have been too fright-ening to contemplate" (pp. 7–8). The effects of such perception and stereotyping on his sense of being, becoming, and belonging no doubt contributed to his sensitivities, sensibilities, and responsive-ness around issues of power relationships throughout his career.

In creating a personal vita of John Ohliger, Hiemstra and Gold-stein (1990) listed the roles of the self-acclaimed radical liberal adult educator who was known to point a "condemning, albeit, subtle fin-ger" at adult education as a field of study and practice (p. 1). These roles include "professor, administrator, author, trainer, speaker, re-searcher, organizer, bibliographer, critic, and volunteer in such as-pects of the field as [social] philosophy, political education [and economy], media, discussion group leadership, university extension, community colleges, liberal arts, and labor education" (p. 1). Hiem-stra and Goldstein might also have added field watchdog, since this is perhaps the role for which Ohliger will be most remembered. For many in mainstream adult education, this role made him a rebel ed-ucator and an irritant. Ohliger (1990a, 1990b) seemed to revel in such categorization, describing himself as a *radlib*, a term Spiro Agnew, disgraced thirty-ninth vice president of the United States, coined to describe someone both radical *and* liberal in political ori-entation. For Ohliger, to be a radlib meant coupling his critique of the dominant culture and a bounded status quo with a call to envi-sion new possibilities for social advancement. His analysis was al-ways guided by a key question: What knowledge has most worth? Ohliger's (1990b) radlib nature is demonstrated in this assessment of what he saw as a burgeoning American culture of practicality:

> The narrow emphasis on practicality is itself *im*practical.
> . . . The exclusively "practical" person is ever a worshiper
> of "business as usual," disliking change, an enemy of
> prophets, but a pal of priests. In addition, the current de-
> mand for practicality confuses feasibility with worth. In
> other words, when we are required to be practical these

days we collapse the difference between what works and
what is worth working. . . . The American streak of over-
emphasis on practicality and over-respect for know-how
has led to our being victimized by the anti-democratic
idea of expertise [pp. 30–31].

For Ohliger (1990a), the difficulty in being a radlib lay in getting the two halves of the notion to stay together: "The halves that
need constant readjustment and delicate balancing are: (1) a belief
that there can be a just social order based on human rationality, and
(2) a belief that there can be a good society that fosters spontaneous
freedom through true community" (p. 5). In explaining what he
meant, Ohliger placed Paulo Freire, who was inspired by Latin
American Christian Marxism, in that half opting for rational order,
and he placed Ivan Illich, who was guided by "a kind of sophisticated fundamentalist Catholicism," in the half opting for spontaneous freedom (p. 5). Ohliger felt that the Freirean perspective
dominated radicalism, at least in leftist academe circa 1990, such
that "radical adult education literature—so-called critical theory or
critical pedagogy—places almost total reliance on rationality" (p.
5). This move disturbed him.

Framing his definition of radical, Ohliger (1990a) believed in
democratic principles brought to life in deliberations that involved
problematizing experience and envisioning a social structure transformed to eradicate the strictures of the dominant exclusionary social. For Ohliger, being a radical meant being committed to and
passionate about transgressive pedagogical and cultural practices to
transform the social. Of course, his chosen work was never easy.
Over time, he had learned life lessons such as, "No one can be a
radical twenty-four hours a day. You'd be dead of exhaustion and
isolation within a week" (Ohliger, 1990a, p. 5). Another life lesson,
which he often did not heed, was that "simple prudence and the
need for social survival often require radicals to be cautious about
coming right out and saying what changes are necessary, even—or

maybe especially—if they are obvious" (p. 5). Indeed Ohliger (1979) could be reckless at times. His passion for social change often drove him to speak out and contest the conformity and conservatism that he felt constricted society and mainstream adult education as a field of study and practice. He challenged his colleagues and adult learners "to be radical in the senses of: 1. trying to get to the root, the essence of issues, and; 2. calling for a basic change in social structure [for the better]" (p. 17). In workshops, he (1979) shaped his notion of radical adult education using the following quoted themes (pp. 17–18):

A. Education-Learning Is a Fragile, Delicate, Subtle Activity Linked to Social Life.

B. Knowledge-Learning Is More the Experience Itself and Less the Classification of Information, the Acquisition of Facts, Techniques, or Skills.

C. The Path to Truth-Knowledge-Learning Is More Personal Exploration or Mutual Political Dialogue and Less Scientific Experimentation or Didactic-Instruction.

D. Education Is Never Neutral, Politically or Otherwise.

E. Standard Brand Adult Education Is the Most Conservative and Reactionary of the Different Levels of Institutionalized Education.

F. Adult Education Is Best Seen, *Not* as a Field, Discipline, or a Profession, But Simply as Those Activities of the Chronologically Mature in Which Learning Is Involved.

Ohliger's prolific and eclectic contributions to adult education cover a gamut of topics. For example, his critiques of mandatory continuing education as a tool of the establishment, of lifelong learning as a mechanism for controlling citizens as learners and workers, and of critical adult education as an idealistic project that is out of touch with modern practice have a timeless quality and value to them. These critiques have been edgy and variously argumentative, deliberative, disruptive, and informative. They provide a foundation for making basic choices about learning for life and work in contemporary times when advanced technoscientism, individualism, competition, privatization, and globalization constitute cultural change forces dictating what learning has most worth (Grace, 2004, 2005). Indeed these change forces provide a basis for socially controlling adult learning through cyclical and mandated forms of lifelong learning (Grace, 2005).

In a world where citizens as learners and workers need to develop and employ skills in critical thinking and analysis, Ohliger's provocative insights and challenges continue to have meaning and merit. This is indicated, for example, in the following use of Ohliger's work in a graduate adult education institute that focused on contemporary practice, its parameters, and the possibilities for its revitalization.

During a recent summer institute, Lifelong Learning in a Global World, held at Mount Saint Vincent University, Halifax, Nova Scotia, Canada, for thirty graduate students, I (André) used a selection of readings from Ohliger's work as a springboard for daily dialogue and communicative learning around themes, concepts, and ideas pervasive in discourses in adult education and lifelong learning. Students liked Ohliger's straight-up and straightforward language as he mediated the politics of adult education and lifelong learning. As they engaged with his writings, they described Ohliger as a committed and passionate educator with pointed perspectives and deep convictions. They liked his attention to contexts and relationships of power as he deliberated mandatory continuing education and other topics with meaning and value for adult education as a field of study and practice. They liked the edginess that often came through in his writing, and they enjoyed his learner-centered approach to adult education that kept learner freedom at the heart of ethical practice. Most important perhaps, they talked about how pieces that Ohliger had written even several decades earlier—pieces like "Adult Education: 1984" (1971) (see Chapter Three) and "Is Lifelong Education a Guarantee of Permanent Inadequacy?" (1974) (see Chapter Four)—still spoke to them in a contemporary context as they grappled with issues and concerns in their university studies and field practices. Through Ohliger's work, students came away with an important sense of the history of struggle that has marked the modern practice of adult education in its attempts to address the frequently competing needs and concerns of adult learners across instrumental, social, and cultural domains.

Perceiving John Ohliger as a Critical Educator

John Ohliger is respected in critical adult education circles, perhaps more so in Australia and Canada than elsewhere. This is paradoxical since Ohliger (1997) was always suspicious of the critical turn that emerged in adult education during the 1980s. He felt that criticalists were disconnected from the kind of everyday radical practice that he considered essential to social transformation. His anger at them mirrored his anger at those he perceived as intellectual (but not organic intellectual or activist) radicalists. In his critique of these radicalists, Ohliger (1979) emphasized that the chief task of radical educators was to act once they came up with their best answer to a key question: What can be done? Although he acknowledged the difficulty of answering this question specifically and concretely, Ohliger nevertheless disclosed, "Sometimes I get mad at people like [Ivan] Illich [who wrote *Deschooling Society*, 1971], Paulo Freire [who wrote *Pedagogy of the Oppressed*, 1972], and [Everett] Reimer [who wrote *School Is Dead*, 1971] because their proposals for action seem so vague, global, impractical, [and] abstract, or because they don't propose starting a movement, group, program, or organization I can join" (pp. 21–22).

Although Ohliger described himself a radical educator and a radlib, we would also describe him as a critical educator, even though he would reject the label. Ohliger generally limited being radical to being involved as a grassroots social educator, activist, ethicist, and cultural worker. However, he can also be considered critical in the sense that he was always concerned with articulating democratic forms of learning, challenging parameters that limited freedom for everyday citizens as learners and workers, and engaging the ethics of just practices for them. It can also be argued that criticalists are like radicalists because they try to get to the root of issues as they work toward social transformation. Thus, in a twist on his own definition, Ohliger is perhaps a *radcrit* whose radical *and* critical social mission was to make the world a better place for all.

In fulfilling this mission, Ohliger proved himself an insightful and innovative social educator who continuously investigated—indeed interrogated—issues of fundamental concern to adult and continuing education as well as lifelong learning. While many of his contemporaries variously chose to promote adult education in ways that aided and abetted what he saw as a status quo quite lacking in social consciousness, Ohliger consistently chose to radicalize the field of study and practice in ways that were transgressive, if not transformative. His radicalism is grounded in what historically have been the critical social purposes of adult education: to build community and assist everyday citizens as learners by advancing an ethical practice of adult education that keeps the political ideals of modernity—democracy, freedom, and social justice—at the heart of learning matters. In radcrit fashion, Ohliger's social philosophy, pedagogy, and practice have been grounded in a critique of instrumentalism that has inextricably linked credentialism and specialization to the professionalization of the field. To his dismay, social and cultural concerns were often sidelined in producing this link.

John Ohliger is easily situated as one of adult education's most prolific writers and, patently, as his work indicates, one of the mainstream field's most intense critics. His career focused on ordinary people mediating life, learning, and work in the face of power and interests. This theme marked the transgressive nature of his writing and work. As a member of the International Adult and Continuing

Education Hall of Fame 2002 housed at the University of Oklahoma, Ohliger is recognized "for his outstanding and innovative contributions to the progress of continuing education" (p. 1). His hall-of-fame profile notes his contributions to diverse aspects of adult education including social critique, most notably prolific in relation to mandatory continuing education. (Other significant contributions and achievements are listed in the chronology in Chapter One.) Ohliger's body of work provides educators and learners with a rich resource for critical analysis and communicative learning regarding two topics of contemporary concern. First, his critique can help us scrutinize the study and practice of adult education in our broadly construed field with its multiple sources of knowledge and competing interests. Second, it can help us investigate the space and place of lifelong learning as an entity with two faces: as an instrument of social control and as a focal point for social education and cohesion.

Ohliger as a Critic of Modern Practice

The modern practice of adult education is usually dated from 1919, the year the Adult Education Committee of the British Ministry of Reconstruction released a report locating adult education as both a permanent national necessity and an inseparable aspect of citizenship (Cotton, 1968; Knowles & Klevins, 1972). This depiction has marked the emergence of modern practice in Canada, the United States, and other countries where adult education is historically linked to such issues as community development, nation building, education for citizenship, and lifelong learning. Our field of study and practice is broadly constituted, and it has developed in reaction and response to many instrumental, social, and cultural change forces. John Ohliger spent much of his career both inside and outside the academy gauging this emergence. Few other adult educators have offered critiques of the field that have been concomitantly as salient and acerbic as Ohliger's challenges to the prescribed parameters and conventions of modern practice. These critiques contain diverse themes and ideas, and they are variously recorded in his memoirs, academic writing, and popular writing. They embody his social philosophy and frame his political and pedagogical project:

• *Theme 1: Building an encompassing, ethical field of study and practice.* Ohliger believed that adult education ought to be an encompassing, ethical, and inclusive field of study and practice. He was constantly concerned with what enables or inhibits building such a field. In this regard, he was realistic about the limits and absences impacting adult education. He (1990b) declared:

> What we're faced with today is a superstitious belief in education as the panacea for all our ills. . . . The tough question is: Why do we have this pervasive superstition? And the even tougher question [is]: Can we find ways of getting beyond this harmful belief that will be equalitarian [sic], democratic, and spiritually honorable? . . . [To do so we have to address] the fundamental crisis [in adult education]: the lack of a coherent set of goals, the lack of an over-arching philosophy that would lead to ethics or morality worthy of being called ethics or morality [p. 29].

• *Theme 2: Shaping a role as an eclectic social educator, activist, and cultural worker.* Ohliger invariably took a stand on issues affecting citizens as learners and workers in the field of study and practice in which he found himself both a critic and a subject of ostracism. He consistently focused on matters of context and relationship, and he suggested possibilities for practice that he linked to the larger community, its needs, and its other constituencies besides education. Here Ohliger (1990b) encouraged educators to be modest: "I don't believe that education or learning is the be-all or the end-all of life. Those who see education as almighty important seem to be tied to a narrow scientific view of knowledge as illumination or enlightenment. And it's a lot more than that. . . . We need to find ways to balance the [educational] process with other activities, to reduce education to its appropriate share of community resources . . . [in] the holistic human community" (pp. 32–33).

• *Theme 3: Rethinking learning for life and work.* Lifelong learning is an old concept. Indeed the 1919 Report of the Adult Education Committee of the British Ministry of Reconstruction put forth the notion that learning in adulthood, by nature and design, should be universal and lifelong for all citizens (Cotton, 1968; Knowles & Klevins, 1972). Since the 1990s, the notion has gained new vigor and become a pervasive global phenomenon (Grace, 2005). This is indicated, for example, by its emphasis in educational policy documents from influential groups such as the Organization for Economic Cooperation and Development (Grace, 2002).

Ohliger's problematization of the concept of lifelong learning, coupled with his critique of mandatory continuing education, can help us explore how we might (re)conceptualize lifelong learning in the new millennium. A turn to Collins's (1998) analysis is useful here. He credits Ohliger with drawing critical attention to the link between mandatory continuing education and lifelong learning. He asserts that Ohliger's work can help us explore ways in which forms of education under the rubric of lifelong learning have become undemocratic, denying learners the possibility of making decisions about their own learning. Ohliger's critique can help us make sense of the ethical and political nature of lifelong learning in contemporary times when the notion has become a commodity whose future prospects are viewed more in economistic terms than in terms of social and cultural possibilities.

Forever the Scribe

John Ohliger's career in adult education began shortly after World War II and continued into the new millennium. The insights and ideas from his radical social philosophy and practice remain valuable to those of us interested in designing and implementing a more encompassing, ethical, and learner-centered practice of adult education. His critique of mandatory continuing education and his interrogation of compulsory forms of lifelong learning that denied learners the freedom to choose remain informative as neoliberalism, privatization, and globalization create new urgencies for those attempting to address instrumental, social, and cultural concerns in the education of adults.

Ohliger (with McCarthy, 1971) believed in the freedom of learners to choose whether they would participate in particular forms of learning and to choose the parameters of that participation—the what, when, why, and how—when they did. He challenged educators to have faith in the capacities and abilities of learners so that education in tandem with action could be a basis for political engagement and social change. In this regard, Ohliger was deeply influenced by Ivan Illich and his radical educational ideas, which he considered logical, sensible, and hopeful. These ideas situated education in political and cultural terms. Illich (1971) predicted the rapid growth of the information society in which knowledge and lifelong learning would be commodities nurtured by an incessant, instrumental vocationalism. In clairvoyant fashion, he wrote in *Deschooling Society*, "If we do not challenge the assumption that valuable knowledge is a commodity which under certain circumstances may be forced into the consumer, society will be increasingly dominated by sinister pseudoschools and totalitarian managers of information" (pp. 49–50).

Ohliger stands as a passionate agitator and a willful adult educator who offered no apologies for his deep commitment to radicalized social education as a way to address this commodification. Still, he has not been an icon. For many academic adult educators, graduate students, and field practitioners, Ohliger is an unknown quantity or just someone known about in a cursory way. He remains an unsung hero as a scholar and grassroots social educator in the modern practice of adult education. Yet there is much inspiration in his work for those who consider the social a vital context in practice. Like much better-known and more visible social educators such as Eduard Lindeman, Moses Coady, Paulo Freire, Myles Horton, and Ivan Illich, Ohliger advocated for students using a learner-centered social pedagogy. And like them, he connected freedom to learn, which he saw as an engagement with substance and context, to possibilities for individual and social transformation that transgress ideology and power relationships. His greatest legacy is perhaps his abundant writing on this and other topics. He was extraordinarily productive, linking the word to the worlds of teaching, learning, activism, cultural change, and community work. Indeed his passion for writing was perhaps matched only by his obsession with books and reading. Ohliger (1997) wrote in his memoir, "Burt Kreitlow [an academic adult educator and a contemporary of John] . . . once gave me this back-handed compliment: 'I'll say one thing for you, John: At least you're the best read professor of adult education I know of'" (Ohliger, 1997, part 2, p. 12). And Ohliger was. The voluminous bibliographies he created and the numerous articles and book reviews he wrote provide testament to his roles as an avid reader and intellectual scribe.

Challenging the Professionalization of Adult Education

The authors contributing to this book fall into two categories. First, there are those who knew John Ohliger personally and worked with him in various capacities. They variously witnessed his passion and commitment, and sometimes felt the lash of his sharp tongue as well. Second, there are those who knew him only through his written work, using elements of his encompassing social philosophy, pedagogy, and practice to inform their own critical, alternative practices of adult education. It is in the dichotomy of these ways of knowing Ohliger that readers of this book will come to know the dichotomous man: the radical who scorned adult education as an exclusionary and undemocratic field of study and practice, and the liberal who loved citizens as learners and workers and worked to free them from the constraints of a bounded existence as they mediated life, learning, and work in a world often marked by injustice.

Although each chapter has a specific focus in relation to Ohliger's educational and cultural work, his radical social theorizing, and his approaches to a social practice of adult education, contributing authors also consider, albeit in various ways and to varying degrees, the meaning and value of Ohliger's work to a contemporary, encompassing practice of adult education.

Since John passed away before he could write a chapter for this book, we have included six of his more poignant writings over the decades to give readers a good taste of essential Ohliger. These pieces (Chapters Three to Eight) comprise Part Two of the book, "In Ohliger's Words: Accent on the Social from a Radical Liberal Perspective": "Adult Education: 1984" (1971); "Is Lifelong Adult Education a Guarantee of Permanent Inadequacy?" (1974); "The Social Uses of Theorizing in Adult Education" (1980); "Lifelong Learning as Nightmare" (1982); "Forum: You Shall Know the Truth and the Truth Shall Make You Laugh" (1990); and "A Cautious Welcome to the New Millennium" (1999). Notes accompanying each piece speak to the relevance of Ohliger's work to contemporary practices of adult education and lifelong learning. The six pieces speak to core themes, including compulsory education and challenging adult educators to engage in public pedagogy to enhance social democracy. Collectively, they provide insights into the utopian world that John Ohliger desired for citizens as learners and workers.

Part Three of this book is entitled "Challenging Professionalization in an Emerging Field of Study and Practice." It focuses on what Ohliger saw as contradictions in modern practice. In Chapter Nine, André Grace situates Ohliger in the times and tides that shaped him, surveying the history of the field of North American adult education amid the social and cultural change forces at play over the course of Ohliger's career. Grace uses this contextual and relational backdrop to provide an analysis of Ohliger's radical social perspectives and political and pedagogical project as an adult educator, social activist, and cultural worker. He explores how Ohliger dealt with the dichotomy of adult education as an emerging professionalized venture and declining social, amateurish adventure for more than five decades. This exploration provides a contextual and relational backdrop as Grace considers Ohliger's assessment of adult education as a field of study and practice in a period dominated by U.S. academic adult education's quest to build professional community and gain cultural space and place for the field.

U.S. adult education grew more professionalized and academicized in the latter half of the twentieth century. Concomitantly, the term *public intellectual* gained renewed attention in the United States, especially after the publication of Russell Jacoby's *The Last Intellectuals* in 1987. In Chapter Ten, David Yamada draws on Jacoby to reflect on the positionality of contemporary public intellectuals. He relates that, interestingly, and perhaps ironically, Jacoby helped to spur an avalanche of articles, panel discussions, and conferences on how we define a public intellectual and who gets to claim the label. Drawing further on Jacoby's arguments, Yamada considers how these highly specialized and credentialed academicians who write for a very narrow audience have usurped the role of the independent, bohemian public scholar and writer. Situating John Ohliger in this latter, historic role, Yamada discusses how Ohliger's life and work stand as an important counterpoint to the current paradigm of a public intellectual. He recounts how Ohliger was an independent scholar and intellectual activist for much of his life, working through various media to encourage public dialogue and raise important questions about society, learning, and current events. Yamada considers how Ohliger's approach was not "top down" and directive, but personal and interactive, embracing the techniques of popular adult education. From this perspective, Yamada examines the role of the public intellectual, using John Ohliger as an ongoing example of how principles and practices of adult education can be employed to redefine and remake this role. He also considers the limitations and trade-offs of being a public intellectual in this alternative mode.

In Chapter Eleven, Tonette Rocco builds a framework for continuing education that is important to contemporary learners across professions. Here she turns to history to contrast Ohliger's views on the voluntary nature of adult learning and self-directed learning with the mainstream views of his mentors and colleagues, notably Cyril O. Houle and Malcolm S. Knowles. Rocco relates how both Houle and Knowles contributed core field knowledge that had a deep impact on the design and practice of adult education at a time when many adult educators were concerned with professionalism and legitimacy across the discipline of education. She discusses what Ohliger saw as an evident contradiction between the field's claim of adults being voluntary learners and the field's complicity in mandating programs that required adult learners to participate in forms of learning that others sanctioned. In doing so, she provides both an overview of mandatory continuing education and Ohliger's social critique of the notion as she considers the debate and contradictions that shaped its meaning and value.

It is difficult to assess John Ohliger's tremendous contribution to adult education without considering his relationship with Ivan Illich, author of *Deschooling Society* (1971). Jeff Zacharakis argues this point in Chapter Twelve. He explores how Ohliger advocated Illich's ideas and philosophy in adult education as he built his radical framework and language to contest compulsory adult education. Zacharakis, contending that Illich was the most influential figure in John Ohliger's career, examines what he construes as an unequal and sometimes tumultuous relationship between two intellectuals who nevertheless admired and respected each other. He provides biographical sketches that reveal great differences between Illich, the consummate intellectual, and John, the outsider academic adult educator. Zacharakis explores why John gravitated toward Illich and not Everett Reimer, the author of *School Is Dead* (1971), who mentored both Illich and Ohliger. He also explores why the relationship between Ohliger and Illich weakened during the 1980s. Zacharakis ends his chapter with a preliminary archaeology of adult education that links what Ohliger learned from his mentors to his understanding of radical liberal education as a fusion of his learning and experiences.

John felt that formal education was delusional about what it could accomplish. At one point he turned to Taoism to frame a focus on the freedom of individuals to learn. In Chapter Thirteen, Michael Collins reflects on John's interest in Taoist insights, which Ohliger linked to a need to *learn to unlearn* in an increasingly professionalized modern practice of adult education. Collins takes up Ohliger's call to adult educators to adopt a practical orientation to activist work and to laugh in the face of the burdens that accompany such work. Collins points out that this call was guided as much by a rejection of what John perceived as the intrusion of critical theory into adult education as it was by any passion for living in a Taoist moment. In this regard, Collins explores Ohliger's critique of critical theory and critical pedagogy. He indicates that the basis for this critique lay in Ohliger's disdain of what he perceived as obscurity and a lack of clarity in critical educational discourse. As Collins explores the tensions Ohliger saw between critical discourse and radical social education, he discusses how themes like liberty and the social in John's work meant that Ohliger actually contributed to critical adult education. Through his analysis in this chapter, Collins indicates how Ohliger's work could influence contemporary critical adult educational practices that attend to ethics, learner freedom, and the politics of everyday practice.

Part Four of the book brings together narrations of key people who remember John Ohliger as a radical social adult educator who worked in informal contexts in diverse community settings. In Chapter Fourteen, Phyllis Cunningham explores this characterization of John as she recounts her personal relationship with him and discusses her radicalist friend's views as an outsider looking in on adult education as a field of study and practice. Noting that John's life as an outsider was not easy, she relates how some mainstream adult educators—perceived as leaders in our field—treated John badly. She contends it was because they resented his criticism and his challenge to their hegemony over the field. Cunningham firmly believes that John's story should be told because it is rather difficult for an adult educator who has once been on the inside to stand on the outside and make a critique. Accordingly, she sets telling John's story as her task, which includes recalling their odyssey together within what was becoming an increasingly professionalized modern practice. In doing so, Cunningham looks at how John defined and practiced adult education in the community. She suggests that he saw all adult education as community education guided by a public pedagogy that assisted learners in building knowledge as a voluntary acquisition. Cunningham's focus speaks to John's real career as a grassroots radical social educator.

Following Chapter Fourteen, André Grace writes a postchapter reflection that links Cunningham and Ohliger as adult educators and cultural workers who shaped learning culture as a critical and radical space in keeping with a politics of caring and justice. Grace considers themes in John's work that Cunningham discusses and speaks to their relevance to critical and other educators who are concerned with escalating privatization of higher education, mounting instrumentalism in adult education, and increasing commodification of lifelong learning, which is often considered to be replacing adult education.

In Chapter Fifteen, Lee Karlovic grapples with a key question: What can John Ohliger possibly offer us in the twenty-first century? Using Ohliger's extensive personal library to focus particularly on John's work in relation to gender, Karlovic explores John's connections with the women who were part of his network of response over the years. Using the idea of communicant, a term that describes a provider or a receiver of information and other gifts, she explores how John the provider aided receivers of his useful knowledge, his gifts. Specifically, Karlovic investigates women as communicants, interviewing ten women who share their perspectives and memories of their connections to John. In doing so, she problematizes the term *feminist* as a positionality, and she explores what community, freedom, listening, sex and gender roles, nonsexist language, exclusion, and the spiritual, the personal, and the political meant as ideas or practices that these women took up in their connectedness to John.

Following Chapter Fifteen, Elizabeth Tisdell provides a postchapter reflection. In speaking to Ohliger's connection to women and feminism, Tisdell positions Ohliger as a labor educator who interrogated capitalism and power relations, and explored connections and relationships among people and in community. She draws on Karlovic's narration to discuss how John spent his life searching for ways to live the tension between reflection and action as a political mediation affected by systemic barriers. She uses the lens of Karlovic's writing to speak to the importance of Ohliger's work to women as adult learners and social activists who should strive to make connections and build community.

In Chapter Sixteen, Stephen Brookfield takes a different tack, comparing the public intellectual life and cultural work of John Ohliger to Paul Robeson. Brookfield discusses ways in which the two activists connect in ambition and experience as he explores Robeson's learning tasks and his cultural work, particularly his attempt to use the Hollywood studio system to promote race pride and present positive images of black life. Brookfield concludes that both Robeson and Ohliger developed a form of collective leadership for social change that centered on grassroots union organizing. He leaves us with lessons that contemporary educators can learn from their lives and public pedagogical practices, including the importance of having a worked-through rationale for critique and practice; the need always to ground critique in local action and specific situations; the belief that a well-lived life is not found wholly within the domain of rationalism but also involves emotion, affect, spirituality, and aesthetics; and the need to raise questions of merit and worth as we assess what we do, for whom, and for what purposes in the scheme of things.

In a postchapter reflection, André Grace considers the profound political differences that made Robeson and Ohliger two different kinds of grassroots activists and cultural workers. Grace presents Ohliger as a devoted American whose dissension could always be linked to his desire to improve the lot of ordinary people and enhance social democracy. Grace examines John's commitment to liberal ideals and his work to link liberal arts education to a practice emphasizing the freedom of adult learners. Here Grace speaks to John's disdain for lifelong education pushers whom Ohliger saw as key players in the professionalization of adult education. Grace considers how the turn to professionalization was a portent of what was to come under neoliberalism. He ends by considering how a turn to revitalized liberal education might help counter some of the ill effects of neoliberalized learning.

While we had originally planned to have John write the last chapter of this book, we are pleased that his wife, Christina (Chris) Wagner, accepted the challenging task of writing this chapter. Her narrative reflection in Chapter Seventeen provides deep insights into John's complex positionality in personal and professional contexts. It locates John as a rebel with a cause: to engage in adult education to build social democracy, enhance learner freedom, and work for social justice. In her chapter, Chris portrays the human and personal side of a complex man, radical scholar, social instigator, and communicator extraordinaire. Reminiscences of John through the eyes of his wife bring essences of his life into focus. Chris recounts John's knack for making all people seem important and his ability to learn from his mistakes. She shares snippets of his relationships with his contemporaries, notably Ivan Illich and Frank Adams. She revisits his critique of mandatory continuing education, and his outreach to citizens as learners and workers through Basic Choices and WORT radio. In the end, what Chris reveals in this chapter is John's legacy to adult education. This legacy is crystallized in André Grace's postchapter reflection.

In sum, John's legacy lies not in his particular accomplishments, but in the social purposes of adult education that he set as challenges for those of us who engage in adult education as a field of study and practice. With John as an inspiration, the task is now ours to engender future forms of adult education that are more democratic, inclusive, just, and ethical for coming generations of adult educators and learners.

References

Basic Choices. (1982). Lifelong learning as nightmare. In R. Gross (Ed.), *Invitation to lifelong learning* (pp. 273–274). Chicago: Follett Publishing.

Collins, M. (1998). *Critical crosscurrents in education.* Malabar, FL: Krieger.

Cotton, W. E. (1968). *On behalf of adult education: A historical examination of the supporting literature.* Boston: Center for the Study of Liberal Education for Adults.

Freire, P. (1972). *Pedagogy of the oppressed.* New York: Herder & Herder.

Freire, P. (1998). *Teachers as cultural workers: Letters to those who dare teach* (D. Macedo, D. Koike, & A. Oliveira, Trans.). Boulder, CO: Westview Press.

Grace, A. P. (2002). Intersecting instrumental, social, and cultural education to build and sustain inclusive lifelong-learning communities. In K. Appleton, C. Macpherson, & D. Orr (Eds.), *Proceedings of the Second International Lifelong Learning Conference, Central Queensland University, Yeppoon, Central Queensland, Australia* (pp. 181–187). Rockhampton, Queensland, Australia: Central Queensland University Press.

Grace, A. P. (2004). Lifelong learning as a chameleonic concept and versatile practice: Y2K perspectives and trends. *International Journal of Lifelong Education, 23*(4), 385–405.

Grace, A. P. (2005). Lifelong learning chic in the modern practice of adult education: Historical and contemporary perspectives. *Journal of Adult and Continuing Education, 11*(1), 62–79.

Hiemstra, R., & Goldstein, A. (1990). *John Ohliger: Personal vita.* Retrieved May 30, 2005, from http://www-distance.syr.edu/pvitajfo.html.

Illich, I. (1971). *Deschooling society.* New York: HarperCollins.

International Adult and Continuing Education (IACE) Hall of Fame. (2002). *John F. Ohliger.* Retrieved July 26, 2005, from http://tel.occe.ou.edu/halloffame/2002/ohliger.html.

Jacoby, R. (1987). *The last intellectuals: American culture in the age of academe.* New York: Basic Books.

Knowles, M., & Klevins, C. (1972). Résumé of adult education. In C. Klevins (Ed.), *Materials and methods in adult education* (pp. 5–15). New York: Kelvens.

Lisman, D., & Ohliger, J. (1978). Must we all go back to school? The pitfalls of compulsory adult education. *The Progressive, 42,* 35–37.

Ohliger, J. (1968). Accent on social philosophy: Lifelong learning—voluntary or compulsory. *Adult Leadership, 17,* 124.

Ohliger, J. (1970). Accent on social philosophy: Dialogue with myself. *Adult Leadership, 18*(8), 250, 265.

Ohliger, J. (1971). Adult education: 1984. *Adult Leadership, 19*(7), 223–224.

Ohliger, J. (1974). Is lifelong education a guarantee of permanent inadequacy? *Convergence, 7*(2), 47–58.

Ohliger, J. (1979, May). Radical ideas in adult education: A manifesto-bibliography. *Radical Teacher,* 17–26.

Ohliger, J. (1980). Searching for balance, coping with threats, looking for opportunities. *Setting the Pace, 1*(1), 22–26.

Ohliger, J. (1987, September). *Partners in adult learning.* Keynote address presented at the joint national conference of the Australian Association of Adult Education and the Library Association of Australia, Ohio State University, College of Education, Columbus, Ohio.

Ohliger, J. (1990a, February 12). What is radical adult education? *Adult and Continuing Education Today,* 5.

Ohliger, J. (1990b). Forum: You shall know the truth and the truth shall make you laugh. *Journal of Adult Education, 19*(1), 25–38.

Ohliger, J. (1997). [My search for freedom's song: Some notes for a memoir]. Third draft. Unpublished raw data.

Ohliger, J. (1999, Fall). Crises in higher education, 1991–98. *College Daze,* no. 1, 15–27.

Ohliger, J., & McCarthy, C. (1971). *Lifelong learning or lifelong schooling? A tentative view of the ideas of Ivan Illich with a quotational bibliography.* Syracuse, NY: Syracuse University Publications in Continuing Education and ERIC Clearinghouse on Education.

Reimer, E. (1971). *School is dead: Alternatives in education.* New York: Doubleday.

Part Two

In Ohliger's Words
Accent on the Social from a
Radical Liberal Perspective

3

Adult Education: 1984

John Ohliger

*Editors' note: John Ohliger was a member of the faculty
at The Ohio State University when this futuristic narrative
was published in* Adult Leadership *in January 1971.
The editor noted that John had previously written on
the tendency toward compulsory adult education in the
journal's "Accent" pages in the September 1968 and
February 1970 issues. Though this is brief, few other
pieces of John's work have had the recognition that his
writing here has had. John speaks eloquently to the
regimentation of life and work prompted by mandatory
forms of education. It has contemporary utility for those
who critique structured but short-lived instrumentalized
forms of learning for adults that emphasize learning for
earning instead of learning for life.*

A child is born in the United States in the year 1984. He can
never look forward to getting out of school. From the "infant
school" he starts attending at the age of six months to the "geriatric
learning center" he dies in, he finds himself going to school all his
life "for the good of society." From "infant school" he goes on to elementary school, then to junior high school. At the point he might
"graduate" from junior high school, he takes a series of tests. These
tests of his mental abilities, social adjustment potential, and motivation determine whether he will go on to a high school which will
prepare him for "higher schooling" and a career as a professional or

whether he will go on to a vocational school which will prepare him for life as a worker. Let's say he is sent to a vocational school. After graduation perhaps he is placed in a job, or perhaps he is sent to a technical school to prepare him as a paraprofessional, or perhaps he is sent to a "job bank school." Many "job bank schools" exist in the late 1900s because there are so few jobs available, since the great strides of automation.

The "permanent school district" in which the young man resides has experts to make the important decisions for him. It is called a "permanent school district," because by 1984 it was recognized that all people must go to school all their lives—permanently. The "permanent school district" is run by a "board of lifelong education" which has some of the characteristics of the old local board of education, the old draft board (because it is now accepted that we will be continually at war fighting "Communism" all over the world), and the old board of regents or board of trustees for what were formerly called universities or colleges. By 1984 there are no more universities or colleges as we know them. Their buildings and remaining funds have all been turned over to the local "permanent school districts," and the institutions have been renamed "higher schools." The private colleges ran out of resources years ago, because few rich people or corporations would contribute money to such "disruptive" and "permissive" institutions. The public universities found they could no longer get appropriations from the state legislatures, for the same reasons. Most of the faculty members of the old universities or colleges have long since been fired, sent to "retraining camps," or to mental institutions for "the good of society."

So let's say our young man, who was born in 1984, is sent to a "job bank school." There he learns, along with some "worthwhile hobbies," some skills that experts think he might just possibly use a few years later, in new jobs that just might exist then. Let's say our young man is lucky, the job he is preparing for does develop. He gets that job, and what is the first thing he does? He goes back to school.

This time the school is in the factory where he works. Though he has learned the skills of the job, he still needs orientation to that particular factory, still needs to learn the unique demands of his particular task in relation to other functions in that factory, and needs to learn how to "adjust" to the men and women and computerized robots working around him.

Suppose he does well at that job after attending the "factory school." He saves up some money and decides he wants to get married. His local "board of lifelong education" gives him permission to marry, provided he and his fiancée attend a "School for Marital Adjustment." After attending the school the couple are married, settle down in a house which they are allowed to purchase after going to a "School for Home Ownership Responsibilities," and decide they want to have children. They apply for permission to have babies and are put on a long waiting list, because there are the necessary controls on births to keep the population within manageable limits.

One of the controls is that every male child, at an early age, has a reversible vasectomy performed on him. Finally after waiting a few years the couple is told they may have *one* baby. But first, before the operation is performed on the husband to reverse the sterilization, the couple must attend a "School for Child Care." After attending the school the couple is permitted to have the baby. Six months after he is born the baby is placed in an "infant school," and the cycle begins all over again.

Meanwhile, the father finds that the job he has been performing is now obsolete. Back to the "job bank school" he must go to prepare for another position the experts predict will exist in a few years. Incidentally, all this time the young man, along with the rest of the adult population, is required to attend a "citizenship institute" as part of his employment, which keeps him up-to-date on current political issues so he can vote intelligently, which is now compulsory.

At the age of 40, our young man, no longer young, is required to attend a "geriatric preparation academy." There he learns how to get ready to "retire," which he must do at the age of 55. At 55 he leaves his job (the seventh one he has held and gone to "job bank schools" to prepare for), and enters a "geriatric learning center" where he is taught the arts and crafts which he is told will keep him "happy" and "out of mischief" until he dies.

When he does die, a minister eulogizes him over his grave. By the way, the minister has gone through a "higher school" and has been required to go back to the "higher school" every two years for refresher courses in order to keep his license to preach. The minister delivers a beautiful eulogy. He points out that this man was very lucky, for he was born in 1984, the first year that the national "Permanent School Law" was in effect. The minister extols the wisdom of the late President Spiro Agnew, who in the last year of his second term of office was able to get such a great law passed. "And so we bid goodbye to this lucky man," the minister chants, "firm in the conviction that he will go to heaven where he will attend a 'school for angels' into infinity."

4

Is Lifelong Adult Education a Guarantee of Permanent Inadequacy?

John Ohliger

Editors' note: This piece was published in 1974 in Conver-
gence, Volume 7, Number 2. An editorial note positioned
Ohliger as a participant, administrator, and professor in the
field of adult education in the United States and Canada
who had been practicing for more than twenty-five years.
The note mentioned that John had been an academic at The
Ohio State University, but he had moved on to become an
independent researcher and writer on the themes found in
this piece. John had presented a speech on these themes at an
international conference, "The Dangers of Permanent Adult
Education," which was held at the Center for Intercultural
Documentation in Cuernavaca, Mexico, during the summer
of 1974. These themes, which have contemporary relevance
to those who work in the nebulous fields of adult education
and lifelong learning, include the inadequacy of adult learners
in the face of continuous and compulsory adult education;
the problem of technological optimism and the crisis of tech-
nology as a crisis of education; the changing nature of higher
education, which is caught up in mass higher education; the
myth of the learning society; and the reduced emphasis on
the personal and the sociopolitical in increasingly mandated
forms of lifelong learning. John originally wrote this piece
with endnotes. Page numbers for particular quotes were not
always provided.

Off and on for five years I have discussed the general topic of this article with Bob Carlson, Associate Professor of Continuing Education, University of Saskatchewan. In a recent letter he did a better job of summarizing what follows than I could: "The speech will deal with your interpretation that adult education is becoming an oppressive force that's beginning to take over people's lives in North America. Into this thesis you will fit UNESCO's *Learning to Be* report, Illich, Freire, the Open University, and educational media as well. You'll also spend time on the dangers of compulsory adult education."

My title, however, comes from a conversation with a young couple, Jan and John, who were about to have a baby and were determined to have it at home whether they obtained a physician's help or not. When we talked about why they had made this decision, about health professionals and the compulsory adult education they are subject to, Jan commented, "If we are forced to go to school off and on all our lives, we'll feel inadequate all our lives" (see Ohliger, 1974a).

Schools, other educational institutions, and now more adult education institutions define people as inadequate, insufficient, lacking, incomplete. You don't know something so you have to go to school for the temporary relief of your inadequacies. Since there is more and more to know in these "technologically complex, crisis ridden days" you have, like it or not, to keep going back to school, whether in the classroom, in front of the computer terminal, or the television set. There is no need to quibble about whether it can only be called a school when there is a classroom. As David Gueulette (1972) has pointed out, the media controlled programs can actually be "super-schools."

The Widening Net

When I first pointed to the growing number of courses which adults were required to take by law, regulation, or pressure, I was told by my colleagues, "Don't waste your time! There's no trend toward compulsory adult education; this is a voluntary field. At the most you're premature, too early" (see Ohliger, 1968a). Now, with the trend glaringly obvious, those same colleagues say, "Don't waste your time! It's too late to stop it. Climb aboard the bandwagon and help make the required courses as good as possible."

Some of the groups now subject to mandatory continuing education in many parts of North America are: traffic offenders and judges; parents of delinquents and public school teachers; illiterates on welfare; nurses; pharmacists; physicians; optometrists; nursing home administrators; firemen; policemen; dentists; psychiatrists; dieticians; pediatrists; preachers; veterinarians; many municipal, state, provincial, and federal civil servants; employees of all types pressured into taking courses, classes, or joining sensitivity training or organizational development groups; and, of course, the military, where most, if not all adult education is compulsory (Ohliger & Rosenberg, 1973).

Is it any wonder that an official of the U.S. Office of Education recently predicted that the "middle-aged dropout may, within 20 years, find himself running from a truant officer" (Eugene Weldon, quoted in McCarthy, 1972). If some educators have their way, the slow tide may become a flood. An ultra-liberal friend of adult education, Dwight Allen, the Dean of the School of Education, University of Massachusetts, was recently asked on television, "Suppose now that state legislatures . . . say . . . that everybody is compelled to go to a state-approved night school once a week, including you, Dr. Allen. Are you in favor of that?" And Dean Allen replied, "If that's the best they can do, then I would rather be there than on my own and not advancing in terms of my human potential" (Allen, quoted in McGhee, 1972).

This attitude of a Dean of a prestigious college of education only carries to extremes the logic of schooling as developed by Comenius and the other founding fathers of our trade. Such a logical possibility may have been what led George Bernard Shaw to declare in 1918, "If the advance of education is to mean nothing more than the widening of the net of the child prison and boy farm until not one of us can escape it, we had better abolish it altogether" (Shaw, 1918). We have not reached the point yet where not one of us can escape it, but the net is certainly widening.

Perhaps surprisingly the net covers the health professions more than any other area at present. I thought it would smother the poor and unemployed before it swept over the healers. A bill proposed by President Nixon would have forced poor adults into compulsory education (Ohliger, 1970). But spending billions to keep poor people poor went out of style. Taking its place were billions to keep sick people sick, and with it mandatory continuing education to insure the inadequacy of the medicine men. These statements aren't as far fetched as they may sound. Most observers agree that throughout the world the gap between the poor and the rich is widening. As more dollars are poured into medical research and treatment, more illnesses are created by medicine itself. We even have a name for these diseases: "iatrogenic" (Illich, 1973a). And several studies show there is no evidence that continuing education improves health practice (Lewis & Hassanein, 1970).

Bob Blakely, former Vice-President of the Fund for Adult Education, has completed a study of continuing education in the health professions for the U.S. government. He concluded that mandatory courses waste what is very precious to us all—time. Thus the requirements actually do harm, *not* good (Blakely & Ohliger, 1972). In Canada, J. Roby Kidd (1973), the Secretary General of the International Council for Adult Education, says he has "some worries about . . . compulsory adult education" (personal correspondence). His Ontario colleague, Professor Alan Thomas (1970) writes: "By and large, men cannot be coerced into learning. They can be bullied and overpersuaded, but fear is a dangerous motive, and its main result is to create in the learner a loathing for the teacher, the subject, and the school. In fact, it cripples any further likelihood of learning."

However, the private enterprise and bureaucratic entrepreneurs aren't concerned about crippling learning as they package their "modules" into what Theodore Roszak (1972) calls "electronicizedindividualized-computerized-audio-visual-multi-instructional con-soles." Each element in that mouthful of a phrase represents many millions of dollars of investments, sales, and government purchases, and with each element goes the promise of a bright tomorrow if we will only get with the technological revolution. It's enticing, it's frightening, it's fun and dangerous, ego massaging and risky. It offers to fulfill our Walter Mitty dreams of power and glory while hurting only the bad, and at the same time it hits us with the spectre of be-coming the devil on earth destroying all that's good with our grubby mind-piercing tools, our slick radio and TV productions, our ma-chines turned into monsters before our eyes. Roszak lays it on the line when he says: "Technological optimism is the snake oil of urban industrialism. Each new application buys time, fast-shuffles the dis-senters, and rubs the addiction to artificiality, deeper into the col-lective psyche."

A Personal and a Social Dilemma

I think we all face a personal *and* a socio-political dilemma. For me, it goes something like this: I believe I have something to say. I am a person; I am present; I want to communicate with others and want them to communicate with me. I need them and I know they need me. But because I don't want to be controlled by others, I both do not want to control them and I do want to control them to keep them from running my life. On a more social level it goes like this: Education or communication is a tender, delicate, subtle, extremely elusive activity. Though learning or dialogue can lie unborn due to a lack of individual nurturing and personal care, it can much more easily be killed off by collective attention, institutionalized control, and instructional manipulation.

For years I advanced the listening group approach as a major po-litical move toward individual freedom and social justice only to see it turned by UNESCO and others into a tool of indoctrination in the name of "development" (Ohliger, 1966). I thought (perhaps naively) that as people attended to specially prepared radio or TV programs and then discussed them, the controversies that arose would help them to gain control over their destinies and to work toward a more human world. That didn't happen. Almost by definition, if such an activity fails it's because it was becoming successful. If it succeeds in stirring up controversy, effectively agitating thoughts, it is killed off. That seems to be one major reason for the death of the famed Canadian Radio Forum, for instance (Ohliger, 1968b).

About three years ago Colleen McCarthy and I (1971) made a series of proposals on behalf of personal dignity and popular power for opposing "all trends toward imbedding adult education further into the structure of the schooling establishment," and for "applying the hee-haw and then the heave-ho to the growing trend toward extending the compulsory principle to adult education."

We suggested "laughing out of the ballpark the drift toward the packaged treatment mode as seen in recent . . . proposals for an 'adult Sesame Street'." Now we find that the producers of Sesame Street, those old purveyors of the TV commercial as the learning unit, have got seven million dollars to prepare a 26-program series for adults aimed at "improving the level of their health" (Veatch, 1970). We also called for "applying well-deserved sarcasm at attempts to smother adults in certification mania as seen in moves [by] college administrators who would develop more 'adult degree' programs." Let's take a look at recent developments in "adult degrees," as they relate to the use of so-called educational media.

Opportunity and Openness

There should be no confusion about why colleges and universities are suddenly excited about "adult degrees," "external degrees," or "open learning." All observers, not just jaundiced radicals, agree that higher education is in deep financial difficulty. Enrolments are leveling off or declining, budgets are tighter, appropriations and gifts are getting harder to obtain, and the institutions are still looked at suspiciously by many citizens as hotbeds of dissent. What better way to get back on a firm dollar base and to smooth the ruffled feelings of the voters than to begin to appear to offer degrees to everyone in the name of equal opportunity?

In the world of grossly unequal distribution of wealth and power ruled by an economic élite, we need to be wary whenever that term "equal opportunity" is flashed. As the great British socialist adult educator, R. H. Tawney, said: "Equality of opportunity is a fraud . . . , the impertinent courtesy of an invitation offered to unwelcome guests, in the certainty that circumstances will prevent them from accepting it" (Terrill, 1973). And in the name of "equal opportunity," external degree programs are burgeoning. Where there were only a few in the 1960s, they now exist at hundreds of universities in the U.S.A. More are being planned every day (Houle, 1973).

The most recent development in the rise of open higher education is a national conference held in mid-January, 1974, at Lincoln, Nebraska. One of its announced goals was to "accelerate the use of technology to bring college courses to the wide variety of potential students." This first annual "National Conference on Open Learning in Higher Education" attracted about 400 participants from 42 states and four foreign countries. All the big shots were there. Observers told me that the conference combined all the high pressure atmosphere of a national sales convention of educational "hard" and "software" salesmen, with the hothouse aura of a national political convention—the big educational media associations were busy putting the arm on participants to get in line and support the national groups.

One of the few interesting papers was "The External Degree: Some Disquieting Ramifications" presented by Herbert Eisenstein (1974) of Penn State University who made a number of points that have been elaborated elsewhere. Though these programs are being touted by many as cost-savers, they may indeed be as expensive if not more expensive than others, especially when media and "start-up" costs are calculated. Adult educators may also lose out on other continuing education programs in universities as the external degrees take over. It is ironic that as educators push external degrees and other so-called "non-traditional" approaches as ways of gaining respectability and power, they may well find themselves subordinated to more sophisticated academic politicians who have better access to the commanding heights of the central administrations, the foundations, the computer terminals, and the government appropriation channels.

Eisenstein's most intriguing belief is that these external degree programs will attract and mentally castrate much of what's left of the disaffected young adult population in the United States. He writes: "The siphoning off of oppositional student talents from campuses throughout any State, and converting them into a shredding out external degree process of self-initiated joy through learning, is highly possible." This view is reinforced in *Change* magazine by Michael Miles (1973); [in] an avowedly leftist critique of external degrees, he notes: "The sale of freedom cannot be regarded as progressive education in any sense, but only as an avant-garde form of alienated education."

Although Eisenstein's paper received little attention, the British Open University was naturally prominent and several sessions were devoted to it. The flood of public relations material has been phenomenal, another example of the obscene language of technological optimism, couched in soft, modest English accents. This makes it difficult to trace the background of the O.U., but it seems to be essentially the outcome of adding the patina of English snob appeal to American developments like the Chicago TV College, with a few new twists thrown in. The O.U. was sold for a long time as a way of providing higher education to the "working classes" of England. After a few years of operation, even those favoring it admit that hasn't happened (Houle, 1973). In a recent interview the Vice-Chancellor said his institution offered "probably one of the most difficult ways of getting a degree yet devised by the wit of man" (Walton, 1973). He did not make this comment to establish the academic respectability of his fledgling college, but as proof that the O.U. is not part of a movement toward an "efficient, inhuman, frightening, Orwellian hell."

Others are not so sure. Two men very active in European adult education circles have expressed their concern over the centralization of control in the O.U., and elsewhere, that is made worse by the combination of media and academic administrative traditions in the name of mass education. They are Professor Ian Lister of York University in England and Professor Hermann Frese of Netherland's Leiden University. Frese has pointed to this and similar European developments in *éducation permanente* as ones which "will reinforce the established social order . . ., controlling and manipulating the destiny of whole populations." David Williams (1973, 1974) at Ohio State University has expressed similar concerns about "permanent education" and adult "career education" as well.

The "in" word for the ed biz media folks seems to be "open"—open learning, open universities, open systems. What we sometimes forget is that the jaws of the alligator and the mouth of the bottomless pit are also "open." There is little doubt that the term "open" as used by educational technocrats is an example of what Michael Marien's (1972) wife Mary Lou calls "edushit." It may all add up to what the great adult educator Eduard C. Lindeman (1926/1961) warned us against almost 50 years ago—"the Americanization of adult education."

The Faure Report

If it is bad to promote technocratic control via media in the false name of equal chances for one nation, it is even worse to propose it for the whole world, but that is the message of the report of UNESCO's International Commission on the Development of Education called *Learning to Be* (International Commission on the Development of Education, 1972). The senior professor of adult education at the University of Chicago, Dr. Cyril Houle, says it may well be the most significant book of the last third of this century. I am inclined to see it as just another example of international bureaucratese although in places the book has a haunting quality strangely akin to a tale of unrequited love.

Time after time the authors pose beautiful dialectic questions only to fall back under the spell of "science" or "technology" or even more alien terms such as "mathetic," "semeiology," "ergonomy" or "psychopedagogy." This loss of heart and nerve leads me to conclude that the authors confuse a dialectical approach with just pointing out opposites or apparent contradictions and then choosing one side over the other with some slight cosmetic modifications. This only compounds the confusion caused by the alternating courage and timidity of the report. For almost every quotation I might offer as proving that *Learning to Be* calls for a kind of worldwide friendly oppression, a supporter of the UNESCO commission could find a quotation indicating the opposite in *abstract* terms. But the concrete comments, and, even more, the omissions and assumptions, tell another story.

For example, perhaps the most significant part of this report is the letter of transmittal in the beginning of the book from the Chairman of the Commission, Edgar Faure, to UNESCO's Director General. They assumed at the start, says Faure, that lifelong education was necessary. Is it any news that after months of work they found enough evidence to decide they were right? It is, of course, no surprise that they, as agents of governments, explicitly assumed "the fundamental solidarity of governments and peoples." It's no surprise, but it's disappointing. We do have a right in these times of basic questioning to expect government agencies to at least consider the alternate possibility that there is a fundamental hostility between the rulers and the ruled.

The book suffers generally from the rigidity and extremism of the moderates, seen most often in gross excesses of prudence. Such defects may simply be evidence of coyness while the educators wait patiently, they think, to take over the reins of power if only behind the scenes like puppeteers. In 1967 John Kenneth Galbraith pointed out that education appeared to be on the way to greater power because economic leaders think it is more and more necessary to provide continuously trained manpower for "the new industrial state" in all its apparent spiraling technological complexity. Now *Learning to Be* finds that "education has become the world's biggest activity as far as overall spending is concerned." But in their educational chauvinism the authors want to see much more spent until we reach the nirvana of the "learning society," really a training society, ruled by educators.

If I must be oppressed, I don't want it to be by educators. Can you imagine what it would be like with educators, such as the authors of this report, running our lives in a "learning society"—especially when they are in league with the technocrats and the scientists? Here are just two examples:

"Contemporary science," says this report, "has made a singular contribution to our knowledge of man by showing that he is biologically unfinished. One might say that he never does become an adult, that his existence is an unending process of completion and learning." That is dangerous talk for educators to make while scientists are listening. Soon an enterprising biologist will produce through genetic manipulation a woman who will bring forth a truly complete human. It will only require a gestation period of 18 years instead of nine months. But this "new man" will be truly complete. He won't have to go through the educational process, which is the title of this book, *Learning to Be*.

It's just possible that we don't have to go through it. It is not unthinkable that at birth a person *is* and is capable of self-motivated and self-disciplined learning. Could it be that there really is no more pornographic question for a so-called child than "What do you want to be when you grow up?" The authors of this book would have us ask this question all our lives and engage in life-long or continual education as they define it.

Here is one of their definitions: "In contrast with traditional school forms of initial education, continual education is becoming a complex cybernetic system, based on a 'responsive-sensitive' situation comprising the following elements: a learner whose behavior may be evaluated and modified; a teacher, functionally speaking the educator; sources of structured knowledge, to be presented to the student or else explored by the student himself; an environment designed specifically for the learner to have access to necessary data; arrangements for evaluating and checking modified behavior, that is to say for recording reaction and the new behavior which it stimulates."

That jargon-filled paragraph contains some keys to understanding why the point of view represented by this book is so dangerous, not so much for what it is as for what it would drive out of human life. It would drive out an alternative conception of learning and knowledge that is absolutely essential to the existence of free human beings now and in a just society of the future. Ivan Illich has been trying to make this point for years.

The Balance of Learning

Illich says that there are at least two views of what learning or knowledge is that go far back in history: they can certainly be found in the Hebrew of the Old Testament (Salczer, 1972). From one point of view learning is "the penetration of naked reality." It is intimacy, intercourse, momentary unrepeatable activity. It is learning *as* experience, not *from* experience. One way of looking at it from this point of view is the expression, "He knew her in the Biblical sense." If true sexual love isn't knowledge *as* experience I don't know what it is. There is a second view of learning or knowledge as "the classification of information." This is what the quoted paragraph from *Learning to Be* describes as "structured knowledge." No one, least of all Illich (1973b), denies that this type of knowledge is important, but to overemphasize it is to destroy what he calls "the balance of learning."

Learning to Be refers to structured knowledge, modules of instruction, interchangeable blocks of information, and units of learning. Those concepts are precisely what Illich is talking about when he laments that all of knowledge is being reduced to a commodity, to what he labels "official knowledge" as opposed to "personal knowledge." "Personal knowledge," Illich (1971) writes, "is unpredictable and surprising with respect to both occurrence and outcome, whereas official knowledge must be anticipated and directed to measurable goals."

It should be obvious by now why some of us become angry when this book and authorities even closer to home speak of the great demands of the so-called "knowledge explosion." Or, as Professor Malcolm Knowles (1964) and others do, about the dangers of man becoming "obsolete." "Explosion" and "obsolescence" refer to "knowledge as a commodity." Such structured knowledge must never be permitted to drive out, as it is beginning to do, the spontaneous, random, chance, unplanned learning that is the great joy and sorrow of our human existence.

It is the possibility of expulsion from this natural garden of man into a technocratic Garden of Eden that concerns many of us. Perhaps because we are so concerned that at times we resort to extreme language about the world as a womb-to-tomb school or about an approaching apocalypse that turns you off. But at least grant us the possibility that such dangers exist. If we grant those of you who deny our point of view the opposite possibility, then perhaps we can begin to reduce our mutual paranoia. Perhaps we can also begin to deal with such ironies as this one: educators who call for "equal chances" for all promote an educational system calculated to kill off chance learning.

In the past, the field of adult education has been for many of us a haven where we could believe that spontaneous and voluntary learning was honored as the most important type of knowledge, although there is increasing historical evidence that the foundations of the present cruel trend were laid many years ago among various budding adult education institutions such as agricultural extension, university extension, and public adult schools (Carlson, 1970). We seem to be moving toward a society in which adults are increasingly told that they must consume "official knowledge" in lifelong education.

Is it any wonder that we say that adult education is becoming an oppressive force and taking over people's lives?

Whatever you think of Illich, try reading almost anything he or Paulo Freire has written with these views in mind. This is what Freire is referring to when he speaks of the "banking" or "depositing" chauvinism theory of knowledge (Hartung & Ohliger, 1972). It's also what J. Roby Kidd (1959) is talking about when he writes of the hole-in-the-head approach to learning.

True Adult Education

While Illich's ideas seem to strike more intellectual fires, Freire's work has attracted more attention from adult educators who are determined to engage in some kind of mutual endeavour to end the domination of oppressive economic, political, and now educational structures. Illich said of Freire's work in Brazil, "True adult education is more dangerous than training guerillas." It is true adult education that we should be practicing in perhaps one of three forms.

First, within standard brand institutions we need to resist, and to loosen, the economic and bureaucratic controls that stifle us all. We need to point out that those who pay lip-service to lifelong learning by proposing lifelong informal curricula are aiding those politicians who would conceal from us the facts of our lives by "making one thing perfectly clear," and are serving those professionals who hoard knowledge while pretending to "disseminate" it (Gross, 1973). Or we may even have to propose to our colleagues and students such slogans as: "Eat, drink, and be merry, for tomorrow you may have to take an inservice education class"; "The time has come to make the world safe from lifelong education"; and "Give me liberty or give me adult education."

Second, outside the establishment, or at its fringes, we need to work with individuals and groups who are moving toward an awareness of political and economic oppression and are acting against it. This is where Freire's approach can be helpful.

Finally, for some who react against "the political path," there is the cultural one that at first glance seems like withdrawal from society, but is not. It involves living/learning as individuals, in small groups, or new communities as examples of, or seeds for, a future society in which what is now called "less" will be recognized as "more." Here the ideas of Ivan Illich's American colleague, Everett Reimer (1971), would be worth attention by adult educators.

In all three of these paths we are making the same statement: We are *not* inadequate, insufficient, or inferior losers, although political, economic, and educational institutions so define us and their leaders try to convince us that we are impotent in the face of rapid change and must adapt to it. We are working perhaps in different ways for a radically new society, directed toward individual freedom without chaos and social justice, without meritocracy—and we are enjoying life as we pursue a humanistic revolution. Finally, we ponder the appropriateness of this line from a poem by Leonard Cohen:

> Every time you use the word "revolution,"
> It gets delayed by seven seconds

Bibliography and References

Blakely, R., & Ohliger, J. (1972). *Conversation on mandatory adult education*. Audio-cassette. Source: Ohliger.

Carlson, R. A. (1970, Winter). Americanization as an early twentieth-century adult movement. *History of Education Quarterly*.

Eisenstein, H. (1974). *The external degree: Some disquieting ramifications*. Paper delivered at the National Conference on Open Learning in Higher Education, Lincoln, NE.

Frese, H. (1970). *Permanent education in the Netherlands*. Strasbourg: Council of Europe. (ERIC Document Reproduction Service No. ED 042 971). See also: Frese, Hermann, "Permanent Education—Dream or Nightmare?" *Education and Culture*, Strasbourg (Summer, 1972). Williams, David C., "The Spectre of Permanent Schooling," Teachers College Record (September, 1974). Williams, David C., "The Impact of Career Education on Adult Education," *Mountain Plains Adult Education Journal* (Spring, 1973).

Galbraith, J. K. (1967). *The new industrial state*. Boston: Houghton Mifflin.

Gross, R. (1973, November 28). Impotence and possibility in continuing education. Presentation to Faculty of the School of Continuing Education, New York University.

Gueulette, D. (1972, September). Accent on social philosophy: Is there school after death? *Adult Leadership*.

Hartung, A., & Ohliger, J. (1972). Quotational bibliography of works by, or on, Paulo Freire. In S. Grabowski (Ed.), *Paulo Freire: A revolutionary dilemma for the adult educator*. Syracuse, NY: Syracuse University Publications in Continuing Education. (ED 068 819)

Houle, C. O. (1973). *The external degree*. San Francisco: Jossey-Bass.

Illich, I. (1971). The breakdown of schools: A problem or a symptom? *Interchange, 2*(4).

Illich, I. (1973a, March/April). Two watersheds: The American public health system. *Social Policy*.

Illich, I. (1973b). *Tools for conviviality*. New York: Harper and Row.

International Commission on the Development of Education. (1972). *Learning to be: The world of education today and tomorrow*. Paris: UNESCO, and London: Harrap.

Kidd, J. R. (1959). *How adults learn*. New York: Association Press.

Kidd, J. R. (1973). Letter to John Ohliger, January 16th.

Knowles, M. (1964). *Growing time: Selected papers from the Michigan State Leadership Seminars*. (ERIC Document Reproduction Service No. ED 031 662)

Lewis, C. E., & Hassanein, R. S. (1970, January). Continuing medical education—An epidemiologic evaluation. *New England Journal of Medicine*.

Lindeman, E. C. (1926/1961). *The meaning of adult education*. Montreal: Harvest House.

Marien, M. (1972). *Beyond the Carnegie Commission*. Syracuse, NY: Syracuse University Research Corporation.

McCarthy, C. (1972). Dissertation proposal on compulsory adult education. Source: Ohliger.

McGhee, P. (Ed.). (1972). Would our kids get a better education if the law didn't force them to go to school? *The advocates*. Boston, MA: WGBH Educational Foundation.

Miles, M. (1973, September). Second thoughts on the external degree. *Change*.

National Conference on Open Learning in Higher Education. (1974). For further information write to Richard L. Spence, Information Coordinator, Great Plains National ITV Library, Box 80669, Lincoln, NE, 68501.

Ohliger, J. (1966). *The listening group in adult education*. Doctoral dissertation, UCLA, Los Angeles, CA.

Ohliger, J. (1968a, September). Accent on social philosophy: Lifelong learning—voluntary or compulsory? *Adult Leadership*.

Ohliger, J. (1968b, Spring). What happened to the Canadian farm radio forum? *Adult Education*.

Ohliger, J. (1970, February). Accent on social philosophy: Dialogue with myself. *Adult Leadership*. (ERIC Document Reproduction Service No. EJ 015 599)

Ohliger, J. (1974a, July–August). Some thoughts on nursing inservice education. *Journal of Continuing Education in Nursing*.

Ohliger, J. (1974b, April). *Bibliography of comments on the Illich-Reimer deschooling theses—or—"Your problem with Illich, Harold, is that you don't understand the Goddam revolutionary mind."* Washington, DC: ERIC Clearinghouse on Teacher Education.

Ohliger, J., & McCarthy, C. (1971). *Lifelong learning or lifelong schooling? A tentative view of the ideas of Ivan Illich with a quotational bibliography.* Syracuse, NY: Syracuse University Publications in Continuing Education. (ERIC Document Reproduction Service No. ED 049 398)

Ohliger, J., & Rosenberg, J. (1973). *Compulsory adult education: A preliminary bibliography.* Columbus: Ohio State University, Center for Adult Education. (ERIC Document Reproduction Service No. ED 079 572)

Reimer, E. (1971). *School is dead.* Garden City, NY: Doubleday.

Roszak, T. (1972). *Where the wasteland ends: Politics and transcendence in postindustrial society.* Garden City, NY: Doubleday.

Salczer, D. (1972, March). *The meaning of the Hebrew verb yada.* Source of paper: Ohliger.

Shaw, G. B. (1918). Introduction. In *Yearbook of the Workers' Educational Association*. London: Workers' Educational Association.

Terrill, R. (1973). *R. H. Tawney and his times: Socialism as fellowship.* Cambridge, MA: Harvard University Press.

Thomas, A. M. (1970). *A brief on the concept of continuing education.* (ERIC Document Reproduction Service No. ED 045 902)

Veatch, J. (1970, April). Review of Sesame Street. *Educational Broadcasting Review*.

Walton, E. (1973, September). Outlook—No. 3: Walter Perry, Vice-Chancellor of the Open University. *Educational Broadcasting International*.

Williams, D. C. (1973, Spring). The impact of career education on adult education. *Mountain Plains Adult Education Journal*.

Williams, D. C. (1974, September). The spectre of permanent schooling. *Teachers College Record*.

5

The Social Uses of Theorizing
in Adult Education

John Ohliger

*Editors' note: This chapter was previously published
in 1980 in* Adult Education, *Volume 31, Issue 1,
pp. 48–53. John Ohliger wrote this journal article as
director of Basic Choices, Inc.: A Midwest Center
for Clarifying Political and Social Options. John notes
that David Lisman, Arthur Lloyd, and Vern Visick
assisted him with this piece. This journal article has
contemporary relevance to those who critique the
knowledge society and the information revolution.
John critiques forms of adult education that reduce
knowledge building to information gathering that does
not promote critical thinking. He calls for forms of
social theorizing that help to shape adult learning as a
collective endeavor where didactic learning is replaced
by self-directed learning as a process of discovery.*

When professionals in a field begin to inquire about the social
conditions for developing theory, it can be both a sign of
a historical crisis and of maturity. A great deal of confusion can
arise from such basic questioning, but extremely fertile and creative
periods can result as well. In this paper we attempt to examine some
of the factors in the social and historical context that influence theory
making.

We are not attempting to survey adult education theorists, but rather to consider some of the significant factors that affect theory making in this field. We suggest that the context for viewing adult education today should be nothing less than education generally in the setting of an advanced high technology society characterized externally by the expansion of multi-national corporations, and internally by the increasing integration of government, industry, and education.

No one would disagree that adult education should be seen against the background of an understanding of the kind of society in which we live. However, there are significant disagreements over how our society should be described and over what our response should be to that description. Generally speaking, present theory in adult education either (1) tries to develop a non-ideological, all-purpose approach separate from the historical context; or (2) accepts the contemporary context as a given that adult educators should help people adjust to, prosper within or ameliorate problems of; or (3) rejects the present context as inhuman and attempts to encourage others to rebel against it. All of these present views, we think, show a lack of critical distance from our society and its ambiguities.

Adult education as we know it is a product of industrial society which made mass education at once possible and necessary. Historically, adult education has taken various forms. In an earlier stage of industrial development, adult education included a combination of technical training for workers and a variety of programs to enrich culturally deprived farmers and workers. More recently, adult education has included such phenomena as vocational and professional continuing education. When engaged in the task of developing theory, adult educators can not escape the impact of industrial society on education.

Our society can be understood in terms of two predominant foci, technical development and the social means by which this development is controlled and directed. By technical development we mean the tools and techniques by which humans attempt to manipulate nature and organize human society. Technical development is employed in the attempt to bring efficient organization to a highly specialized work force and productive system and to provide a vast network of social services. It is the proliferation of these tools and their support systems that lies at the root of the differences between our society and earlier Western societies. These differences have great implications for education.

For example, if life in modern society is defined in technological terms, and techniques appear to be constantly changing and developing, education will be swept up in the same vortex of change and development. Furthermore, if the corporate, government, and professional institutions created to produce and control these techniques grow apace and if access to the fruits of technology is gained only through these organizations, education inevitably becomes almost totally dependent upon this process. We see these forces operating in the increasing requirements for technical education tied to a specialized job market.

The growing dependence upon a technological capitalistic system has created a crisis for liberal education with which many leaders in adult education are familiar. This crisis became evident during the campus turmoil of the sixties. We recall the considerable literature of that period pointing to the fact that rather than serving the liberal purposes of enlightening and humanizing its students, higher education was in truth serving the interests of what was characterized as the military-industrial complex. Needless to say, this has put professors of adult education, for example, in a dilemma, on the one hand still espousing a need for liberal education and on the other hand serving the interests of the economic system.

As a response to the general crisis of liberalism, we see emerging a form of technocratic liberalism which has been especially prevalent in the natural sciences, the social sciences and engineering. Technocratic liberalism retains unbounded confidence in the liberal idea of transforming society through education, but now in place of ideals and values as the means of transformation it substitutes a reliance on the methods of the natural sciences and the latest innovations in technology.

Most adult education literature follows the mainstream view that American society is a basically strong and healthy one—its problems may be complex but are technically solvable. In this view the need for equal opportunities for minorities, for example, can be met by increasing access to adult classes employing the latest and best techniques, including unilateral needs assessments. Literacy is viewed as a technical problem, to be solved by adult basic educational methods rather than as a symptom pointing to the need for fundamental social change. Thus it is not surprising that much theory in adult education views maturity as technical competence and sees adult education's role as helping people to fit into technical systems of development and control.

Among technocratic liberals there is little cynicism about the dependence of education on the dominant economic system because there is a rather uncritical faith that the economic system itself is dependent upon still greater technological forces that human beings and their institutions can shape if only they can master the requisite knowledge.

For adult education, this view is further reflected in the practical effort to service whatever the social order requires. For example, the legitimate understanding of adult education as self-initiated lifelong learning is being converted into the concept of lifelong schooling. Combined with the processes of credentialling and licensing, this trend, with the support of many adult educators, is reinforced by the increasing demand for mandatory continuing education (Lisman & Ohliger, 1978).

Theory Making

Theory making in adult education is frequently influenced by the social sciences. Social sciences attempt to appropriate from the natural sciences a high degree of precision, a reliance on quantification and on models of explanation. In effect they use the language and concepts of the physical and natural sciences as appropriate to the human sciences. In adult education such influences are seen, for example, in the proliferation of demographic surveys, the dependence on structural-functional sociology, and the increasing appeal of behavioral objectives. As Christopher Lasch has observed, the social sciences have appropriated as evidence of social determinism the fact that people are controlled by certain economic realities. Such economic realities are not reducible to the realities of physics; rather they point to disturbing features of political and economic life (Lasch, 1977).

In theory making, technocratic liberalism often uncritically accepts such slogans as "the knowledge explosion." (By knowledge explosion we refer to the view that knowledge includes an unbounded proliferation of valuable data and information and the accelerating expansion of quantifiable facts.) But in our view this concept contributes to the notion that people in such a complex society are permanently inadequate, that is, they need adult education programs. Furthermore, such a concept in adult education does not encourage critical thinking. The concepts of wisdom and learning are converted into knowledge as information gathering, increasingly conceived not as a process of self-initiated discovery in conjunction with other learners, but as the transfer of information from technical experts (adult educators) to learners viewed as rather passive receptacles for such information.

In contrast to various liberal approaches, one response to the crisis of liberal education has been the rejection of the whole system. Few adult educators would explicitly place themselves in this category. Perhaps some who would locate themselves in what used to be called the counterculture and a few others, disillusioned by constant failures at meaningful reform, would raise the banner "resist the state." This rejection of the system is, in our view, a form of reductionism. It is seen in the exclusive preoccupation with development of "positive" approaches without regard for the necessity of dealing politically with the "negative" aspects of the present society or in the exclusive preoccupation with opposing such "negative" aspects. Compulsory adult education under any social conditions is thus dogmatically opposed. Free learning centers, learning exchanges and free universities, to mention but a few of the nontraditional approaches, have sometimes arisen out of a simple rejection of standard educational systems with their overemphasis on credentials and certificates. Although these nontraditional approaches have genuine educational value and may pioneer innovative educational reforms, standard brand adult education continues to prevail. But those who hope to see educational and other more basic social change need to encourage dialogue between the traditional and nontraditional groups.

If academic adult education overlooks the manner in which its "clients" are structured by the socio-economic order, then advocates of some of the radical alternatives are sometimes guilty of believing that by fostering education as an institution less dependent on that order, people can thereby be liberated from the effects of that order. But the fact remains that so long as people must earn their livelihood in this society, regardless of what kind of exotic education they may seek, they are still subject to many of the same kinds of pressures and conditioning that force adults back to school for certification, lead them to the endless pursuit of courses in self improvement, and support their continued dependence on specialists. Like a specter over the cultural horizon, the pervasive technological and economic order clouds even the most Utopian aspirations for education.

Why indeed do we want to develop theories of adult education, anyway? Good theory helps clarify and give coherence to our perspectives on the purposes and functions of adult education in its institutional manifestations. Theory helps facilitate communication and understanding among educators and others concerned about adult learning. Theory helps illuminate the shape and scope of adult education. It promotes better understanding of the activities in which adult educators are engaged, in order to influence the direction that adult educators, their publics, and the broader society take. Theory suggests means of testing such questions as the optimal conditions under which adults learn, what subject matters they learn best, and how to convey various kinds of necessary information. Finally, and perhaps this reason should be scrutinized more critically, theory serves to legitimate adult education in order for adult educators to gain the respect of allied colleagues and groups and to obtain funding to establish the field as a unique one in its own right.

In the pursuit of theory, adult educators, instead of ignoring or succumbing to the crisis of liberal education, could better recognize that they do indeed have important contributions to make. Adult educators are in a position to help adults respond to or cope with the society in which they live by raising questions about its present directions and future possibilities.

Unfortunately, in their search for legitimacy, many adult educators translate their desire to do a good "professional" job all too easily into the desire to make their clients into professionals, that is, to help adults acquire the credentials to "make it" in the system or to fulfill the institutional requirements of society. Adult educators will gain greater legitimacy, we believe, by working with adults than from promoting the educator's own self-interest or the interest of the institutions they represent. Working as equals with other adults to understand better the social and political context in which, for instance, skills are developed and employed will, we believe, in the long run have greater benefits for adults than merely helping them to acquire skills. The overemphasis on acquiring skills, in our view, reduces adult education to vocational training.

Also, we believe adult educators have an opportunity, perhaps not shared as readily by other academics, to influence the society at large. This is especially evident when dealing with groups seeking adult education. As groups seek guidance, for example, on how to deal with community problems, adult educators are in a position not only to help them deal with their social problems, but also to work with them to change their basic situation. Along with other organizations, Basic Choices, Inc., has begun to experiment with this approach in the attempt to help groups to better understand and respond to the social context in which they live.

Turning more specifically to the academic and professional context, we believe that adult educators will find it in their long range self-interest to confront that context as it exists today. To cite one example, some of us have been involved in trying to understand the underlying causes and institutional aspects of the development of compulsory adult education in the health sciences and other areas where further schooling is becoming necessary for certification and relicensing. In the short run it may appear that it is in the economic and professional interest of adult educators to encourage trends toward mandatory education. After all, will it not provide more jobs and greater security for adult educators and increase the competence of those receiving such training? However, many adult educators and professionals in allied fields are beginning to have second thoughts. They are coming to realize that, along with government and business elites, the leaders of the professional organizations mandating such education for credentials are the very ones who control the whole process and who ultimately will be its major beneficiaries.

Another area of concern to adult educators as they seek to develop theory is a trend which might be called the imperialism of the established academic disciplines. In their search for new markets, that is, their need for more students, these disciplines are increasingly moving into university extension programs. To the extent that these disciplines gain control over such programs it is only reasonable to suppose that these academics will treat adult education programs as mere extensions of the approach taken to undergraduate or graduate education, that is to service the adults in much the same way as younger students, especially as it relates to credentialling. Where does this leave the adult educators who emphasize the unique characteristics and needs of chronologically mature persons?

We insist that one of these unique characteristics is the manner in which the adult is part of the social context. By attempting to understand this reality, while striving to develop educational programs which help adults lead more productive lives and to challenge the oppressive conditions that make our human environment alien to us, adult educators stake out a more powerful claim to legitimacy than when they merely promote the development of administrative competency in educational programming. We thus have the opportunity to truly contribute to the growth of adult education in its most meaningful sense—in the search for authentic adulthood for all. Moreover, in the face of the very real crisis of liberalism, adult educators may have a significant role to play in promoting change toward a more humanizing and democratic way of life.

In conclusion, it is clear that once the task is begun of facing the social-historical context, adult educators developing theory need further to penetrate to the basic questions concerning this context. We should continually ask such questions as: Is the technical definition of adulthood adequate to a healthy concept of human maturity? If not, what can and should be done about developing more comprehensive definitions? Is the immersion of the person in ever more complex specialization, hierarchical organization, and the drive toward domination helpful or harmful in working toward some sort of a more fully human society? If it is harmful, can adult educators join with others in working to reduce or eliminate such immersion? Given the present level of technical development, are the unrestrained global expansion of multi-national corporations and the increasing national integration of government, industry, and education adequate larger goals for society? Can they provide the means for restoring technology, knowledge and education to the people whose interests they presumably exist to serve? If not, how might better goals be realized, socially as well as educationally?

References

Lasch, C. (1977). *Haven in a heartless world: The family besieged.* New York: Basic Books.

Lisman, D., & Ohliger, J. (1978). Must we all go back to school? The pitfalls of compulsory adult education. *The Progressive, 42*(10), 35–37.

Lifelong Learning as Nightmare

John Ohliger

Editors' note: This piece originally appeared in 1978 in the first issue of Second Thoughts, *the newsletter published by John's center, Basic Choices, which was set up to advance radical social education for adults. This version was reprinted in Ronald Gross's edited text,* Invitation to Lifelong Learning *(Chicago: Follett Publishing, 1982). In stating principles that undergirded the center's articulation of radical social education, John and his Basic Choices associates challenged adult educators to question their roles and the social purposes of adult education amid the move to increasingly mandated or involuntary forms of continuing education.*

The most provocative issue in the field of adult education for the last five years has been mandatory continuing education. Should adults be pressured to participate in learning experiences, whether through social or economic pressure, certification require-ments, or legal coercion?

Many adult educators have embraced the trend. "It seems that we are pathetically pleased to be wanted, to be recognized even for the wrong reasons," comments Roby Kidd, "and we have been quick to see that in the short run there may be money to be made by of-fering programs to people who are legally compelled to attend."

But a growing countermovement within the field has been led by John Ohliger, a veteran adult education philosopher working out of Basic Choices, a think tank in Madison, Wisconsin. "Millions of adults are currently being compelled to go back to school by a burgeoning jungle of laws, regulations and social edicts," Ohliger asserts. "If those who are pushing this trend have their way, it will proliferate until all Americans find themselves forced to enroll in courses all their lives. Already some distinguished leaders in adult education and powerful interest groups like the American Federation of Teachers are advocating policies leading to this direction. Unless something is done to counter the trend, the child born in the United States in the year 1984 will never look forward to getting out of school. From the 'parent-infant development center' which she starts attending at the age of two months with her mother, to the 'geriatric learning center' in which she dies, she will find herself going to school all her life 'for the good of society.'"

The struggle continues, and each of us in the field is confronted with this inevitable question in our program planning and in our thinking: Which side am I on?

Voluntary Learning and Living for a Free Society

A proclamation put forth for comment and commitment by a group of adult educators convened by Basic Choices:

We are a group of adult educators and others who try to put the following beliefs into practice in our daily lives:

- The primacy of voluntary learning.
- The basic value of free and open discussion intimately integrating thoughts and feelings, reflection and action.
- Working together toward a just society with more democratic control and mutual self-reliance, and less hierarchy, bureaucracy, and external authority.
- Working together toward a world with the best possible balance between maximum free learning and minimum

instruction, with a significant place for activities not publicly defined as job-related *or* as learning.

We are encouraged by the activities of many striving to move the world toward these shared beliefs, but we are concerned about certain trends in other directions:

- Adult education is increasingly becoming compulsory by law or social pressure, accompanied by a drive for more certification, credentialing, and professionalization. These trends are burgeoning within political and economic structures dominated by a small minority. Within this framework, knowledge is defined as worthwhile only if it is technical or scientific. Professional elites are increasingly securing monopoly control over access to this knowledge and its development.

- More time and money is being spent on adult education in the name of lifelong learning. Yet these efforts are presently paying off in less economic benefits for most people, less valuable learning, and a decreasing ability to lead the good life.

- Greater specialization and fragmentation of work continue while increasingly complex technical development is encouraged in the name of greater personal control over our daily lives. In the face of these trends it becomes clear that we need instead to encourage greater *general* questioning and an examination of the whole and *not* just the specialized parts. We need to control technology and other forces supporting it to foster a better life and to remove some of the growing and unnecessary constraints on our liberties.

To work toward the durable better society which we seek and to counteract these trends we therefore propose to join together, and invite others to join us in these activities:

- Research on the extent of these trends and the structural basis for their growth through new forms of critical analysis, examining especially the links between the political, economic, technological, and cultural dimensions.

- To search for, encourage, and work with positive alternatives for human learning at every level: individual, friendship, family, neighborhood, institutional, local, state, national, and international.

- To engage in collective political action and work with others. This action should include raising basic issues for public discussion in these and other contexts:

  1. Opposing laws and pressures for mandatory continuing education in general, and certification, credentialing, and professionalization in adult education.

  2. At the same time working toward true public accountability and the growth of genuine personal and social competence.

7

Forum: You Shall Know the Truth and the Truth Shall Make You Laugh

John Ohliger

Editors' note: John composed this forum, drawing on talks he had given in various forms to the Northern Illinois University doctoral program for community college administrators, De Kalb, Illinois, August 1990; the Abraham Lincoln Unitarian Universalist Fellowship, Springfield, Illinois, August 1990; the Prairie Unitarian Universalist Fellowship, Madison, Wisconsin, April 1989; and the California State University, Northridge, California, February 1989. It was published in 1990 in the Journal of Adult Education, Volume 19, Number 1. *John's central message in the forum is that fundamental change is needed in approaches to knowledge building and learning in mainstream adult education. This message has contemporary value as we think about the parameters of adult education today. In the forum, John provides a critique of technological progress, suggesting that the upshot of this progress has been increasingly mandated learning to acquire the credentials necessary for the changing occupations emerging as a consequence of this progress. The article has contemporary relevance to those interested in exploring ethics in the modern practice of adult education amid technological progress and efforts to hone the field to comply with economic agendas to the detriment of meeting social and cultural needs.*

If this were a regular sermon in a conventional church, to set the tone it might be preceded by a brief reading from the Bible. I have a reading; it's not from the Bible, but it's from a recent bestselling novel that draws heavily on Biblical themes. The book sold over two million copies and became the major motion picture *The Name of the Rose*. Here's our reading:

"Perhaps the mission of those who love humankind is to make people laugh at the truth, *to make truth laugh*, because the only truth lies in learning to free ourselves from insane passion for truth" (Eco, 1984).

I'm going to contend this morning that we need a fundamental change in our uncritically worshipful attitude toward truth, knowledge, and information as well as toward the education, schools, universities, teaching, and learning that support them.

There's no way that I can prove this contention to you scientifically. Science—or scientism—is part of the problem. But I can quote a prominent scientist, the quantum physicist David Bohm, who states, "Our civilization is collapsing because of too much knowledge" (Krishnamurti & Bohm, 1985; Ohliger, 1987a).

Nor will I be able to convert you to my viewpoint from standard scholarly or educational sources. These sources are caught up in trying to keep up with what they call the "knowledge explosion" or the "information revolution." But I can quote the prominent educational scholar Brian Winston. Winston is the Dean of the School of Communication at Penn State University, who declares: "The information revolution is an illusion, an expression of profound ignorance. The hectic visions of the information revolutionaries have nothing to sustain them but the outpourings of industrial public relations officers or the jeremiads of discombobulated social observers" (Winston, 1986; Ohliger, 1987c). Quite a mouthful.

If you're more taken, as I am, with literature and arts, I won't be able to convince you from a conventional aesthetic point of view either. The leading arts and humanities are firmly enmeshed in belief in the almighty value of knowledge and schooling. But I can quote the current Poet Laureate of the United States, Howard Nemerov, who says this in a poem, addressed to his young son:

> I don't know what you will do with the mean annual
>   rainfall
> Or Plato's REPUBLIC, or the calorie content
> Of the Diet of Worms, such things are said to be
> Good for you, and you will have to learn them
> In order to become one of the grown-ups
> Who sees invisible things neither steadily nor whole,
> But keeps gravely the grand confusion of the world
> Under his hat, which is where it belongs,
> And teaches small children to do this in their turn.
> (Nemerov, 1962)

This 25-minute talk is a distillation of thoughts from the minds of a lot of people (including my own mind). It's a tapestry of views about the need for fundamental change in our approaches to knowledge and education. Some of the ideas from other minds I really don't claim to completely understand and some of the assertions that I'll make I can't completely account for. But these ideas and the assertions are put forward to encourage your exploration of some crucial questions. What are the crucial questions? In my view there are at least three of them:

First, how do we know and what do we do with that knowledge?

Second, how do we spend money for what is sometimes called knowledge production and transmission?

And third, what are our overall educational goals, our philosophy, purpose, ethics, morality?

Three little questions.

Albert Einstein said, "Whoever undertakes to set himself up as a judge of Truth and Knowledge is shipwrecked by the laughter of the gods" (Scott, 1955). We'll deal in more detail later with the laughter of the gods *and* with the laughter of human beings, but Einstein's view leads us right into question number one:

1. How do we know and what do we do with that knowledge? As scarce as truth is, the supply is always in excess of the demand. That was said by the 19th century American humorist Josh Billings (Billings, 1865). But just take a look at this invaded land since Columbus and the Puritans came to these shores (McGinn, 1979; Nisbet, 1987). From Europe they brought with them the germs of the total belief in judging truth and knowledge on straightforward rationality, falsely narrowed to logic and science (Weizenbaum, 1976). That remains our current way of judging knowledge, and gods laugh. The *many* paths to truth are reduced to one. If you don't believe me, consider what a teacher's reaction would be if a student footnoted a paper saying, "My mother told me that" or "I had a dream last night that revealed this truth to me" (Jackson, 1987; McKnight, 1988). Descartes had a dream in 1619. And that led to much of the basis for today's high technology. But Descartes was very careful not to announce his dream-inspired revelation as a footnote on a term paper (Davis & Hersh, 1986; Maritain, 1944).

We have narrowed knowledge to facts. But a fact is like a cat. You look a cat straight in the eye and it turns away. And so facts elude our hard stare (Marchand, 1989). But we use facts to build a learning society, proclaiming that "learning never ends" (Ohliger, 1981). We climb the shaky ladder of "factual" statistics and polls. As more and more facts pile up we say they explode—a knowledge explosion propelling us into the information age (Ohliger, 1986a; Roszak, 1986). Have we come through the knowledge explosion without a scratch? The very noise of the explosion during the past two centuries has deafened us to such basic questions as these: Why all this technology? To what ends? Within what priorities? Under what controls? With what consequences? With what effects on human beings? Instead of asking these basic questions, we have been taking so-called "technological progress" as a given, passively acquiescing in its demands and adjusting ourselves to it (Sibley, 1971).

We decide that the cure for the inevitable problems of technology is more technology. But the problems keep mounting. There are—for instance—The Exxon Oil Spill ("Greed and Neglect Set Course Toward Disastrous Oil Spill," 1989), Chernobyl, Challenger, the greenhouse effect (McKibben, 1989), the devastation of the forests, Bhopal, miscarriages from VDTs, and computer viruses. These are just a few examples of the underside of high-tech.

Joseph Weizenbaum at the Massachusetts Institute of Technology was once called "The High Priest of Artificial Intelligence." But now he's labeled "The Turncoat of the Computer Revolution." He states: "We cannot recover (from technological intoxication) without the help of a miracle. By a miracle," Weizenbaum concludes, "I don't mean bread falling out of the sky. I mean the sort of thing that happened when Rosa Parks refused to leave the front of the bus in Alabama and ignited the civil-rights movement" (Long, 1985; Rosenthal, 1983).

That miracle should help us recover from the misguided notions of the "knowledge explosion" and the "information revolution"? They are misguided because the sheer quantity of data available has very little to do with our ability to think wisely or act effectively (Jackson, 1987; Ohliger, 1986b; Winner, 1986). I keep telling myself that's true as I read more and more books and gather more and more information.

II. The second question in education concerns how we spend our money for it and the scale we spend it on. To put it bluntly, we are confronting a mass superstition. Since early in the 20th century we have been swept away on a flood-tide of public policy and popular sentiment into an expansion of schooling that is grossly wasteful of wealth and effort and does positive damage to those enmeshed in it (Goodman, 1964).

Schooling of all types is rapidly emerging as the third reservoir for absorbing unemployment right after the military and the bureaucracy. The army of teachers and administrators increases daily. Time in school or training programs gets longer and longer as requirements grow for more qualifications and credentials in occupations and other aspects of social life. Thus, education hides massive unemployment and many other intractable social problems as well (Kohr, 1978).

But schooling *for youth* is only a relatively small part of the problem. Over half the *adult* population is now required to go back to school to keep jobs or professional licenses, to get promoted, to stay out of jail, to stay on the welfare rolls, to stay in this country, or to remedy some other "defect." This forced adult schooling is what Ivan Illich calls "the final solution to learning opportunities" (Illich, 1983; Ohliger, 1983).

Adult education—and that's my field—is the invisible sleeping giant of American society. More money and personnel are devoted to it than to all other areas of education combined—elementary, secondary, and higher (Bowsher, 1989; Ohliger, 1983). One area alone, of the hundreds in adult education—corporate training—involves as many dollars—over 60 billion of them—as are spent on all the instruction in America's colleges and universities every year (Eurich, 1985). Besides the immense military training, there's the General Motors of adult education, the United States Agricultural Extension Service (Power, 1987). And now, in what's been touted as the 20th "Century's Biggest Adult Education Effort," a half billion dollars has recently been appropriated by Congress compelling a million so-called "undocumented aliens" to take citizenship classes (Draves, 1989).

Even when attendance is not compulsory, there's a frenzy about getting involved in adult education activities that is so well illustrated by the many conferences and workshops that elicit the complaint of "seminar stiffness" from characters in Lily Tomlin's wonderful comedy *The Search for Signs of Intelligent Life in the Universe* (Ohliger, 1986c; Wagner, 1986).

We're rapidly moving in the direction of forcing everyone to lead a life spent in the never-ending pursuit of learning. But if learning never ends, does living ever begin? When would there be time for doing, feeling, and just being? (Ohliger, 1981).

What we're faced with today is a superstitious belief in education as the panacea for all our ills (Blumberg, 1989). But *none*—none of these education programs are solving the social ills for which they've been prescribed. The tough question is: Why do we have this pervasive superstition? And the even tougher question: Can we find ways of getting beyond this harmful belief that will be equalitarian, democratic, and spiritually honorable (Ohliger, 1989b)?

The great Lewis Mumford said: "If anything can arrest the total disintegration of world civilization today it will come through a miracle: the recovery of 'the human scale'" (Sale, 1980).

III. Now on to the third and last crucial question in education. It relates to our overall goals, our philosophy, our purpose, our ethics, our morality. Here we see the *fundamental* crisis: The lack of a coherent set of goals, the absence of an over-arching philosophy that would lead to ethics or morality worthy of being called ethics or morality. The appropriate note for the present was set in the past century and a half, and it converges from such disparate viewpoints as those of Carlyle, John Stuart Mill, Matthew Arnold, and the Marxist Antonio Gramsci (Joll, 1978). Arnold (Allott & Super, 1986) expressed their consensus when he declared we are:

> wandering between two worlds, one dead,
> the other powerless to be born.

Though in this view there is a crisis in every field of human endeavor, our charge here is to focus on education and knowledge. The root meaning of "knowledge" is often misunderstood. "Knowledge" is generally accepted as the equivalent of enlightenment acquired in connection with reading. But the word, in its old form, "know-leche," was in common use long before books were accessible. "Know-leche" implies a grace received, the gift of knowing. The second syllable, "leche," is a form of the Anglo-Saxon "lac," a gift. It's also seen in the word "wed-lock."

If knowledge is a gift then—like all such blessings—there's a natural but immeasurable limit to the gifts each person or group appropriately receives. That it isn't always wise to pursue knowledge is touched on in a few places in Western literature. In the Bible, in Ecclesiastes for instance, it says, "He that increases knowledge increases sorrow." And in the Acts of the Apostles we find, "Much learning doth make thee mad." Shakespeare wrote in *Love's Labour's Lost*, "Too much to know is know naught but fame." And our own President Teddy Roosevelt said, "A man who has never gone to school may steal from a freight car; but if he has a university education, he may steal the whole railroad."

Questioning the value of continually pursuing knowledge is much more common in the East. Just one example: In the legendary ancient work of the 5th century B.C. Chinese philosopher, Lao Tzu. His *Tao Teh Ching* has been translated more times than any other work except the Bible and is the second biggest seller in the world next to the Bible. This is one of Lao Tzu's passages:

> Happy the land that is ordered so
> That people understand more than they know.
> (Ohliger, 1984)

In other words, "knowledge without being is dangerous" (Freeman, 1990).

I believe we are in the dangerous position today of having too much knowledge but insufficient social being. And no—*no* educational program is going to solve *that* problem. The dilemma is to find a better approach, one that's more modest and more natural. But that better approach, I believe, can only be found within the context of a better overall path.

IV. What is to be done? So now we're faced with what used to be called the sixty-four thousand dollar question. What is to be done? What should you do? It would be presumptuous, arrogant, and just plain stupid of me to suggest what I think you should do. Especially since I don't know. But I can conclude with a few thoughts about what I'm finding helpful these days. And I hope that these ideas will stimulate some good discussion afterwards (Rosenthal, 1983).

First, is the problem of the constant and insistent demand that whatever suggestions are made, they must be instantly "practical"—like instant coffee. I'm *not* suggesting a retreat into the ivory tower or the monastery, but the narrow emphasis on practicality is itself impractical. Just witness the current dire straits of this world locked in the rigid embrace of those who see little else but "nuts and bolts" practicality and the ideologies behind the construction and sale of those nuts and bolts (Ohliger, 1989a).

Had we waited on the so-called "practical" person, who is a mechanic at best, human beings would still be plowing with crooked sticks and writing with split feathers. The exclusively "practical" person is ever a worshiper of "business as usual," disliking change, an enemy of prophets, but a pal of priests (Hall, 1925; Newman & Oliver, 1967).

In addition, the current demand for practicality confuses feasibility with worth. In other words, when we are required to be practical these days, we collapse the difference between what works and what is worth working (Gilman, 1989). A lot of gadgets that are, at the very least, a hideous waste of time and money work. And they're sold as practical. For instance, nuclear power is certainly one of these useless gadgets.

The next time people interrupt your criticisms of the status quo by asking you what your practical solution is, try this. Ask them if they agree with your criticisms before going on. Usually you'll learn that they don't agree with your criticisms, or at the very least, your criticisms are making them uncomfortable so they want to change the subject.

The American streak of over-emphasis on practicality and over-respect for know-how has led to our being victimized by the anti-democratic idea of expertise (Halsey, 1977). But there is another American streak, and it goes something like this: If you can't do something about it, do something with it. In other words: If life hands you a lemon, make lemonade.

Once you've started to make lemonade, you discover that the question "What should we do?" leads right back into the rigid insistence on practicality. The more fruitful questions are "How shall we be? How shall we be with each other?" (Johnson, 1987; Ohliger, 1987b). Obviously all of life is a mixture of "doing" and "being." We can't have one without the other. Since we greatly overemphasize "doing" these days, why not bring "being" to the fore and ask how it can benefit our personal, social, and political relationships with each other. At least then we won't be running around helter-skelter all the time trying to justify our existence—our "being"—by "doing." Remember, we call ourselves "human beings," not "human doings."

I believe we can move closer to balancing being and doing by telling ourselves: You shall know the truth and the truth shall make you laugh. Remember what I quote from the novel *The Name of the Rose* at the beginning of this talk? "Make people laugh at truth, *make truth laugh*, the only truth lies in learning to free ourselves from the insane passion for truth" (Eco, 1984). In other words, we have a fiendishly sober view of what truth is and what it will do for us. That deathly serious view drags us down and we become, as this novelist says, "slaves of our ghosts" (Eco, 1983; 1984).

Here's where the laughter of humans—and the laughter of the gods that Einstein spoke of—comes to the rescue. We bless the blossoming of our sense of humor.

But humor is one of the hardest of all subjects to study (Schaeffer, 1981). The extensive literature on it repeatedly emphasizes the impossibility of even defining it satisfactorily (Ohliger, 1989c).

And generally nothing is more deadly than a discussion of humor (Hunt, 1988). I'm going to be very brief. Any attempt to isolate it trivializes it (Updike, 1976). It eludes mass production just as do knowledge and education. As the American humorist Ogden Nash (1957) said:

> I wish hereby to scotch the rumor
> That I'd attempt to write on humor,
> For those who do, fall into groups
> Of solemn pompous nincompoops
> By whom a joke must be enjoyed
> In terms of Bergson or of Freud.
> Portentously they probe and test,
> And in the jargon lose the jest.
> True humor can't be taught in schools,
> For wayward humor knows no rules.

Well, humor *can* be seen as the mood where we're conscious at the same time of our importance and of our insignificance (Kaufman & Blakely, 1980). Another more fashionable way of putting it is that when you laugh at yourself you become aware that you never let your right brain know what your left brain is doing (Jacoby, 1975).

What surprised me in looking at the literature on humor was how frequently authors concur with the philosopher Schopenhauer who wrote, "A sense of humor is the only divine quality in human beings" (Luke, 1987). Those roughly agreeing include the psychologist Jung (Luke, 1987), the Sufi teacher Rumi (Shah, 1977), the feminist author Rita Mae Brown (Brown, 1988), the sociologist Peter Berger (Berger, 1970), and the prolific science-fiction writer Isaac Asimov (Asimov, 1982).

Without humor we cannot experience the fresh breeze of friendly laughter that renews our strength to keep working for fundamental change while giving our day-to-day work a sharp new focus. We will be liberated from the frenzied pursuit of knowledge and truth in spontaneous humor (Jacoby, 1975). We could start right now—I could start right now—with a little light laughter at myself and my pretension to know the truth, the whole truth, and nothing but the truth (Shaw, 1924).

I've been involved in education for over forty-five years, well almost sixty if you go as far back as kindergarten, where despite what the fulsome Reverend Fulghum, the friendly Unitarian minister author of the best seller, wrote, I doubt that I *really* learned all I need to know in kindergarten—or in school at all (Fulghum, 1988). But I don't believe that education or learning is the be-all or the end-all of life. Those who see education as almighty important seem to be tied to a narrow scientific view of knowledge as illumination or enlightenment (Ohliger, 1982; Panikkar, 1980). And it's a lot more than that. Education is, however, one of life's fundamental energy domains. It needs conservation to survive, just as our fragile earth and its environment need conservation. As with most efforts, conventional learning requires the expenditure of unrecoverable energy, so don't we need to find ways to balance the process with other activities, to reduce education to its appropriate share of community resources?

Recognizing the ecological community in the world of nature helps us to work toward the holistic human community. Education in the best and more modest sense is a part of that community. The ecological community offers one example for the human community (Parris, 1989).

Learning is a delicate but durable plant. It should be nurtured respectfully, tenderly, and with a warm sense of humor (Eliot, 1934). But today, sledge hammer approaches in our schools, universities, and adult programs are destroying the real but limited value of education, learning, knowledge, and truth itself (Kundera, 1984; Ohliger, 1985; Popkewitz, 1989; Rifkin & Howard, 1989).

Well, I've been weaving three themes—or what some people call "dualities"—into this talk: knowledge/understanding, doing/being, sober solemnity versus a sense of humor. I've been calling for more understanding and less knowledge, more being and less doing, more humor and less deadly seriousness.

I believe that these three themes are all basically elusive. I keep in mind what Lily Tomlin says: "At the point you can comprehend how incomprehensible it all is, you're about as smart as you need to be" (Wagner, 1986). But exploring these themes may be helpful to you as it has been to me in finding a way through the maze of too much knowledge and too much education in a world crying out for modesty and balance, especially when viewed from fresh perspectives. I'll conclude with a few thoughts from one of those fresh perspectives.

Eduard Lindeman was a close friend and colleague of the philosopher John Dewey. An eminent social philosopher in his own right, he was also an Emerson scholar, devoted social worker, and the most universally respected adult educator in American history.

According to two recent books on him (Brookfield, 1987; Stewart, 1987) and in the words of his daughter, Betty Leonard (1990), Lindeman stressed:

> A "habit of humor" is an important ingredient to a happy family life, as well as a condition of democracy. He (himself) had a captivating and irresistible sense of humor. He loved puns, clever witticisms, and had an inexhaustible repertoire of jokes to fit almost any occasion. (In his many public speeches) he stressed the relationship between humor and democratic experience.

For example, here's what Lindeman said in his eulogy for the son of a prominent Unitarian minister at a memorial service in a Philadelphia Unitarian Church:

> Sympathy and humor must somehow be blended in (people) of goodwill. If (you) cannot feel for those who suffer, for those who are exploited and debased, (you)

will never enlist in the struggle for justice. But if (you) cannot see the foibles of those defended, (you) can never become a "happy warrior." And if (you are) incapable of admitting that (you yourself) may at times play the harlequin's role, (you) will remain forever a harsh partisan. "Radiancy of humor is a basic ingredient of (people) of goodwill." (Gessner, 1956)

About the same time, Lindeman said:

I believe that ultimately the world will belong to those who are able to see life as a kind of drama. Sometimes it's a drama in which the outcome is sheer tragedy and sometimes it's a kind of melodrama without much sense and sometimes it's comedy, nonsense. But there is a relationship between nonsense and sense. . . . I'm now talking about genuine humor, the humor which comes out of life and out of experience. (Stewart, 1987)

Lindeman concludes: "I do not know whether or not humor is teachable but I feel certain that the adult teacher who is lacking in this quality will make of adult education, not a happy adventure of the mind, but, rather, a grim despondency of the spirit" (Lindeman, 1947).

Finally, to put this whole talk in a nutshell: In the words of one of Lindeman's contemporaries, the American poet E. E. Cummings (1972):

I'd rather learn from one bird how to sing
than teach ten thousand stars how not to dance.

References

Allott, M., & Super, R. H. (Eds.). (1986). *Matthew Arnold*. New York: Oxford University Press.

Asimov, I. (Ed.). (1982). *Laughing space*. New York: Houghton Mifflin.

Berger, P. L. (1970). *A rumor of angels*. New York: Doubleday/Anchor.

Billings, J. (Henry Wheeler Shaw, 1818–1885) (1865). *Josh Billings: His sayings.* In J. Bartlett, *Familiar quotations* (14th edition). Boston: Little, Brown, 1968.

Blumberg, P. (1989). *The predatory society: Deception in the American marketplace.* New York: Oxford University Press.

Bowsher, J. E. (1989). *Educating America: Lessons learned in the nation's class-rooms.* New York: Wiley.

Brookfield, S. (Ed.). (1987). *Learning democracy: Eduard Lindeman on adult education and social change.* London: Croom Helm.

Brown, R. M. (1988). Revisiting Rubyfruit jungle (15th ann. ed.). In *Rubyfruit jungle.* New York: Bantam.

Cummings, E. E. (1972). *Complete poems.* New York: Harcourt Brace Jovanovich.

Davis, P. J., & Hersh, R. (1986). *Descartes' dream: The world according to mathematics.* San Diego, CA: Harcourt Brace Jovanovich.

Draves, W. (1989, March 17). Century's biggest adult ed effort on tap: Training required for illegal aliens. *Adult & Continuing Education Today,* 1–2.

Eco, U. (1983). *Postscript to the name of the rose.* New York: Harcourt Brace Jovanovich.

Eco, U. (1984). *The name of the rose.* New York: Warner Books. (Originally published in 1980 in Italian)

Eliot, T. S. (1934). *The Rock.* A pageant play, Chorus from Act I: Where is the life we have lost in living? Where is the wisdom we have lost in knowledge? Where is the knowledge we have lost in information?

Eurich, N. (1985). *Corporate classrooms.* Princeton, NJ: The Carnegie Foundation for the Advancement of Teaching.

Freeman, R. (1990). *From Freeman's unpublished translation and commentary on Lao Tzu.* Yellow Springs, OH.

Fulghum, R. (1988). *All I really need to know I learned in kindergarten.* New York: Ivy Books.

Gessner, R. (Ed.). (1956). *The democratic man: Selected writings of Eduard C. Lindeman.* Boston: Beacon Press.

Gilman, E. W. (Ed.). (1989). *Webster's dictionary of English usage.* Springfield, MA: Merriam-Webster.

Goodman, P. (1964). *Compulsory miseducation and the community of scholars.* New York: Vintage Books.

Greed and neglect set course toward disastrous oil spill (1989, April 9). *State Journal-Register* (Springfield, IL), p. 66. (From the Associated Press)

Hall, C. (1925). In defense of dreaming. In P. Buhle et al. (Eds.), *Free spirits: Annals of the insurgent imagination.* San Francisco: City Lights Books, 1982.

Halsey, M. (1977). *No laughing matter: The autobiography of a WASP.* New York: J. B. Lippincott.

Hunt, G. W. (1988, May 21). Of many things. *America, 158*(20), 1.

Illich, I. (1983, April). *Eco-pedagogics and the commons.* Cuernavaca, Mexico: Tecno-Politica.

Jackson, W. (1987). *Altars of unhewn stone: Science and the earth.* San Francisco: North Point Press.

Jacoby, R. (1975). *Social amnesia: A critique of conformist psychology from Adler to Laing.* Boston: Beacon Press.

Johnson, S. (1987). *Going out of our minds: The metaphysics of liberation.* Freedom, CA: The Crossing Press.

Joll, J. (1978). *Antonio Gramsci.* New York: Penguin Books.

Kaufman, G., & Blakely, M. K. (Eds.). (1980). *Pulling our own strings: Feminist humor and satire.* Bloomington: Indiana University Press.

Kohr, L. (1978). *The overdeveloped nations: The diseconomies of scale.* New York: Schocken Books.

Krishnamurti, J., & Bohm, D. (1985). *The ending of time.* San Francisco: Harper & Row.

Kundera, M. (1984). *The unbearable lightness of being.* New York: Harper & Row.

Leonard, E. L. (1990). *Eduard Lindeman: Friendly rebel.* (For information on this manuscript contact the author at 3G Lyndhurst Village Court, Savoy, IL 61874)

Lindeman, E. C. (1947, July). Adult education and the democratic discipline. *Adult Education Journal, 6,* 112–115.

Long, M. (1985, December). Turncoat of the Computer Revolution. *New Age Journal,* 47–51, 76–78.

Luke, H. M. (1987, November). Laughter at the heart of things. *Parabola, 12*(4), 6–17.

Marchand, P. (1989). *Marshall McLuhan: The medium and the messenger.* New York: Ticknor & Fields.

Maritain, J. (1944). *The dream of Descartes.* New York: Philosophical Library.

McGinn, B. (1979). *Visions of the end: Apocalyptic traditions in the Middle Ages.* New York: Columbia University Press.

McKibben, B. (1989). *The end of nature.* New York: Random House.

McKnight, J. (1988). *Things that take time.* Talk to a conference on *time* as it works in communities. (Tape available for five dollars from Education for Community Initiatives, 187 High Street, Holyoke, MA 01040)

Nash, O. (1957). *I couldn't help laughing: Stories selected and introduced by Ogden Nash.* Philadelphia: J. B. Lippincott.

Nemerov, H. (1962). To David, about his education. In *The next room of the dream*. Chicago: University of Chicago Press.

Newman, F. M., & Oliver, D. W. (1967, Winter). Education and community. *Harvard Education Review*, 61–106.

Nisbet, R. (1987, March). America as Utopia: The city upon a hill. *Reason*, 33.

Ohliger, J. (1981, July). If 'learning never ends,' does living ever begin? *Second Thoughts*.

Ohliger, J. (1982). *Adult education in a world of excessive riches/excessive poverty*. Talk delivered September/October for the University of British Columbia, Athabasca University, University of Alberta Extension, University of Calgary, Ramah-Navajo School Board (New Mexico), & University of Wyoming.

Ohliger, J. (1983). Reconciling education with liberty. *Prospects (UNESCO)*, 13(2).

Ohliger, J. (1984). The Tao of adult education. *The Learning Connection*, 5(1).

Ohliger, J. (1985). The final solution to learning opportunities. *Tranet*, 37.

Ohliger, J. (1986a, December 8). Review of *The cult of information: The folk-lore of computers and the true art of thinking*. *Adult & Continuing Education Today*, 16(24).

Ohliger, J. (1986b, December 8). Beyond Challenger and Chernobyl? *Adult & Continuing Education Today*, 16(24).

Ohliger, J. (1986c, December 22). Our newest addiction? *Adult & Continuing Education Today*, 16(25).

Ohliger, J. (1987a, January 19). Review of *The ending of time*. *Adult & Continuing Education Today*.

Ohliger, J. (1987b, August 31). Beyond Left and Right. *Adult & Continuing Education Today*, 17(17).

Ohliger, J. (1987c, November 23). Review of *Misunderstanding media*. *Adult & Continuing Education Today*.

Ohliger, J. (1989a). Alternative images of the future in adult education. In P. Cunningham & S. Merriam (Eds.), *The 1990 handbook of adult and continuing education*. San Francisco: Jossey-Bass.

Ohliger, J. (1989b, November 22). Education summit lacks conviction: The ecology of education. *Adult & Continuing Education Today*, 19(22), 6.

Ohliger, J. (Ed.). (1989c). *Bibliography of wit and humor in adult education and reading list on wit and humor*. Springfield, IL: Basic Choices, Inc.

Panikkar, R. (1980, Winter). A philosophy of liberation. *Cross Currents*, 454–455.

Parris, H. E. (1989). Social adjustment in the late industrial age: *The contradiction*. Unpublished manuscript.

Popkewitz, T. (1989, April). *Educational research and its social context*. Keynote address given at the annual Adult Education Research Conference, Madison, WI.

Power, H. (1987). *Empowerment, no! Advocacy, yes!* (Available from Hilton Power, 50 Shawmut Street, Lewiston, ME 04240)

Rifkin, J., & Howard, T. (1989). *Entropy: Into the greenhouse world*. New York: Bantam Books.

Rosenthal, E. (1983, August). Joseph Weizenbaum: A rebel in the computer revolution. *Science Digest*.

Roszak, T. (1986). *The cult of information: The folklore of computers and the true art of thinking*. New York: Pantheon Books.

Sale, K. (1980). *Human scale*. New York: Coward, McCann & Geoghegan.

Schaeffer, N. (1981). *The art of laughter*. New York: Columbia University Press.

Scott, J. (1955). *Political warfare: A guide to competitive coexistence*. New York: John Day.

Shah, I. (1977). *Special illumination: The Sufi use of humor*. London: Octagon Press.

Shaw, G. B. (1924, April 13). Shaw on Saint Joan. *New York Times*, sec. 8, p. 2.

Sibley, M. Q. (1971). *Technology and Utopian thought*. Minneapolis, MN: Burgess Pub.

Stewart, D. W. (1987). *Adult learning in America: Eduard Lindeman and his agenda for lifelong education*. Melbourne, FL: Robert E. Krieger Publishing.

Updike, J. (1976). *Humor in fiction. Picked-up pieces*. New York: Random House.

Wagner, J. (1986). *The search for signs of intelligent life in the universe*. New York: Harper & Row.

Weizenbaum, J. (1976). *Computer power and human reason: From judgment to calculation*. San Francisco: W. H. Freeman.

Winner, L. (1986). *The whale and the reactor: A search for limits in an age of high technology*. Chicago: University of Chicago Press.

Winston, B. (1986). *Misunderstanding media*. Cambridge, MA: Harvard University Press.

8

A Cautious Welcome to the New Millennium

John Ohliger

Editors' note: This chapter was published previously as an editorial or perspective piece in the Canadian Journal for the Study of Adult Education (CJSAE). *It was part of a special issue (Vol. 13, No. 2, November 1999) entitled* The New Millennium: Realities, Possibilities, and Issues for Adult Education. *The writing is vintage Ohliger, and we thank CJSAE and its editor, Tom Nesbit, for permission to include this perspective piece here. In writing this perspective, John revisited notions like compulsory education, spoke about bibliographies (a key legacy of his writing), and provided us with a lived example of his public pedagogy to enhance social democracy: a correspondence forum that he conducted on the millennium and its possibilities. As usual, John networked to write this editorial, and he gratefully acknowledged the following colleagues who offered comments, criticisms, and suggestions on earlier drafts of this personal perspective: David Brightman, Vicki Carter, Webster Cotton, Richard Freeman, David Kast, Jim McCarthy, Helen Modra, Fritz Ohliger, Tonette Rocco, Kody Ryan, Michael Trend, Christina Wagner, Linda Warner, Harvey Wheeler, and David Yamada.*

Abstract: This personal perspective takes a broad view of the impact of the millennium on adult education. It is based on many years of considering millennium issues in conjunction with a shared correspondence forum among adult educators, an extensive millennium bibliography, and development of The Millennium Survival Kit in 1990. Caution flows from ideas expressed by these adult educators, as well as ideas about utopia, and trends in society. Positive approaches include recognition that the millennium and time itself have a variety of meanings; understanding that the year 2000 is of interest to only a minority of the world's population; recognition that time moves in a variety of directions, coupled with the realization that time itself can be a great adult educator; and recognition that healthy movements toward a truly democratic society are expressed by those authors who write powerfully of their visions within different time vistas.

Instead of the typical enthusiastic welcome to the millennium, I propose only a cautious one. Cautions flow from five sources: the concerns of 100 adult educators participating in a correspondence forum; an exploration of the adult education implications of Edward Bellamy's utopian classic *Looking Backward: 2000–1887* published in 1888, which envisioned a peaceful and economically equal society in 2000; a critical look at how the coming of the millennium generates both hopes and fears; examination of the implications of the "Y2K" problem; and the growing commercialized interests in society, as illustrated in a variety of religious and higher-education responses surrounding both the millennial year and the Y2K problem. To overcome this ominous potential of the coming millennium, I issue a call to see time as a series of landscapes, not just a linear progression. If this call is accepted, there is the possibility of a wholehearted welcome during the new millennium for worthwhile social change.

A Cautious Welcome by Adult Educators Participating in a Correspondence Forum

In the 1950s, while engaged in graduate work, I began to believe that adult education is best seen not as a field, a discipline, or a profession (see Grattan, 1955), but simply as those activities of the chronologically mature where more than random learning is involved (Ohliger, 1975).

In the 1980s, when I began reading the hype about the coming millennium, I started encouraging exploration of related adult education questions. For three years I conducted a forum via shared correspondence, while giving speeches, preparing bibliographies, and writing articles on the issues (see Cunningham & Ohliger, 1989; Milfred, 1999; Ohliger, 1987a, 1987b, 1989, 1990a, 1990b, 1999). Ultimately I published *The Millennium Survival Kit*, offering a wide range of divergent opinions (Ohliger, 1990c). In his books on the millennium, Schwartz (1990, 1996), Senior Fellow with the Millennium Institute, concluded that our efforts (the shared letters, the bibliographies, the Kit, etc.) "take to heart the ideal of a corresponding community of scholars" (p. 244; 126).

Adult education professor Von Pittman led off the correspondence forum in 1987 with the first sign that there should be, at most, only a cautious welcome to the millennium: "It is one of our old habits in continuing higher education to have conference themes like 'preparing for the challenge of the 80s' to start each decade. I shudder to think what it will be like at the turn of the century. We will undoubtedly bring a new meaning to the word 'trite.' By 'we,' I mean our professional organizations."[1] Similarly Karen Wilson at the University of Victoria in British Columbia inferred this caution with her wording, "regarding the ominous approaching year of 2000."

The millennium begins in 2001, not 2000, several correspondents noted. Mark Rogness, with The Kindred Community in Des

Moines, Iowa, added: "2001 is a better year to celebrate anyway. After all the media hoopladeda and sickeningly stilted millennium-in-review specials; alternative people can, from a lofty view, pick apart the predictions that fell flat and the common media views. I think I might be a hermit for a year." Kody Ryan, one of several respondents who were very helpful in thinking about millennial questions, contributed 15 letters. Ryan's views loosened up my thinking process. She helped me recognize that conventional definitions of controversial terms such as *antinomianism, anarchism,* and *nihilism* are skewed to leave out the positive aspects and to overemphasize the negative connotations. Gaining such understanding led me to a more tentative perspective on adult educational, political, and cultural issues. More important for the millennium, she introduced me to the "ageless tradition," the view that healthy social approaches to living can be timeless—that is, without being cemented to a particular century or culture.

Looking Backward

Many of the items in the bibliographies for the correspondence forum dealt with the educational impact of one book, Bellamy's (1888/1996) *Looking Backward: 2000–1887.* First published in 1888 and still in print, it is the most popular, controversial, and politically influential American utopia ever written. More predictions have been made about the year 2000 than any other time in history (The 2000 Group, 1998). Bellamy's book stands out among them all. In his novel, Bellamy looks back from the year 2000, when the United States is a peaceful nation practicing equality.

But as 2000 arrives the United States is *not* a peaceful nation and does *not* practice the economic equality Bellamy envisioned (Barnes, 1996; Singer, 1999; Vidal, 1998). As the 19th century drew to a close, a significant number of utopian works dealt with the possibility of social fruition at the end of the 20th century (see Schwartz, 1990). Of these, only Bellamy's work survived. Furthermore, over

150 adult discussion groups met to further the goals of Bellamy's book. These groups lasted into the middle of the 20th century (2000 Group, 1998; Sadler, 1944; Shurter, 1939). By the end of the 20th century, we North American adult educators are left without a popular "postmodern" vision comparable to Bellamy's utopia to help lead us into a better world in the 21st. As Jacoby (1999) points out in *The End of Utopia*, "In an era of political resignation and fatigue the utopian spirit remains more necessary than ever. It evokes neither prisons nor programs, but an idea of human solidarity and happiness. The effort to envision other possibilities of life and society remains urgent and constitutes the essential precondition for doing something" (p. 181).

In 1897 Bellamy published a sequel to *Looking Backward*, prophetically titled *Equality*. In a chapter called "Lifelong Education" (1897/1955), he wrote: "The graduation from the schools at the attainment of majority means merely that the graduate has reached an age at which he [sic] can be presumed to be competent, and has the right as an adult to carry on his further education without the guidance or compulsion of the state. Thanks to an economic system, which illustrates the highest ethical idea in all its workings, the youth going forth into the world finds it a practical school for all the moralities" (pp. 124–125). But, contrary to Bellamy's vision and to the basic principle of voluntary adult learning, North American society is entering the year 2000 with most adult education compelled by the state and by an economic system that lacks the "highest ethical idea." Such a sad state of affairs, brought about by the power of corporatism, is certainly an important reason to only cautiously welcome the millennium (Ohliger, 1994).

Millennial Hopes and Fears

Don Toppin is (or was) the chair of The Committee on Toronto/2000, initiated in 1980 by The Toronto Futurists Group in association with the Department of Adult Education at the Ontario Institute for Studies in Education and the Planning Commission of the City of Toronto. In our forum Toppin maintained: "The Third Millennium AD can become The Great Millennium: one thousand years of peace and well being for all the inhabitants of the global village. Never before has a guiding image of this magnitude been viable. Now the vision is clear, realizable and urgent" (see Toppin & Laxer, 1989, p. 2).

Combine Toppin's hopeful views with Pittman "shuddering to think what it will be like at the turn of the century" and Wilson viewing the approaching year 2000 as ominous. A similar range of beliefs encompasses much of the literature on the coming millennium (Adams, 1992; Bunson, 1999; Heard, 1999). Frequently one person or group holds the extremes of both views at the same time. Even U.S. President Clinton, who predicts a happy bridge into the 21st century, recognizes "the hopes and fears this time presents" (White House Millennium Council, 1998). Let popular psychologist Joyce Brothers have the last word here: "We often celebrate to hide our fears, which is why we'll celebrate the millennium" (cited in Thorton, 1997, p. 14).

"Y2K: Is End Near?"

The American Federation of State, County, and Municipal Employees (1999) poses the question "Y2K: Is end near?" (p. 1). The most salient current reason for cautiously welcoming the millennium is "Y2K," the problem of converting two digits on computers to recognize two zeros in the date as the year 2000 not 1900. By the mid-1970s computer experts were converting banks' and others' computers to handle this problem (Welsh, 1999). But not until the mid-1990s was the general public alerted. Even then, they were not getting the information they needed—or sometimes getting misleading information (Squeo, 1998). By now the estimated final costs of conversion and lawsuits have reached 4.6 *trillion* dollars (Newman, 1998). Meanwhile, computer makers and vendors are raking in the cash selling their correction programs, while governments get ready to quell any panics or riots (Gleick, 1999).

Though our correspondence forum was not even aware of the Y2K issue in the 1980s, now there is more literature on it than on any other aspect of the millennium. And there are more organizations dealing with Y2K preparedness than with any other millennium activities. The U.S. Government created more committees, action weeks, budget reports, Presidential councils, Presidential orders, Congressional acts, and Web pages for Y2K than for AIDS and global warming combined (Gleick, 1999).

When our correspondence forum thrived, some of us kept at it as a way of counteracting the uncritical praise of the future of high technology. At the end of the 20th century the techno-literature continues that praise (Hensley, 1998). As serious as the Y2K problem is, there is one reason to be pleased. It has put a damper on some of the technological optimism about computers and other supposedly time-and-money-saving devices. Y2K could encourage those previously uncritical of high-tech to put their minds to broader perspectives instead of seeing technology as a solution to every problem (Atlee, 1999; Foote, 1999; Scanlon, 1998).

The Yearlong Christmas: Selling the Millennium

Groups benefiting from Y2K almost as much as profit-seeking businesses are the religious ones. Some conservative Protestants have capitalized on the recent interest in videos for their religious adult-education programs. Reverend Jerry Falwell's $28 video, *A Christian's Guide to the Millennium Bug*, sold close to 2,000 copies in five months. On the tape Falwell says Y2K may "be God's instrument to humble this nation" into a spiritual awakening. Other prominent Protestants such as Pat Robertson with his Christian Broadcasting Network, Jack Van Impe with his video *2000 Time Bomb*, and the associate publisher of one of the world's largest religious publishing firms with his book *The Millennium Bug: How to Survive the Coming*

Chaos, share Falwell's concern about the bug (see "Doom and Dollars," 1999, review of the book).

Conventional wisdom has until recently seen scientific technology and religion as totally separate and opposed domains. But since the current concern with Y2K by church leaders "suddenly, technology has become intertwined with theology" (Bullers, 1999). However, a professor of history at York University in Toronto contends technology and theology have actually been enmeshed since the early days of Christianity: Noble (1998) presents a great deal of evidence that technology really advanced only when it was linked with the belief in Christian redemption, often tied in by both scientists and theologians with predictions about the coming millennium as well as support for elitist, anti-democratic goals.

Among American Catholics, there is a small but growing apocalyptic subculture, which combines Biblical millennialism with right-wing political conspiracy theory (Allen, 1998). But the dominant Catholic view follows Pope John Paul II. One of the pope's first acts was to declare the year 2000 a full year's Christmas celebration (O'Brien, 1994). Freburger (1986) commented in the liberal, Catholic *National Catholic Reporter*: "Given the propensities of our consumer economy, the mind boggles at the commercial activities surrounding an official yearlong celebration of Christmas" (p. 19). According to Monsignor Illich (1970): "The Roman Church is the world's largest non-governmental bureaucracy. It employs 1.8 million full-time workers—priests, brothers, sisters, and laymen. These employees work within a corporate structure, which an American business consultant firm rates as among the most efficiently operated organizations in the world. The institutionalized Church functions on a par with the General Motors Corporation and the Chase Manhattan Bank" (p. 71).

The Vatican is expecting 30 million visitors because the year 2000 will officially be the bi-millennium of Christ's birth (see "Zero-Based Celebrations," 1998). The pope is calling for a great jubilee to celebrate the occasion. He sees the jubilee as a time for reexamination and recommitment to the faith, not as a time of apocalypse (Dulles, 1995). At least nine books are being specially published and sold for adult education purposes about the Catholic millennial celebration (Tickle, 1997).

Like many churches, colleges and universities are succumbing to commercial pressures. As 2000 dawns, large private for-profit universities are listed on the stock exchange. They invade the budding distance-learning arena. And many universities, both for-profit and non-profit, are turning faculty into part time "adjunct" peons without security or benefits. Now the very definition of higher education is compromised (Ohliger, 1990a, in press-a, in press-b). Thus, another reason for cautiously welcoming the millennium is its effect on increasing the commercial and corporate domination of religion, higher education, and all other aspects of society. A few months before he was assassinated, as the American Civil War was winding down, Abraham Lincoln wrote a letter to one of his officers: "I see in the near future a crisis approaching that unnerves me and causes me to tremble for the safety of my country. As a result of the war, corporations have been enthroned and an era of corruption in high places will follow. The money power of the country will endeavor to prolong its reign by working upon the prejudices of the people until all wealth is aggregated in a few hands and the Republic is destroyed" (1864/1999, p. 78).

Some deny Lincoln wrote that letter (Boller & George, 1989), but there is no denying that corporate power has spread, concentrated, and internationalized until today it is the single strongest force in the world (Brosio, 1998; Derber, 1998; Ohliger, in press-a; Saul, 1994, 1997; Singer, 1999; Vidal, 1998).

The Landscapes of Time

I agree with O'Brien (1994) that the millennium "should be an occasion for self-questioning" (pp. 165–166). The years of self- and mutual-questioning I have been engaged in about the millennium have led me to the tentative conclusion that time itself has a variety of meanings, not just the linear one. Murdoch (1994) calls time that "strange medium we live in" (p. viii). It is the same with the term *millennium*, which means, among other things, a period of exactly one thousand years, or "an indeterminate length signified by a symbolic denomination of a thousand" (McGinn, 1996, p. 3).

The year 2000 as the millennium means little to the majority of the world's population, including those following the different Chinese, Japanese, Muslim, Buddhist, Hebrew, Indian, Persian, or Baha'i calendars as well as those for whom *any* calendar plays no part in their lives (2000 Group, 1998; Lee, 1999).

Moving back and forth across the invisible line between literal and symbolic reality makes it possible to discover that time does not just march forward in a straight line; it stops, it speeds up, it slows down, it circles, it weaves itself into a thousand landscapes. Calling the clock the only way of experiencing time is like calling American money the only real money. Labeling differing views of time as *landscapes* assists in viewing time as "place" and gives it more concrete meanings other than the oversimplified linear one. Those, like some of the poor and indigenous populations, who are not trapped in the view that time moves only ahead bit by bit, are freer to live in these different places, these landscapes. And there are many popular and classic examples of these landscapes in fiction, drama, movies, television, painting, and poetry (Ohliger, 1990c). These various ways of understanding time often accord with striking events in people's lives when, for instance, they experience love, or encounter beautiful nature.

Also consider investigating the hundreds of examples where time is the chief adult educator—for instance poet Carl Sandburg's (1936) "Time is a great teacher, / Who can live without hope?" (p. 286).

Exploring *all* these landscapes of time offers a measure of peace and serenity instead of the hectic feelings of pressure brought on by the crushingly constricted movement forward of one moment following inexorably after another. It is one way of moving from only a cautious view of the year 2000 toward welcoming the millennium wholeheartedly in the context of worthwhile social change. Such a wholehearted welcome meshes with other similar views of time that include, but also go beyond the narrow straight line one. For instance, think of time as a "funnel, meaning a place where the 'here and now' and the 'there and then' can live side by side" (Hiss, 1999, p. 19). Study those who write powerfully to encourage democratic social action within different time vistas (Collins, 1994; Gorz, 1989; Priestley, 1962; Rifkin, 1987).

And don't neglect those who write with literary quality and expressive clarity about the different time perspectives *within* the linear one. In his new book *Whose Millennium? Theirs or Ours?* Singer (1999) points to the significance of both historical time and personal time as he seeks "a realistic utopia" (p. 6). Such masters of prose as Gore Vidal, Studs Terkel, Barbara Ehrenreich, and Eduardo Galleano endorse the accomplishment and importance of his writing. Singer concludes his book with this stirring summons to a fundamentally improved 21st century:

> We are at a moment, to borrow Whitman's words, when society "is for a while between things ended and things begun," not because of some symbolic date on the calendar marking the turn of the millennium, but because the old order is a-dying, though it clings successfully to power, because there is no class, no social force ready to push it off the historical stage. The confrontation between the old and the new—the sooner it starts the better—will now have to be global by its very nature. On the ground littered with broken models and shattered expectation, a new generation will now have to take the lead. Chastened by our bitter experiences, they can advance with hope but without illusions, with convictions but without certitudes, and, rediscovering the attraction and power of collective action, they can resume the task,

hardly begun, of the radical transformation of society. But they cannot do it on their own. We must follow their lead and, to the dismay of the preachers and propagandists shrieking that the task is impossible, utopian, or suicidal, and to the horror of their capitalist paymasters, proclaim all together: "We are not here to tinker with the world, we are here to change it!" Only in this way can we give a positive answer to the rhetorical question asked in this book: whose millennium, theirs or ours? It is also the only way in which we can prevent the future from being *theirs*—apocalyptic or, at best, barbarian. (p. 279)[2]

Notes

1. All non-referenced quotations in this paper are taken from unpublished contributions to the correspondence forum.

2. From *Whose Millennium? Theirs or Ours?* by D. Singer, New York: Monthly Review Press. Copyright 1999 by Monthly Review Press. Reprinted with permission.

References

The 2000 Group. (1998). *Uncle John's indispensable guide to the year 2000.* Ashland, OR: Bathroom Reader's Press.

Adams, C. (1992). *California in the year 2000: A look into the future of the golden state as it approaches the millennium.* Palo Alto, CA: Pacific Books.

Allen, J. (1998, April 3). Gimme that end-time religion: Seer harmonizes apocalyptic views, catechism, Pope. *National Catholic Reporter, 34*(22), 3–5.

American Federation of State, County, and Municipal Employees. (1999). Y2K: Is end near? [Banner headline]. *AFSCME Reports, 9*(64), 1. (Available from AFSCME, Madison, WI)

Atlee, T. (1999, February 4). *Some of the big questions about Y2K and life [an update to the Transforming Y2K web site].* Available: www.earley.org/Y2K/y2k_frame.htm.

Barnes, R. (1996). *Military legitimacy: Might and right in the new millennium.* London: Frank Cass & Company.

Bellamy, E. (1955). Lifelong education. Reprinted in J. Schiffman (Ed.), *Selected writings on religion and society* (pp. 124–128). New York: The Liberal Arts Press. (Original chapter published in 1897)

Bellamy, E. (1996). *Looking backward: 2000–1887*. New York: Signet Classics. (Original work published 1888)

Boller, P., & George, J. (1989). *They never said it*. New York: Oxford University Press.

Brosio, R. (1998). End of the millennium: Capitalism's dynamism, civic crises, and corresponding consequences for education. In H. Shapiro & D. Purpel (Eds.), *Critical social issues in American education: Transformation in a postmodern world* (2nd ed.) (pp. 27–43). Mahwah, NJ: Lawrence Erlbaum Associates.

Bullers, F. (1999, February 11). Y2K bug creates a religious schism. *Knight–Ridder/ Tribune News Service*.

Bunson, M. (1999). *Prophecies 2000: Predictions, revelations, and visions for the new millennium*. New York: Pocket Books

Collins, D. (1994). *Time and the Priestleys*. Phoenix Mill, England: Alan Sutton Publishing.

Cunningham, P., & Ohliger, J. (Eds.). (1989). *Radical thinking in adult education*. Syracuse, NY: Syracuse University Kellogg Project.

Derber, C. (1998). *Corporation nation: How corporations are taking over our lives and what we can do about it*. New York: St. Martin's Press.

Doom and dollars. (1999, January 16). *The Economist, 344*, 30.

Dulles, A. (1995, December 9). John Paul II and the advent of the new millennium [Cover Story]. *America, 173*(19), 9–16.

Foote, T. (1999). Forget Y2K! *Smithsonian, 29*(11), 45.

Freburger, W. (1986, March 28). A siecle with 14 years left is no joke. *National Catholic Reporter, 22*, 19.

Gleick, J. (1999, January 24). Fast forward. *New York Times*.

Gorz, A. (1989). *Critique of economic reasoning*. New York: Verso.

Grattan, C. H. (1955). *In quest of knowledge: A historical perspective on adult education*. New York: Association Press.

Heard, A. (1999). *Apocalypse pretty soon: Travels in end-time America*. New York: W. W. Norton & Co.

Hensley, D. (1998). *Millennium approaches*. New York: Avon Books.

Hiss, T. (1999). *The view from Alger's window: A son's memoir*. New York: Knopf.

Illich, I. (1970). *Celebration of awareness: A call for institutional revolution*. New York: Doubleday.

Jacoby, R. (1999). *The end of utopia: Politics and culture in an age of apathy*. New York: Basic Books.

Lee, L. (1999, January 8). Millennium hoopla muted among Asians. *Wall Street Journal*, p. B8.

Lincoln, A. (1864). Letter to Colonel William F. Elkins, November 21. In
    M. Bunson, 1999, *Prophecies: 2000 predictions, revelations, and visions for
    the new millennium* (p. 78), New York: Pocket Books. Also in C. Derber,
    1998, *Corporation nation: How corporations are taking over our lives and
    what we can do about it*, New York: St. Martin's Press.

McGinn, B. (1996). *The meanings of the millennium*. Washington, DC: Inter-
    American Development Bank.

Milfred, S. (1999, January 1). Year 2000 fever is starting to go around. *Wisconsin
    State Journal* [Madison], pp. 1A, 3A, 11A.

Murdoch, I. (1994). Foreword. In D. Collins (Ed.), *Time and the Priestleys* (p. viii).
    Phoenix Mill, England: Alan Sutton Publishing.

Newman, J. (1998, October 9). Chipping away at the dreaded Y2K. *Wisconsin
    State Journal* [Madison], p. 1.

Noble, D. (1998). *The religion of technology: The divinity of man and the spirit of
    invention*. New York: Alfred A. Knopf.

O'Brien, C. C. (1994). *On the eve of the millennium: The future of democracy
    through an age of unreason*. New York: Free Press.

Ohliger, J. (1975). *Radical ideas in adult education*. U.S. Department of Education.
    (ERIC Document Reproduction Service No. ED 121 979). (Revised and
    reprinted in National Free University Network, August 1976, National
    Free University News; Radical Teacher: A Newsjournal of Socialist Theory
    on Practice, May 1979; International Council for Adult Education,
    December 1989, Formation Newsletter.)

Ohliger, J. (1987a). *Millennia: The past, the present issues, and the future of adult
    education*. Madison, WI: Basic Choices.

Ohliger, J. (1987b). The millennium: Are you ready for it? *Adult & Continuing
    Education Today, 17*(25), 6.

Ohliger, J. (1989). Alternative images of the future in adult education. In
    S. Merriam & P. Cunningham (Eds.), *Handbook of adult and continuing
    education* (pp. 628–639). San Francisco: Jossey-Bass.

Ohliger, J. (1990a). *Higher education "crises": Part One (1921–1990)*. Madison,
    WI: Basic Choices.

Ohliger, J. (1990b, September). Straight time and standard brand adult educa-
    tion. *New Horizons in Adult Education, 4*, 1–4.

Ohliger, J. (1990c). *The millennium survival kit*. Madison, WI: Basic Choices.

Ohliger, J. (1994). It never ends: The problem of mandatory continuing educa-
    tion. *Growing Without Schooling, 94*, 34–36.

Ohliger, J. (1999). *Prepare your own millennium survival kit*. Madison, WI: Uni-
    versity of Wisconsin Extension.

Ohliger, J. (in press-a). *Corporatism: A quotational bibliography*. Madison, WI: Basic Choices.

Ohliger, J. (in press-b). Higher education "crises": Part Two (1991–1998). *College Daze*.

Priestley, J. (1962). *Margin released*. New York: Harper & Row.

Rifkin, J. (1987). *Time wars: The primary conflict in human history*. New York: Henry Holt.

Sadler, E. (1944). One book's influence: Edward Bellamy's *Looking backward*. *The New England Quarterly, 17*, 530–555.

Sandburg, C. (1936). *The people, yes*. New York: Harcourt, Brace, & World.

Saul, J. R. (1994). "Corporatism." In *The doubter's companion: A dictionary of aggressive common sense* (pp. 74–79). New York: Free Press.

Saul, J. R. (1997). *The unconscious civilization*. New York: Free Press.

Scanlon, M. (1998, December). Nerve tonic for the year 2000. *Mother Earth News*, 4.

Schwartz, H. (1990). *Century's end: A cultural history of the fin de siecle from the 990s through the 1990s*. New York: Doubleday.

Schwartz, H. (1996). *Century's end: An orientation manual toward the year 2000*. New York: Doubleday.

Shurter, R. (1939). The writing of *Looking backward*. *The South Atlantic Quarterly, 38*, 255–261.

Singer, D. (1999). *Whose millennium? Theirs or ours?* New York: Monthly Review Press.

Squeo, A. (1998, October 5). FTC says consumers need info on Y2K bug. *Bloomberg News*.

Thorton, J. (1997, February 10). Sentiments of gloom. *U.S. News & World Report, 122*(5), 14.

Tickle, P. (1997, January 13). Pope declares 2000 "year of jubilee," and the books follow. *Publishers Weekly, 244*(2), 40.

Toppin, D., & Laxer, D. (1989). *Toward the great millennium*. Toronto: World Millennium Network. (Available from Don Toppin, Toronto 2000, 390 Bay St., Toronto, ON, Canada M5H 2Y2)

Vidal, G. (1998). *The American presidency*. Monroe, ME: Common Courage Press.

Welsh, R. (1999). *The year 2000 (Y2K) disaster survival guide: How it happened, why it happened, what you can do*. Barneveld, WI: Y2K Consulting.

White House Millennium Council. (1998). *Honor the past: Imagine the future*. Washington, DC: Author.

Zero-based celebrations. (1998, April 18). *The Economist, 343*, 81–84.

Part Three

Challenging Professionalization in an Emerging Field of Study and Practice

9

Contesting Adult Education as a Venture
John Ohliger's Critique of Modern Practice

André P. Grace

As U.S. academic adult education emerged after World War II, it worked to configure the field of study and practice as an enterprise with acknowledged expertise useful to assist the technoscientific and economic advancement of postwar culture and society (Grace, 1999, 2000a; Verner, 1964a, 1964b; Griffith, 1970; Wilson, 1995). Conceptually, the term *enterprise* integrates two ideas that encompass the ambition of U.S. academic adult education to gain space and place as it performed in a postwar change culture of crisis and challenge. First, it incorporates the idea of adult education as a venture designed to attain cultural currency in professional terms. Adult education as a venture inextricably linked the emergence of a professionalized field of practice to the emergence of a field of study where developments in theory, research, and method usually aligned with the regulatory culture of technoscience and the attendant rise of technical intellectualism. Second, enterprise includes the idea of adult education as an adventure designed to help adult learners negotiate new and unfamiliar life, learning, and work terrains. This idea was hooked to a field history valuing an amateurish spirit nurturing transformative social and cultural forms of adult learning. In the postwar period, adult education as an adventure became a struggling adult learning terrain that attempted to keep the ideals of liberal education alive as the field attempted to address the new instrumental, social, and cultural learning needs of citizens as learners and workers. In keeping with its historical role, adult education as an adventure emphasized context, relationship, and learner freedom in community settings. This role often put it at odds with the emerging idea of adult education as a venture, which seemed more concerned with the rigors of professionalism and occupying prime cultural space as the field navigated its way along new economic and cultural terrain.

It was during this period of change in adult education that John Ohliger assumed roles as both an adult educator and an adult learner. Having gained some experience as an adult educator during his time in the U.S. Army (1945–1948), Ohliger, like many other veterans, took advantage of the GI Bill of 1944 to complete his undergraduate university education, receiving a bachelor of arts in 1951 from Wayne State University in Detroit, Michigan. He completed a master of arts in adult education in 1957 and an educational doctorate in 1966, obtaining both degrees from the University of California, Los Angeles. Ohliger was a graduate student at a time when universities appeared to support increased space and place for adult education, and academic adult education experienced tremendous growth (Grace, 2000b). The flow of veterans into the university after World War II affected not only day programs but also, and strongly, adult education, including continuing education and extension (Portman, 1978). The veterans were mature, vocationally oriented learners focused on catching up; they recast the higher education population as a heterogeneous and more "adult" body (Riesman, 1981). They even changed some academics' minds about the space and place of adults in the university.

The assimilation of millions of veterans was the predominant characteristic of U.S. higher education from 1946 until the early 1950s. As a result of the Veterans Administration higher education (GI Bill) programs, veterans doubled college and university enrollments in this period, which led to a doubling of their numbers as employees in government and corporations (Portman, 1978). Aronowitz and DiFazio (1994) recount that the GI Bill legislation guaranteed income and tuition, which allowed veterans to pursue secondary and higher education in such swollen numbers. The veterans, they wrote, became "the cadre of the postwar knowledge class" of technical intellectuals (p. 41). They conclude, "In retrospect, the GI Bill was, perhaps, the most dramatic material basis in American history for the American ideology of exceptionalism and, particularly, the belief in [class] mobility" (p. 41).

Although the GI Bill helped advance adult education as a venture, and indeed his own career, Ohliger did not believe that government-enabled adult education assisted class mobility. He felt that class remained an issue in modern practice: "The invisible but unyielding class barrier remains. Adult education hasn't been able to remove it. Does the field con people into believing . . . that through individual educational efforts not only can one person find economic salvation but that through the same path the class barrier itself can be eliminated?" (Ohliger, 1989, p. 6). Ohliger later criticized the GI Bill as actually marking a move toward mass training instead of mass education in the United States (Ohliger, 1999a). He believed that political expediency undergirded this move in which indoctrination and instruction prepared citizens as learners and workers to meet the needs of the post–World War II U.S. economy (Ohliger, 1999a).

As a graduate student in the 1950s, Ohliger became committed to the ideal of learner freedom and choice. He approached adult education not as a field, a discipline, or a profession but, in the spirit of adult education as an adventure, as a set of activities, at least somewhat organized for the chronologically mature (Ohliger, 1999b). He agreed with Eduard Lindeman, who cautioned in 1952, "There is ultimate danger that the professional leadership in this [adult education] movement might get itself in the same box as has the professional leadership in our conventional [public school] education" (quoted in Ohliger, 1991, p. 15). With Colleen McCarthy, Ohliger (1971) described this box and its problems: "Many students . . . intuitively know what the schools do for them. They school them to confuse process with substance. Once these become blurred, a new logic is assumed: the more treatment there is the better are the results: or, escalation leads to success. The pupil is thereby 'schooled' to confuse teaching with learning, grade advancement with education, a diploma with competence, and fluency with the ability to say something new. . . . School has become the world religion of a modernized proletariat" (pp. 9–10).

Always leery that adult education would become another version of this world religion, Ohliger, as a graduate student and in his subsequent field roles, interrogated the capacity of modern practice to make basic choices that would benefit citizens as learners and workers whom he placed at the heart of adult education as an adventure. The essence of his critique is captured in two questions that he posed in the first issue of the newsletter *Media/Adult Learning* in December 1967: "Is education designed to maintain and establish the existing system on a firmer foundation, giving support to the prevailing values? Or is the educational system designed to stimulate the potential and the capacity for change, not only in the individual but [also] in the society?" (1982a, p. 46). These questions dichotomize adult education into its possible positionalities as a venture and an adventure. Ohliger believed the true purpose of adult education (as adventure) lay in a positive answer to the second question.

In this chapter, I consider how John Ohliger dealt with the dichotomy of adult education as a venture and adventure for more than five decades. I examine his assessment of adult education as a field of study and practice in a period dominated by U.S. academic adult education's quest to build professional community and gain cultural space and place for the field.

The Struggle of Academic Adult Education in a Post–World War II Change Culture of Crisis and Challenge

As citizens negotiated new life, learning, and work terrains after World War II, change appeared to be the only constant. U.S. academic adult educators felt the turbulent times provided both circumstance and opportunity for the field to articulate the parameters

of a technoscientized professionalism designed to assist adult learners faced with technological change, worker obsolescence, complex
domestic problems, and civic and political unrest (Axford, 1969;
Hallenbeck, 1960; Liveright, 1968). Indeed, in this period, U.S.
academic adult education experienced tremendous growth, which
occurred amid dramatic cultural and economic change forces that
profoundly reconfigured U.S. culture and society (Houle, 1964,
1970; Verner, 1964a, 1964b; Smith, Aker, & Kidd, 1970). These
change forces manifested themselves in "turbulence born . . . [of]
prosperity [that] brings in its wake new anxieties, new strains, new
urgencies" (Bell, 1960, p. 94). They contoured life, learning, and
work in new and unfamiliar ways and, in effect, constituted the pre-
conditions for a transition in the functional system of capital.

Fredric Jameson (1991) has viewed this transition as a move to
a new stage of capitalism. This stage, which he called late capitalism, emerged as technology transformed capitalism. Jameson contends that the basic technology necessary to sustain it existed in the
United States by 1945. He locates the economic precondition for
establishing the new system in the 1950s, when escalating consumerism and expanding new-product production were the predominant features of the changing U.S. economy. He situates the
cultural precondition for continuing the development of this new
functional system in the 1960s when social upheaval and genera-
tional rupture radically altered U.S. culture and society. While he
believes that this periodization represents the more proper location
of each precondition, Jameson is not suggesting that economic and
cultural impacts occurred separately in the postwar period. They
were just not particularly synchronized.

In Daniel Bell's (1960) earlier opposing view, this transition in
the functional system of capital represented a rupture rather than a
transformation of capitalism: An unprecedented expansion of capitalism into postwar U.S. culture led to the emergence of what he
called postindustrial society. Bell (1967) considered the years 1945
to 1950 as the symbolic birth years of this society distinguished
by "the rise of the new elite whose status is based on [specialized

knowledge, planning abilities, and] skill" (p. 165). As C. Wright Mills saw it, these elitists or technical intellectuals constituted a constrained new middle class that was potentially significant yet disastrously dependent on its procreators, science and government (Aronowitz & DiFazio, 1994). Their cultural worth was generally a measure of their technoscientific expertise (Said, 1994). Perennially worried about the ascendancy of the expert and the concomitant control of knowledge production, exchange, and distribution, Ohliger (1990) formulated "three little questions" whose answers he felt would provide a "tapestry of views about the need for fundamental change in our approaches to knowledge and education" (p. 26): "First, how do we know and what do we do with that knowledge? Second, how do we spend money on what is sometimes called knowledge production and transmission? And third, what are our overall educational goals, our philosophy, purpose, ethics, [and] morality?" (p. 26).

As adult education appeared to gain new impetus as a vehicle assisting postwar cultural adjustment and advancement (Kempfer, 1955; Knowles & DuBois, 1970), many U.S. academic adult educators promoted professionalism as the domain of the expert and the guarantor of U.S. culture. This strategizing amounted to constructing professionalism as the "right" cultural attitude. Said (1994) explains, "By professionalism I mean thinking of your work . . . as something you do for a living . . . with one eye on the clock, and another cocked at what is considered to be proper, professional behavior—not rocking the boat, not straying outside the accepted paradigms or limits, making yourself marketable and above all presentable, hence uncontroversial and unpolitical and 'objective'" (p. 74). However, academic adult education still lacked the rudiments of a professionalized practice. The field of study needed to set parameters clarifying its role and purpose, controlling entrance to the field, and delineating a domain of specialized knowledge and competency (Thomas, 1963; Verner, 1964a, 1964b). It had to transcend a haphazard approach to method, which meant academic adult educators not only had to build theory and expand research efforts, but they also had to overcome a field penchant for faddism. In a reflection on trends in post–World War II modern practice, Malcolm S. Knowles (in Jarvis, 1987), who entered the field in 1935, intimated that faddism had become engrained as a laissez-faire modus operandi: "Our field has had a lot of fads. . . . In the 40s it was audio-visual aids. In the 50s it was group dynamics. In the 60s it was programmed instruction. . . . Well I jumped on board every one of those fads, but as a new fad came along, and I jumped aboard that one, what I found was that then I put the previous one in a lower perspective" (p. 6).

To advance professionalism in the field of study and practice, many U.S. academic adult educators sought to fulfill two longstanding goals: to have adult education recognized, respected, and valued as a profession and to have academic adult education as a field of study achieve a more valued presence in the university and the larger culture. Here the field of study as a "discipline" would shape the field of practice as a technoscientized and more precise venture with worth in the emerging knowledge-and-service economy (Verner, 1963, 1978). However, professionalization had been a concern throughout the modern practice of adult education, and distinct moves toward it can be traced back at least to the 1930s (Cotton, 1968). In 1953, Paul H. Sheats, Clarence D. Jayne, and Ralph B. Spence called for professional standards of behavior and agreed-on ethical principles to guide the emergence of an enterprise emphasizing adult education as a venture. Ohliger always questioned what the emphasis on professionalism was achieving. Instead of creating a just and equitable learning society that has "greater control over its destiny" (p. 37), Ohliger (1975) argued that by the mid-1970s, the professionalization of modern practice had created a credentialing society that moved everyone "closer to a rigid, standardized, calcified, ossified, vocationalized world" (p. 39).

Indeed U.S. adult education as a venture did promote credentialism as the kind of cultural capital needed in an emerging postwar culture driven by consumerism (everybody needs to have it) and the desire for upward mobility (everybody can have it) (Aronowitz & DiFazio, 1994; Griffith, 1970; Verner, 1964a, 1964b). Using credentialism as a means to achieve a more professionalized modern practice is an expression of a move toward specialization (Verner, 1964a, 1964b; Wilson, 1995). Said (1994) recounts that specialization, revolving around the rituals of technical intellectualism, was a pervasive phenomenon in postwar education and culture: it meant the elevation of expertise and the cult of the expert, recognition by certification, control over particular knowledge, ownership of a particular language to transmit that knowledge, and claim to a specific domain in which to act. While specialization cultivated professionalism, Said argues that it was a kind of professionalism linked to instrumental pressures to perform and produce. Various critical adult educators have suggested that this turn to instrumentalism limited the ability of the modern practice of adult education to be socially and culturally inclusive and encompassing (Collins, 1991; Hart, 1992; Welton, 1995). Thus, advancing specialization as a means to enhance professionalism amounted to a diminishment of amateurism, which had historically given the field of practice its social character that kept the political ideals of modernity—democracy, freedom, and social justice—at the heart of adult education.

Amateurism can be understood as the driving force of adult education as an adventure and social education for adults. It is "the desire to be moved not by profit or reward but by love for and unquenchable interest in the larger picture, in making connections across lines and barriers, in refusing to be tied down to a specialty, in caring for ideas and values despite the restrictions of a profession" (Said, 1994, p. 76). It is the field's amateur spirit that has nurtured adult education as a vocation (Collins, 1991). Still, amateurism and, concomitantly, social education declined with the ascendancy of professionalism. Ohliger (1982b) bemoaned this decline, noting that in earlier days in the history of the field of practice, an amateur spirit marked social education, valuing the entrepreneurial, the experimental, the experiential, learning in community, and learner freedom. Such a spirit permeates his perspective on the social form that adult learning ought to take: "It is often said that without knowledge of the proper techniques, adult educators are condemned to dilettantish and ineffective amateurism. Everyone affirms the importance of a job well done. But the techniques themselves just cannot be separated from the social milieus in which they are learned. . . . [Moreover, we cannot overemphasize] words, ideas, and intellect to the detriment of feelings, experience, and personal human relationships" (Ohliger, 1982b, p. 68).

For a contingent of U.S. academic adult educators that included prominent social educator Paul Bergevin, the devaluation of amateurism raised a key question. It is framed here using Said's words: Should adult education move forward in the dominant culture "as a professional supplicant or as its unrewarded, amateurish conscience?" (1994, p. 83). Although social educators were inclined to acknowledge that specialization seemed necessary to advance adult education in a postwar change culture of crisis and challenge, they remained committed to a culture of learning that would be driven by maintaining the historical commitment to amateurism as the social conscience of adult education. In words in keeping with the philosophy of Eduard C. Lindeman, who believed that "true adult education is social education" (1947 in Brookfield, 1987, p. 55), Bergevin (1967) laid out the role and purpose of adult education: "Adult education should make a continuing attack on ignorance, disease, superstition, and enslavement of mind and spirit. Its purpose is to liberate people; to provide creative opportunities for utilizing their talents and energies; to help them learn to play their roles as dignified human beings and as citizens in a society in which they can have some control of the social forces operating on them; and to show them how to do all this with the intelligence and decorum that befit human dignity" (p. 170).

Although the spirit of amateurism drove some academic adult educators to question any strengthening of the emphasis on professionalism in adult education (Griffith, 1970), professionalism nevertheless became a cultural tour de force in the field. In the Foreword to the 1948 *Handbook of Adult Education in the United*

States, Alain Locke had heralded the arrival of the corporate age of adult education. The parameters of a more professionalized practice became clearer in subsequent decades as indicated, for example, by a "forms, function and future" (p. 1) focus emphasizing technoscientism and professionalism in the 1970 handbook. Ohliger (1975) saw this professional turn in the field of study and practice as a reaction by adult educators to what they perceived as their "political impotence and insecurity in the face of other forces in the world" (p. 39). Such acerbic opinions positioned Ohliger as a thorn in the side of many colleagues who wanted to advance adult education as a venture.

Ohliger's caustic comments often overshadowed his commitment to adult education as an adventure at a time when he perhaps should have been taken more seriously instead of being relegated to a dark, radical box. Like Lindeman and John Walker Powell, social educators and philosophers who were well received in mainstream modern practice, Ohliger (1969) saw education as a practice directed toward social justice and social change. The freedom of learners to choose was at the heart of this practice. He declared, "There were two routes to freedom—action and education, inextricably intertwined. The [civil rights and liberation] action route is the responsibility of us all. . . . But the education route is your special concern" (p. 417). As Ohliger saw it at the time, it was the duty of every adult educator to use liberal education to assist learners to know what to do with freedom. Here he drew on social philosopher Robert J. Blakely, who maintained that a liberal education ought to focus on studying individual and communal concerns with existence, time, and space; relationships between one individual and another and between the individual and society; and critical concepts like truth, justice, freedom, responsibility, and peace. As Blakely put it, "Liberal education does *not* mean a particular school, method or content. It *does* mean the process of free and responsible thought; it *does* mean the product of free and responsible citizenship" (cited in Ohliger, 1969, p. 418).

U.S. Academic Adult Education and the Notion of Community

Field history has shown the persistence of the concept of adult education (Verner, 1960, 1964a). The notion has encompassed education for occupational, vocational, and professional competence; personal or family competence; social and civic competence; and for self-realization (Liveright, 1968). Despite these eclectic purposes, adult education has had a history of marginalization in the United States, and the field has never been a united movement or a common endeavor (Knowles, 1962/1977). This history suggests that adult education should more properly remain an adventure: "There has been a continuing lack of agreement as to whether or not there is such a thing as an adult education movement, the counter hypothesis being that adult education in this country is—and should properly be—a *patternless mosaic of unrelated activities*" (Knowles, 1962/1977, p. viii). Historically, it has proven quite difficult to find common ground to build community in U.S. adult education. After World War II, the diffuse, episodic, peripheral, and exclusionary nature of adult education worked against the creation of a lasting national umbrella organization that would represent the entire field and create a strong public image for adult education as an enterprise (Axford, 1969; Liveright, 1968; Sheats et al., 1953). Although the American Association for Adult Education and the Department of Adult Education of the National Education Association merged to create the Adult Education Association of the U.S.A. in 1951, interest in such mergers was not commonplace (Charters, 1971).

Still, period literature in U.S. academic adult education indicates that those in the field of study worked hard to build a professional community after World War II (Cotton, 1968; Jensen, Liveright, & Hallenbeck, 1964; Knowles 1962/1977). Academic adult educators attempted to develop common goals and state common beliefs predominantly in keeping with the idea of adult education as a venture. The postwar growth and development of graduate adult education, the increasing technoscientization and professionalization of the field, the promotion of lifelong learning as a way to become a skilled and contributing citizen, and the development of a growing body of knowledge and research specific to adult education exemplify efforts to build community (Houle, 1964; Knowles, 1960; Smith et al., 1970; Verner, 1964a, 1964b). In his 1965–1966 study of adult education in the United States, A. A. Liveright (1968) indicated that academic adult educators had improved the quantity and quality of field research: The journal *Adult Education* (introduced in 1950) clearly focused on reporting adult education research while the Educational Resources Information Center (ERIC, established in 1967 at Syracuse University) provided a collection site for information about adult education research and programming.

However, if community is built in John Dewey's (1916/1944) sense as a place where people come together "in virtue of the things which they have in common" (p. 4), then the field's task was an onerous one. Ohliger observed two camps: one could be seen to support adult education as a venture, while the other nurtured adult education as an adventure. Remembering Paul H. Sheats, Cyril O. Houle, and Malcolm S. Knowles as venture camp advocates, Ohliger, in a 1987 interview, recalled the rage he felt because he had not been critical of them when they asserted that professionalized adult education had a voluntary modern practice (Brennan, 1987). Ohliger (1974) felt that much of adult education as a venture was associated with the wrong kind of education, often mandated, that interfered with learner freedom and learner capacities to communicate, deliberate, and engage. He believed such interference worked against both individuality and sociality, and it created dilemmas personal and sociopolitical in nature. Ohliger concluded, "Though learning or dialogue can lie unborn due to a lack of nurturing and personal care, it can much more easily be killed off by collective attention, institutionalized control, and instructional manipulation" (p. 48). In addition, Ohliger (1991) viewed the incursion of psychology into adult educational practice as divisive, making common guidelines for practice impossible. He contrasted the disparate views held by andragogy guru Malcolm S. Knowles and adventure camp advocate and social philosopher Robert J. Blakely: "While Blakely favored a liberal adult education issue-oriented approach centered in philosophy, Knowles believed in group dynamics derived from psychology as a way of helping adults to learn how to get along better with each other. There was value in both approaches, but the split in views kept social philosophers divided and kept our umbrella organizations ineffective in working for democratic social change" (p. 15).

The field of study's move toward increasing professionalization disturbed Ohliger. Although he seemed to understand the economic and cultural pressures that dictated the moves of field kingpins, he found it difficult to comprehend their underlying motivations. His antagonism toward Houle seemed to be cemented during Ohliger's period of advanced study with him during the late 1950s. Ohliger (1982b) asserted that his "worst experiences resulted from Houle's unwillingness to engage his students in gut-level discussions and our inability to get him to be frank with us" (pp. 69–70). In a reflection on another postwar field kingpin, Ohliger recounted a letter that Coolie Verner wrote to him in the mid-1970s about professionalism. In it, Verner, approaching retirement, links his commitment to professionalism to his lifelong passion to make adult education something separate and special:

At the beginning at least, the desire for professional status in adult education was still imbued with some kind of a shining social purpose as vague—as vague as it might have been. Though professionalism has turned out to be irrelevant to the social and personal concerns of the [19]80s, in those dark [19]50s and early [19]60s, it might have looked like the saving grace. It might not only end the marginal status of the field, but [also] make it possible for adult educators to do really good work in secure surroundings. In the mid-[19]70s I sensed a whiff of this hope and faith turned sour by the years after the early [19]60s in a letter Coolie Verner wrote me: "I'm glad that I am approaching retirement and can leave our field and profession," Coolie stated. "Heretofore I've never doubted the validity and viability of either, but now I begin to wonder if it was all worthwhile. Too many people have become academics in adult education without any real commitment to it or any sense of responsibility to the development of the discipline or the profession. We are not just another arm of an already obsolete educational system, but the new members seek to make us that. Adult education cannot be a viable alternative to a decadent educational system when those in it see it only as an extension of that system, rather than as a unique opportunity to create a new learning alternative. I know that I am *persona non grata* for these views and that's why I shall be glad to get out. Someone else can fight the good fight" [Ohliger, 1982b, p. 6].

Building community remained an elusive project in the U.S. field of adult education in the decades following World War II. Moreover, academic adult education failed to become an acceptable and accepted part of the university community. Although the GI Bill of 1944 gave university participation an adult face, academic adult education remained the "stepchild of the American university" (Riesman, 1981, p. 113). Despite significant growth in the number of graduate adult education programs with a corresponding increase in research production (Houle, 1964; Kreitlow, 1960, 1970; Verner, 1964a, 1964b), academic adult education suffered from the field's history as extension, which created an image of the enterprise as little more than a service activity that had to be self-supporting. Adult education was not valued like "regular" university teaching and research. At a time when the research university was ascendant and professionalism, valuing research over education, had increasing cultural status (Kerr, 1995), academic adult education remained on the margins of the university. Other factors exacerbated this marginal status in higher education, contributing to its confusion of purpose (Portman, 1978). For example, many academics (including educators with responsibility for the schooling of children) were reluctant to consider adult education as important as other forms of public education (Harrington, 1977). And in a time of increasing social turmoil, adult education remained a predominantly white, male, middle-class enterprise that was not available (that is, relevant and affordable) to every citizen (Liveright, 1968). In the late 1960s, A. A. Liveright (1968) asserted that the time had come for academic adult educators and field practitioners to change the field's perennial locatedness as "an ancillary and peripheral component in the individual and social development of the country" (p. 138). He related, "Adult educators, in 1968, are clearly in the position where they must make a better case for the relevance of adult and continuing education to the crucial social and individual problems confronting the United States at this time. . . . The future of adult and continuing education and the extent to which adult educators will play a crucial role in the life of the country are clearly dependent upon professional adult educators themselves" (p. 138).

John Ohliger's Political and Pedagogical Task

In 1971 John Ohliger received the Ivan D. Illich Dystopia Award for his poignant critique of lifelong schooling in his article *Adult Education: 1984* (Chapter Three in this book). In the article, Ohliger (1971) provided dark prophecy suggesting that children born in 1984 would find themselves in a world where compulsory learning for life and work is normalized. They would be sentenced to school for life by their "board of lifelong education" in the "permanent school district" in which they reside (p. 223). Even in death, these apparently Christian souls would "attend a 'school for angels' into infinity" (p. 224). In this world, there would be no learner freedom; schooling would be a matter of fact rather than a matter of choice.

This pivotal piece in Ohliger's career as a radical social educator encapsulated his political and pedagogical task: to resist forms of compulsory lifelong learning and to enable learners to be free to make choices. This freedom in personal and communal learning contexts was the cornerstone of a politics of hope and possibility that Ohliger (1987) trusted would bring citizens as learners and workers into closer communication, communion, and co-creativity in "the relaxing and stimulating climate of human fellowship" (p. 6). Although he realized that hope was a problematic concept and "sloppy sentiment" for many cold, hard realists (p. 6), Ohliger deemed hope as essential to a way out and a way forward for humankind. At age sixty, he reflected, "I find I want to concentrate on a few enthusiasms that encompass their own contradictions . . . [such as my] 'enthusiasm for adult learning outside of institutional control'" (Ohliger, 1987, p. 3).

This desire was caught up in Ohliger's (1988) belief that institutionalized adult education had moved outside hope to the point that the principle of compulsion was winning and spontaneity was losing in late 1980s U.S. adult education. He provided this rationale: "Over half the adult population is now required to go back to school to keep a license to practice, to stay out of jail or on the welfare rolls, to get promoted, or to remedy some deficit. Adult education is the invisible sleeping giant of American society where more money and personnel are devoted to it than all other areas of education—elementary, secondary, and higher—combined" (pp. 7–8).

Ohliger's political and pedagogical task often put him at odds with the mainstream field. For example, suspicious of the emergence of lifelong learning as a necessity, he (1974), apparently conflating European lifelong education with Americanized lifelong learning (Boshier, 2000; Grace, 2005), positioned Edgar Faure's 1972 UNESCO Report entitled *Learning to Be* as "just another example of international bureaucratese" (p. 52). He concluded, "*Learning to Be* refers to structured knowledge, modules of instruction, interchangeable blocks of information, and units of learning. Those concepts are precisely what [Ivan D.] Illich is talking about when he laments that all of knowledge is being reduced to a commodity, to what he labels 'official knowledge' as opposed to 'personal knowledge' (p. 54). *Learning to Be* made Ohliger angry. He used his critique of it to vent his rage at American colleagues like Malcolm S. Knowles, whom he felt had developed andragogy in ways that linked instrumentalism to learner control and the advancement of official knowledge. He was also quite critical of Cyril O. Houle, who called *Learning to Be* the most significant book of the last third of the twentieth century. Ohliger felt that Houle and his work exemplified much of what was wrong with adult education as a venture.

For years after its publication, Ohliger (1982b) continued to question the legitimacy, indeed the very notion, of *Learning to Be*: "I remember when I was an early adolescent being pushed into thinking about and deciding what I wanted to 'be' when I grew up. There is no more questionable question for a so-called child than 'What do you want to be when you grow up?' UNESCO adult educators and others continue to push 'Learning to Be,' when we already 'are,' and need no educational program to legitimize our existence" (p. 64). Ohliger's resistance to the formalization of the process of learning finds expression in his notion of radical education that focuses on the freedom of citizens as learners and workers to make choices based on who they are. Ohliger felt that adult learners were puzzled and puzzling beings who could not have parameters set to their learning for life and work. Concomitantly, he considered adult educators to be "relatively unique and definitely obscure" (p. 64), which he said is the characterization that drew him to the field in the first place. As he perceived them, adult educators did not teach inside the box.

Irritated and dismayed with academic adult education and numerous field colleagues, Ohliger left the academy in 1973. He set up Basic Choices, Inc., in Madison, Wisconsin, in 1976 as a center for exploring and deliberating social and political ideas and actions in radical adult education. His critiques of professionalism, the commodification of adult education as a venture, and the compulsory participation of learners in mandated forms of lifelong learning continued with new and unrelenting vigor. What bothered him most about lifelong learning was the concept's incorporation as an integral part of professionalism (Ohliger, 1981). He worried that this would lead to a monopoly for institutionalized learning at the expense of self-initiated and self-directed learning in individual and community contexts. In the hope of avoiding this possibility, Ohliger (1981) challenged adult educators to reject mandatory continuing education. He wanted them to embrace voluntary learning as a way to address "the basic problems of finding good work, being mutually accountable, and living a worthwhile life" (p. 5). He asked them to recognize that "knowledge and the education that fosters it are almost always subtle, indirect, intangible, unmeasurable, illusive, delicate, and, above all, not amenable to the sledgehammer approach" (p. 7). Ohliger maintained this would mean more freedom for both adult educators and learners to choose because the sledgehammer approach destroyed historically cherished liberal educational values.

Ohliger's work with Basic Choices focused on education as the practice of liberty expressed as learner freedom to make choices. Ohliger (1983) made learner freedom a focal point in his social educational and cultural work because he believed that much of Americanized lifelong learning left liberty behind, devalued the modest but real value of education, and amounted to a compulsory engagement in "therapeutic education to remedy a deficiency" (p. 161). In his usual fault-finding fashion, he positioned Americanized lifelong learning as a social movement inhabiting "the crest of institutionalized adult education" (p. 163):

The trend toward compulsory lifelong schooling is due to a social movement which denies it is one. This movement is fed by the twin growing giants of industrialized technology and capitalistic economics. Its most salient focus is the formalizing education dimension of professionalism. The movement pushes its unending creation of wants masquerading as needs into the shadows by spotlighting scientific knowledge as the only legitimate way to know. Scientific knowledge claims to offer the only realistic panacea to the world's problems, though many of them were created by the movement now demanding the mandate to solve them [p. 162].

Beck (1992) would later dub this society the *risk society*, where science offers itself as a solution to the problems it creates. In this risk society, reconciling education with liberty is no mean feat. As Ohliger (1983) put it, "The tough problem . . . becomes, in part, one of devising educational approaches that foster self-expression with an absolute minimum required involvement in structures that cloud it" (p. 172). He maintained that balancing value-oriented, self-initiated, and self-directed social learning with more structured, results-focused, and specialist-directed learning requires adult educators to be wary of technoscientism and the commodification of knowledge production and to attend to feelings and intellectual clarity. In the 1989 U.S. *Handbook of Adult and Continuing Education*, Ohliger made it clear that mainstream adult educators had failed in this regard. He exposed their technical intellectual myopia focused on "the splendor of the now" (p. 634):

Mainstream adult educators generally stick to the straight-and-narrow path. They frequently confidently predict what they think will happen. Worthwhile alternative or off-center educators are more tentative and eschew bliss about the future for the steady stare at the present. Mainstream protagonists foster the enhancement and extrapolation of present dominant technological trends, for instance, the so-called knowledge explosion, the information revolution, or the specter of human obsolescence. . . . [However,] the splendor of the now may not be enough. It leaves unanswered some of the questions raised by the massive accumulation of the past— the past recognized as the history of oppression. The splendor of the now leaves unresolved the dilemma of the future that appears to remain stubbornly resistant to fundamental change [pp. 630, 634].

When he focused specifically on academic adult educators, Ohliger's tongue became even sharper. For example, writing about them in 1991, Ohliger used this barb to describe those in the field of study as unworldly and unworthy: "Intellectual authorities in adult education don't recognize realities beyond those that can be expressed via written or spoken words. This problem is only compounded by the difficult, boring, or lifeless style in which most of them write" (p. 15). The subtext here is that academic adult educators are armchair intellectuals disengaged from the world and action in their preoccupation with the word. Ohliger was just as scathing when he critiqued field literature: "Standard adult education literature is filled with . . . cliches [like learning how to learn] that are mines in themselves, but don't explode with the lack of meaning because they're so immersed in gloom. The standard adult education literature represents the rage in my view of most adult educators who are spreading their rage thin by writing boring materials" (interview excerpt in Brennan, 1987, p. 56). Ironically, Ohliger, admired as an exemplar of radical and liberal thought by many critical adult educators, was even more cutting in his criticism of criticalist literature in adult education. In 1987 he jeered, "Grim and cheerless, but currently proposed, constructs such as *critical pedagogy* and *theories of resistance* offer little" (p. 635). Later, Ohliger (1999a) gibed, "So many tomes on higher education put us to sleep" because "they are often deliberately written in obscure language in order to give the appearance of profundity and in order to secure academic positions for the authors . . . bitten by the critical theory bug" (p. 17). The subtext throughout is that both standard and critical adult education literature are neither substantial nor meaningful. Ironically, Ohliger's acerbic comments smack of an anti-intellectualism that one would not expect from such a devotee of books. His cutting words obviously did little to build community with contemporaries in academe. Perhaps they are a testament to the deep hurt and bitterness he still felt long after he left his academic position at Ohio State University.

Ohliger's resistance to compulsory forms of lifelong learning and his ambition to enable learners to be free to make choices never waned. In the late 1990s, he (1999a) declared that training had overshadowed true education, with learning for profit outdistancing education for any kind of social transformation. A question crucial to adult education as an adventure—What knowledge has most worth?—no longer seemed to be asked. Instead another question important to adult education as a venture took precedence: "How quickly can we get on this training bandwagon?" (Ohliger, 1999a, p. 16). Ohliger thought that society would become less humane as colleges and universities succumbed to corporate models of education that eroded their social power. In "A Cautious Welcome to the New Millennium" (Chapter Eight in this book), Ohliger (1999b) critically examined the increasing commercialism in society influencing higher education's hope-and-fear responses to the new century and the much anticipated Y2K problem. On the upside, he saw the Y2K problem as a damper on technological optimism and a counterpoint to the "uncritical praise of the future of high technology" (p. 11). Still, commercialism had induced a proliferation of private for-profit colleges and universities that promoted learning in economistic terms while placing faculty security at risk. Ohliger felt this turn in higher education had compromised its very definition. He wondered if it was a harbinger of the end of adult education as an adventure.

Concluding Perspective: Ohliger's Thoughts on a Turn to Theorizing

Ohliger (1980) believed that a turn to theorizing could be a sign of either a field maturing or a field in crisis. More than twenty-five years ago, he depicted conditions that situated the field of study and practice within "an advanced high technology society characterized externally by the expansion of multinational corporations, and internally by the increasing integration of government, industry, and education" (p. 48). These conditions were in many ways a response to another profound post–World War II condition, the knowledge explosion, which Ohliger felt located citizens as permanently inadequate learners and workers. As he saw it, all of these conditions set the stage for mandatory lifelong schooling wed to a credentialing society that devalued personal and social forms of self-initiated lifelong learning. In sum, they had import for theory development in adult education, which he placed into three categories: "Generally speaking, present theory in adult education either (1) tries to develop a non-ideological, all purpose approach separate from the historical context; or (2) accepts the contemporary context as a given that adult educators should help people adjust to, prosper within or ameliorate problems of; or (3) rejects the present context as inhuman and attempts to encourage others to rebel against it" (p. 48). These three categories of theorizing can be respectively described as ahistorical, universalistic standard theorizing; technorational instrumental theorizing; and historico-critical social theorizing. Each competing form of theorizing is found in the present, in which its currency is related to the conditions of the times and the value placed on it by its adherents.

Ohliger (1980) considered all three categories of theorizing problematic, asserting that they showed "a lack of critical distance from our society and its ambiguities" (p. 48). As he critiqued it, ahistorical, universalistic standard theorizing ignored the impact of technoscientific development and how the proliferation of its tools and support systems historically changed the nature of work and societal well-being. Technorational instrumental theorizing equated field maturity with technical competence, sidelining the liberal purposes of adult education: enlightening and humanizing adult learners. Historico-critical social theorizing seemed idealistic and out of touch with the everyday realities of citizens as learners and workers. However, this critique appears to exemplify once again Ohliger's tendency toward an anti-intellectualism that forgets the mutuality of the theoretical with the practical and realistic. His own words suggest this characterization is apt and that he tended to succumb to the very gloominess he often associated with criticalist literature:

> Advocates of some of the radical alternatives are sometimes guilty of believing that by fostering education as an institution less dependent on . . . [the socioeconomic] order, people can thereby be liberated from that order. But the fact remains that so long as people must earn their livelihood in this society, regardless of what kind of exotic education they may seek, they are still subject to many of the same kinds of pressures and conditioning that force adults back to school for certification, lead them to the endless pursuit of courses for self-improvement, and support their continued dependence on specialists. Like a specter over the cultural horizon, the pervasive technological and economic order clouds even the most utopian aspirations for education [p. 51].

Still, in times when neoliberalism, privatization, and globalization or "Americanization of the world economy" (Ohliger, 1999a, p. 22) have a deep impact on the contemporary practice of adult education (Grace 2004, 2005), Ohliger continues to remind us of the difficulties facing adult education as it attempts to mediate the contemporary twists and turns of the economic and the cultural. His critique of categories of theorizing should not be taken as a dismissal of theorizing per se. Rather, it is meant to teach us to problematize theorizing as we think about theory in terms of the matters of context, disposition, and relationship that shape it, as well as in terms of the modern practice of adult education with which it is mutually informative. When we do so, we bring the intellectual and the real world together in ways that John Ohliger and other radical educators like Paulo Freire, Eduard Lindeman, and Ivan Illich would have wished.

References

Aronowitz, S., & DiFazio, W. (1994). *The jobless future: Sci-tech and the dogma of work*. Minneapolis: University of Minnesota Press.

Axford, R. W. (1969). *Adult education: The open door*. Scranton, PA: International Textbook Company.

Beck, U. (1992). *Risk society* (M. Ritter, Trans.). Thousand Oaks, CA: Sage. (Original work published 1986)

Bell, D. (1960). *The end of ideology*. New York: Free Press.

Bell, D. (1967). The post-industrial society: A speculative view. In E. Hutchings & E. Hutchings (Eds.), *Scientific progress and human values* (pp. 154–170). New York: American Elsevier.

Bergevin, P. (1967). *A philosophy for adult education*. New York: Seabury Press.

Boshier, R. (2000). Running to win: The contest between lifelong learning and education in Canada. *New Zealand Journal of Adult Learning, 28*(2), 6–28.

Brennan, B. (1987). Conversation with John Ohliger. *Australian Journal of Adult Education, 27*(3), 52–56, 65.

Brookfield, S. (1987). *Learning democracy: Eduard Lindeman on adult education and social change*. London: Croom Helm.

Charters, A. N. (1971). *Report on the 1969 Galaxy Conference of Adult Education Organizations*. Syracuse, NY: Syracuse University Publications in Continuing Education.

Collins, M. (1991). *Adult education as vocation: A critical role for the adult educator*. New York: Routledge.

Cotton, W. E. (1968). *On behalf of adult education: A historical examination of the supporting literature*. Boston: Center for the Study of Liberal Education for Adults.

Dewey, J. (1944). *Democracy and education*. New York: Free Press. (Original work published 1916)

Faure, E. (1972). *Learning to be: The world of education, today and tomorrow*. Paris: UNESCO.

Grace, A. P. (1999). Building a knowledge base in U.S. academic adult education (1945–1970). *Studies in the Education of Adults, 31*(2), 220–236.

Grace, A. P. (2000a). Canadian and U.S. adult learning (1945–1970) and the cultural politics and place of lifelong learning. *International Journal of Lifelong Education, 19*(2), 141–158.

Grace, A. P. (2000b). Academic adult education in Canada and the United States (1917–1970): A chronology of their emergence and a conspectus of their development. *PAACE Journal of Lifelong Learning, 9,* 65–78.

Grace, A. P. (2004). Lifelong learning as a chameleonic concept and versatile practice: Y2K perspectives and trends. *International Journal of Lifelong Education, 23*(4), 385–405.

Grace, A. P. (2005). Lifelong learning chic in the modern practice of adult education: Historical and contemporary perspectives. *Journal of Adult and Continuing Education, 11*(1), 62–79.

Griffith, W. S. (1970). Adult education institutions. In R. M. Smith, G. F. Aker, & J. R. Kidd (Eds.), *Handbook of adult education* (pp. 171–189). New York: Macmillan.

Hallenbeck, W. C. (1960). The function and place of adult education in American society. In M. S. Knowles (Ed.), *Handbook of adult education in the United States* (pp. 29–38). Washington, DC: Adult Education Association of the U.S.A.

Harrington, F. H. (1977). *The future of adult education.* San Francisco: Jossey-Bass.

Hart, M. U. (1992). *Working and educating for life: Feminist and international perspectives on adult education.* London: Routledge.

Houle, C. O. (1964). The emergence of graduate study in adult education. In G. Jensen, A. A. Liveright, & W. Hallenbeck (Eds.), *Adult education: Outlines of an emerging field of study* (pp. 69–83). Washington, DC: Adult Education Association of the U.S.A.

Houle, C. O. (1970). The educator of adults. In R. M. Smith, G. F. Aker, & J. R. Kidd (Eds.), *Handbook of adult education* (pp. 109–119). New York: Macmillan.

Jameson, F. (1991). *Postmodernism, or, the cultural logic of late capitalism.* Durham, NC: Duke University Press.

Jarvis, P. J. (1987). *An interview with Malcolm Knowles.* Interview conducted at the Eighth International Seminar on the Education of Adults. Surrey, UK: Department of Educational Studies, University of Surrey.

Jensen, G., Liveright, A. A., & Hallenbeck, W. (1964). Adult education. In G. Jensen, A. A. Liveright, & W. Hallenbeck (Eds.), *Adult education: Outlines of an emerging field of study* (pp. iv-xi). Washington, DC: Adult Education Association of the U.S.A.

Kempfer, H. (1955). *Adult education*. New York: McGraw-Hill.

Kerr, C. (1995). *The uses of the university* (4th ed.). Cambridge, MA: Harvard University Press.

Knowles, M. S. (1960). Historical development of the adult education movement in the United States. In M. S. Knowles (Ed.), *Handbook of adult education in the United States* (pp. 7–28). Washington, DC: Adult Education Association of the U.S.A.

Knowles, M. S. (1977). *A history of the adult education movement in the United States*. Malabar, FL: Krieger. (Original work published 1962)

Knowles, M. S., & DuBois, E. E. (1970). Prologue: The handbooks in perspective. In R. M. Smith, G. F. Aker, & J. R. Kidd (Eds.), *Handbook of adult education* (pp. xvii-xxiii). New York: Macmillan.

Kreitlow, B. W. (1960). Research in adult education. In M. S. Knowles (Ed.), *Handbook of adult education in the United States* (pp. 106–116). Washington, DC: Adult Education Association of the U.S.A.

Kreitlow, B. W. (1970). Research and theory. In R. M. Smith, G. F. Aker, & J. R. Kidd (Eds.), *Handbook of adult education* (pp. 137–149). New York: Macmillan.

Liveright, A. A. (1968). *A study of adult education in the United States*. Boston: Center for the Study of Liberal Education for Adults.

Locke, A. (1948). Foreword. In M. L. Ely (Ed.), *Handbook of adult education in the United States* (pp. ix-x). New York: Institute of Adult Education, Teachers College, Columbia University.

Ohliger, J. (1969, April). Adult basic education programs and the liberal arts approach. *Adult Leadership, 17*, 417–419.

Ohliger, J. (1971). Adult education: 1984. *Adult Leadership, 19*(7), 223–224.

Ohliger, J. (1974). Is lifelong education a guarantee of permanent inadequacy? *Convergence, 7*(2), 47–58.

Ohliger, J. (1975). Prospects for a learning society. *Adult Leadership, 24*(1), 37–39.

Ohliger, J. (1980). The social uses of theorizing in adult education. *Adult Education, 31*(1), 48–53.

Ohliger, J. (1981, October). *Must we all go back to school?* Public lecture given at the annual Minnesota Education Association Convention. Madison, WI: Basic Choices.

Ohliger, J. (1982a). Is J. Edgar Hoover a virgin? *Media/Adult Learning, 4*(1), 46–52.

Ohliger, J. (1982b). *Adult education in a world of excessive riches/excessive poverty*. Madison, WI: Basic Choices.

Ohliger, J. (1983). Reconciling education with liberty. *Prospects, 13*(2), 161–179.

Ohliger, J. (1987, September). *Partners in adult learning*. Keynote address at the joint national conference of the Australian Association of Adult Education and the Library Association of Australia, Ohio State University, College of Education, Columbus.

Ohliger, J. (1988, October). *Some thoughts on knowledge and power*. Keynote address delivered to the Eighth Annual Convocation of the Meiklejohn Education Foundation, University of Wisconsin, Madison.

Ohliger, J. (1989). Alternative images of the future in adult education. In P. Cunningham & S. Merriam (Eds.), *Handbook of adult and continuing education* (pp. 628–639). San Francisco: Jossey-Bass.

Ohliger, J. (1990). Forum: You shall know the truth and the truth shall make you laugh. *Journal of Adult Education, 19*(1), 25–38.

Ohliger, J. (1991). Social philosophy: Its past, present, and future. *Adult Learning, 2*(8), 15.

Ohliger, J. (1999a, Fall). Crises in higher education, 1991–98. *College Daze*, no. 1, 15–27.

Ohliger, J. (1999b). A cautious welcome to the new millennium. *Canadian Journal for the Study of Adult Education, 13*(2), 7–18.

Ohliger, J., & McCarthy, C. (1971). *Lifelong learning or lifelong schooling? A tentative view of the ideas of Ivan Illich with a quotational bibliography*. Syracuse, NY: Syracuse University Publications in Continuing Education and ERIC Clearinghouse on Education.

Portman, D. N. (1978). *The universities and the public: A history of higher adult education in the United States*. Chicago: Nelson-Hall.

Riesman, D. (1981). *On higher education*. San Francisco: Jossey-Bass.

Said, E. W. (1994). *Representations of the intellectual*. New York: Pantheon.

Sheats, P. H., Jayne, C. D., & Spence, R. B. (1953). *Adult education: The community approach*. New York: Dryden Press.

Smith, R. M., Aker, G. F., & Kidd, J. R. (Eds.). (1970). *Handbook of adult education*. New York: Macmillan.

Thomas, A. M. (1963). The making of a professional. In J. R. Kidd (Ed.), *Learning and society* (pp. 336–344). Toronto: Canadian Association for Adult Education.

Verner, C. (1960). The literature of adult education. In M. S. Knowles (Ed.), *Handbook of adult education in the United States* (pp. 162–175). Washington, DC: Adult Education Association of the U.S.A.

Verner, C. (1963). Basic concepts and limitations. In J. R. Kidd (Ed.), *Learning and society* (pp. 229–240). Toronto: Canadian Association for Adult Education. (Original worked published 1961)

Verner, C. (1964a). Definition of terms. In G. Jensen, A. A. Liveright, &
    W. Hallenbeck (Eds.), *Adult education: Outlines of an emerging field of
    study* (pp. 27–39). Washington, DC: Adult Education Association of
    the U.S.A.
Verner, C. (1964b). *Adult education*. New York: Center for Applied Research in
    Education.
Verner, C. (1978). Organizing graduate professional education for adult educa-
    tion. In J. R. Kidd & G. R. Selman (Eds.), *Coming of age: Canadian adult
    education in the 1960s* (pp. 132–141). Toronto: Canadian Association for
    Adult Education. (Original work published 1969)
Welton, M. R. (1995). The critical turn in adult education theory. In M. R.
    Welton (Ed.), *In defense of the lifeworld: Critical perspectives on adult learn-
    ing* (pp. 11–38). New York: State University of New York Press.
Wilson, A. L. (1995). The common concern: Controlling the professionalization
    of adult education. In S. B. Merriam (Ed.), *Selected writings on philosophy
    and adult education* (2nd ed., pp. 147–172). Malabar, FL: Krieger.

10

The Adult Educator as Public Intellectual

David Yamada

In a unique way, John Ohliger was a public intellectual, a learned individual who addressed "a general audience on matters of broad public concern" (Perlstein, 2002, p. A19). The term *public intellectual* has been the subject of considerable discussion since the appearance of Russell Jacoby's *The Last Intellectuals* (1987). Jacoby opined that highly specialized and heavily credentialed academicians who write for a very narrow audience have usurped the role of the independent, bohemian public scholar and writer. High urban rents, he explained, have made it difficult for creative minds to congregate and build intellectual communities. In addition, affiliations with universities, with their requirements for dissertations and tenure, have discouraged the creation and nurturing of intellectuals who communicate with the general public on topics of the day.

In the wake of *The Last Intellectuals* has come an abundance of commentary not only debating Jacoby's thesis (*Nation* Forum, 2001; Honan, 1990; Krupnick, 1987), but also examining how we define a public intellectual and who can claim the label (Melzer, Weinberger, & Zinman, 2003; Small, 2002; Posner, 2001). Amid this discussion, it would seem natural to link our conceptions of the public intellectual with our ideas about adult education. After all, public intellectuals are adult educators, in that they are sharing information, opinions, and even artistic work with a largely mature audience.

Despite all that has been said about public intellectuals in recent years, however, there has been little effort to frame their work within the context of adult education.

As a short response to that void, this chapter examines the roles of public intellectuals as adult educators. I posit that most public intellectuals operate in an instructional, pedagogical mode and that virtually every consideration of their role tacitly assumes this. In addition, today's leading public intellectuals have been accorded celebrity status, whereby public exposure has often supplanted public education as an end result of their work.

By contrast, John Ohliger modeled an unconventional public intellectual role by conducting his work in a largely facilitative, andragogical mode, particularly through Basic Choices, the independent center he cofounded in 1976. After he left a tenured position as an associate professor in adult education at Ohio State University in the early 1970s, Ohliger created a niche for himself as an educator, writer, and intellectual activist. He did so in a personal and engaging manner that fostered friendships in addition to intellectual exchanges, an approach sufficiently distinctive that I refer to it as the "Ohliger method" of being a public intellectual. Even his most publicly visible campaign of direct advocacy—the fight against mandatory continuing education—was grounded in a commitment to voluntary learning in smaller-scale, noninstitutional settings. Ohliger's practice of inquiry, outreach, and dialogue may have cost him some of the fame conferred on more conventional public intellectuals, but he left a legacy worth studying and emulating.

The Instructive, Pedagogical Public Intellectual

To understand the significance of Ohliger's work, we should first consider the practices of mainstream public intellectuals. Notwithstanding differing political ideologies, areas of specialization, and media outlets, the tie that binds most contemporary public intellectuals is that they deliver information and opinions drawn from their expertise. Books (usually nonfiction), op-ed pieces, and media interviews (print and electronic) are their typical venues. Public lectures and keynote addresses may add to the mix. In most instances, public intellectuals have limited opportunity (and, often, equally little desire) for ongoing exchanges with their audiences. A letter to the editor, an unsolicited e-mail, or perhaps a question or comment during the Q&A portion of a talk is usually the extent of the active feedback. Thus, the public intellectual's role is similar to that of a college lecturer who is addressing a group of students in a large hall.

As adult educators, public intellectuals operate primarily in a pedagogical mode. The "pedagogical model assigns to the teacher full responsibility for making all decisions about what will be learned, how it will be learned, when it will be learned, and if it has been learned" (Knowles, Holton, & Swanson, 1998, p. 62). Granted, the typical milieu of the public intellectual—the print and electronic media—may suggest that "students" have some degree of choice in the manner and means of their personal learning, and they (obviously) do not face a final examination at the end of the article or interview. Regardless, the "teacher" retains virtually complete control over the content and mode of its delivery. In terms of outcomes, the public intellectual seeks mainly to inform, and at times to persuade, the audience.

This is not necessarily a bad thing. We should be pleased when individuals who have closely studied a topic share the fruits of their intellectual labor in an accessible manner. The world benefits from the dissemination of specialized knowledge and insight gained through the blending of intelligence and hard work. A thoughtful book, lecture, or op-ed column promotes understanding, stimulates thinking, and nurtures an open society. Although the typical public intellectual delivers content in a more or less instructional format, so long as means exist to preserve it, it can be the catalyst for learning and discussion months or even years after its original appearance, even if the author is not present.

Public Versus Intellectual?

Even in the realm of intellectual work, the cult of celebrity has joined with the content of the message. Today's prominent public intellectuals do not fit the mold of the bohemian independent scholar. Instead, they "tend to be academic celebrities, professors who write regularly for magazines like *The New Yorker* or television pundits who churn out opinions on topics from campaign finance to 'The Sopranos'" (Cohen, 2000, p. A16). Those who are members of the professoriate may enjoy a certain visibility on campus that makes them the envy of less publicized colleagues. This fame can be heady stuff for holders of graduate and professional degrees who never imagined gaining such notoriety as they toiled in classrooms and libraries.

Conventional public intellectuals have also become very marketable commodities in an information age that places a premium on snappy quotes and sound bites. Jurist and legal scholar Richard Posner has listed leading public intellectuals by counting "media mentions, web hits, and scholarly citations" (Posner, 2001, p. 194), while curiously bemoaning how some have become all-purpose pundits for the media by supplying commentary on topics well beyond their areas of expertise. University of Chicago scholar Jean Bethke Elshtain has observed that a public intellectual risks becoming more public and less intellectual, meaning "less reflective, less inclined to question one's own judgments, [and] less likely to embed a conviction in its appropriate context with all the nuance intact" (*Nation* Forum, 2001, p. 28). Similarly, Columbia University sociologist Herbert Gans acknowledged that today's public intellectuals have become "quote-suppliers" for members of the media who are looking for the right words to plug into a news story (*Nation* Forum, 2001, p. 30).

Anyone who has faced the task of boiling down years and pages of research for a media interview or an op-ed column knows what this means. A public intellectual's visibility often depends on taking sharp, memorable positions and vigorously defending them with the brevity of a PowerPoint slide. Lengthy explanations and analyses virtually ensure that one's words will end up in the recycling bin or on the cutting-room floor. Scholars who emphasize the gray areas of important public issues are likely to be passed over in favor of those who can supply a quick turn of the phrase, even if it means sacrificing important depth and nuance.

Furthermore, public intellectuals are tempted to assume the role of all-knowing pontificators. Reporters working on a tight deadline are more likely to go back to previous sources who have supplied them with good quotes. Given the pleasing prospect of seeing one's name in print or face on television, it takes character (or, some might say, foolishness) for a public intellectual to respond to a media request by saying that a topic is outside his or her realm of expertise.

The University and the Public Intellectual

In a twist on Jacoby's thesis, it now appears that the modern academy has seen the light on the value of having public intellectuals on faculties, but not necessarily because of a renewed commitment to public dialogue and civic education. Rather, the current obsession within higher education over institutional reputation has made it desirable for universities to hire and support publicly visible scholars. Columbia's Gans observed that public intellectuals "are beloved by their [university] employers, because they get these employers publicity," adding that when universities get publicity, "they think they're getting prestige, and if they get prestige, that may help them get students or grant money" (*Nation* Forum, 2001, p. 30).

The Ivy League schools are not the only ones playing this game. For example, the media relations office of DePaul University in Chicago advises professors and administrators that a "timely, well-written and provocative piece can establish the writer as an expert on a particular topic and gain national media recognition for the author and DePaul University" (DePaul University Media Relations, n.d.-a). DePaul staff are further reminded that "when a reporter calls, cite your affiliation with DePaul University and ask that

you be identified as a DePaul professor or administrator in the story"
(DePaul University Media Relations, n.d.-b).

Lest this be seen as unfairly singling out one school, it should be
added that DePaul deserves credit for demystifying media processes
for its academicians. However, DePaul's materials demonstrate how
universities now regard faculty work as a commodity that can be
used for institutional self-promotion in the academic marketplace,
regardless of the content or social value of that work. For schools
like DePaul, a well-regarded regional university with national ambitions, this becomes an important function in the drive toward
greater recognition.

In sum, the renewed attention to the roles of public intellectuals
has coincided with a further retreat from the notion of an independent, interactive intellectual life. The paradigmatic public intellectual has embraced both authority and celebrity. The modern
university, while perhaps complicit in failing to support independent public intellectuals, understands that publicly visible faculty
can attract attention that will enhance its reputation. The media
has helped to create public intellectuals who are part of an entertainment culture of punditry and personality. The end product is a
"system" designed to meet the market needs of today's knowledge
society.

The Facilitative, Andragogical Public Intellectual

John Ohliger was a different kind of public intellectual, one whose
methods were more facilitative than instructional, more andragogical than pedagogical. Although he spent a number of years teaching at traditional universities, much of his most compelling work
was done without a full-time academic affiliation. In the years that
followed his resignation from Ohio State University, he engaged in
many activities related to adult learning. These included cofounding and directing Basic Choices; cofounding WORT, a public radio
station in Madison, Wisconsin; and hosting the "Madison Review

of Books," a WORT radio program that invited members of the public to conduct on-air reviews of books of their choosing. He also taught on a part-time and visiting basis at several universities, though he would never again be a permanent faculty member.

Theories about andragogy abound (Grace, 1996), but the conceptualization that best fits Ohliger's methods and philosophy was formulated by the Nottingham Andragogy Group. They defined it as "an attempt to assist adults to become the originators of their own thinking and feeling" (Brookfield, 1986, p. 100). The group identified twelve features "essential to the andragogic process": "a non-prescriptive attitude, issue-centered curricula, problem posing, praxis, continuous negotiation, shared responsibility for learning, valuing process, dialogue, equality, openness, mutual respect, and integrated thinking and learning" (p. 100). Ohliger, a man given to strong opinions about the world around him, nevertheless produced a remarkable body of work that reinforced these values. It is particularly noteworthy that although his political views placed him to the left of center, his writings were largely free of ideological browbeating. Even his frequent use of the term *radical* suggested more a general distancing from mainstream technocratic and consumer culture than a rigid sociopolitical and economic worldview. Rather, he offered a truly kinder and gentler vision for a society of tomorrow:

> My picture is of a future where we live more relaxed and more modest lives with an abundance of unmeasurable and infinitely available non-material (or better, trans-material) resources. All the travail and pressure we're going through right now may be paving the way for that future. This future could be one where we will have a choice of "goodies"; *not* ones requiring scarce energy, minerals, or dollars; or ones permitting some people to get rich while others go hungry, but choices that we create with our own hearts and heads and hands among people we know and care for [Ohliger, 1981, p. 7].

This vision was entirely consistent with Ohliger's own lifestyle and his outlook on the future of adult education. Ohliger chose to live modestly. He once remarked that before he began living with his wife, Chris Wagner, he occupied what in her words was a "hovel." He expressed guilt over using a car, saying, "I felt less of a sinner when I lived cheaper without an auto." (It should be emphasized that the two hardly lived indulgently, even with a car and a habitable home.)

On a more scholarly note, Ohliger appealed to the work of adult educators Michael Marien and Phyllis Cunningham in recognizing two competing visions of the future for society and adult education (Ohliger, c. 1982). One vision was that of a "technological, top-down, service society" that defined "the 'good life' as affluence and leisure with high-tech big technology solving problems which lead to mastery of the environment" (Ohliger, c. 1982, p. 1). The other vision saw the "good life" as embracing "useful work, peace, self-fulfillment, and appropriate technology leading to harmony with the environment" (Ohliger, c. 1982, p. 1). Ohliger (c. 1982) conceded that most adult educators, including himself, exist "in both worlds of adult education and interact daily with people who have the two contrasting visions of the future" (p. 1).

Ohliger and Basic Choices

In 1976, Ohliger and fellow Madison intellectual activists founded Basic Choices, which they styled "A Midwest Center for Clarifying Political and Social Options" (Basic Choices, 1977, p. 1). Basic Choices began with lofty rhetoric, detailing broad crises in America's social, political, and economic infrastructure and calling on those "who share a vision of a more humane, democratic society" to work for social change (p. 1). This new center, its founders reasoned, would advance that vision in ways that existing, inadequate social institutions could not. It is through Basic Choices that Ohliger would hone his role as a public intellectual in an alternative mode, and much of his work would reflect the essential features of the andragogic process.

In addition to embracing an overarching commitment to progressive social justice, each of the core founders of Basic Choices brought specific issues and projects to this new initiative. Ohliger's main issue was mandatory continuing education. Vern Visick, a Methodist campus minister, had a special interest in "student development and the question of governance in higher education" (Basic Choices, 1977, pp. 5–6). Art Lloyd, an Episcopalian campus chaplain, examined "alternate styles of work in modern society" (p. 6). John Hill, a Catholic priest, concentrated on "the practical organization and financing of alternate voluntary organizations" (p. 6). (It is ironic that Ohliger, who wrestled with questions of religion and spirituality throughout his adult life, chose to collaborate with three men of the cloth.)

Basic Choices secured modest space in Madison, which housed an office and a resource center containing materials about education, politics, and public affairs. The resource center featured a notable collection pertaining to the works of Paulo Freire and Ivan Illich. The small headquarters hosted meetings of Basic Choices volunteers and visits from researchers.

It is fair to say that Basic Choices never reached the level of its founding aspirations. By the mid-1980s, the core participants were questioning whether they should continue to work together within this structure. Eventually most of them went their separate ways, but Ohliger's success was in maintaining the center largely as a one-person operation.

During the early years of Basic Choices, Ohliger concentrated his efforts on opposing mandatory continuing education (MCE). It is on this issue that Ohliger assumed a more traditional public intellectual role. His objective was to persuade educators, policymakers, and the general public that MCE was undesirable. Ohliger's argument opposing MCE was grounded in the conviction that adult learning should be voluntary rather than coerced and imposed in perpetuity.

Ohliger received national attention for that work. A coauthored piece in the *Progressive* helped to establish him as a leading opponent of MCE. He edited and coauthored an internationally circulated newsletter, *Second Thoughts*, that was devoted to the fight against MCE. He also participated in many conferences focused on MCE, including a memorable 1979 gathering at the Highlander Center in Tennessee, which served as a national organizing meeting for educators and activists committed to voluntary adult learning.

Aside from his crusade against MCE, Ohliger's signature body of work under the Basic Choices label was a collection of unique bibliographical essays on a wide range of topics, often linked by a common theme of adult learning. A typical piece consisted of an opening essay containing observations and statements, followed by dozens, even hundreds, of brief annotations on relevant books and articles. Many of the essays appeared (without annotations) as guest columns in *Adult and Continuing Education Today*, and Ohliger invited readers to send in for the full versions. Ohliger's intention was clear: to facilitate our understanding by inviting us to dig deeper and draw our own conclusions. It is quite a balancing act to both share strong opinions and enable others to think for themselves, but Ohliger often succeeded.

For example, in *Radical Ideas in Adult Education* (c. 1990), Ohliger put forth "a series of tentative statements" about the social and political underpinnings of adult education, which he divided into three categories: "ideas about people," "ideas about society," and "ideas about adult education" (p. 1). The underlying messages emerging from these statements were that everyday people were very capable of learning and making important decisions, that the world was run by an elite few, and that conventional adult education was too conservative and inattentive to personal development and human interaction. The heart of the piece is a lengthy series of annotated sources linked to the major statements in the opening essay by an index. It takes little effort to discern Ohliger's progressive, populist leanings, but his complete transparency about the materials that informed his viewpoints allows curious readers to consult the sources and draw their own conclusions.

The very term *public intellectual* conjures up images of earnest people talking about earnest things. Ohliger could be very serious, but he could just as easily be intellectually playful, inviting us to learn from popular culture. For example, his article "Billy Joel: The Fire, The Facts, and The Story" parsed the performer's hit song "We Didn't Start the Fire," a musical "roll call" of 120 historical "persons, places, and events" (Ohliger, 1990a, p. 1). Ohliger suggested that adult educators could use the song as a basis for discussion, and his sixty-five-item bibliography provided background information on its historical references.

Similarly, in his article "Mystery, Crime, and Adult Education," Ohliger (c. 1993) took an oft-maligned literary genre, mystery and crime fiction, and wrote, "Reading or watching the right stuff, you'll learn a lot about the world *and* about adult education" (p. 1). He noted that mysteries cover different historical eras; engage religious, political, and legal issues; and even portray educational settings. His annotated bibliography included dozens of recommendations of quality mysteries.

Ohliger and WORT Radio Station

In the Madison, Wisconsin, area, Ohliger is best remembered for his ongoing devotion to WORT, the community radio station that he cofounded in 1973. It bears mentioning that his WORT activities also help us to understand Ohliger's public-intellectual role. WORT would be the most enduring of Ohliger's many contributions to noncommercial radio, which began in 1940 and included a stint as news director of the Pacifica Foundation's public radio stations in California during the early 1960s.

Like Basic Choices, WORT began with the efforts of a small volunteer collective of Ohliger and four other Madisonians who wanted to start a listener-supported radio station. For two years, they did much of the necessary spadework to create WORT. After singer-songwriter Bonnie Raitt performed a benefit concert that helped to raise enough money to begin broadcasting, WORT finally went on the air in December 1975.

Ohliger's most significant on-air programming contribution was serving as founder and host of "The Madison Review of Books," which he described this way in his memoirs: "We obtained thousands of review copies of new books from publishers and offered *anyone* in the community a chance to review them. You didn't have to be an 'expert,' just interested. Hundreds of people did take the opportunity. The idea spread to cable television in Madison, spawned a newsletter, and caught on in other communities as well. One of our theme songs for 'The Madison Review of Books' was The Beatles' 'Paperback Writer'" (1997, p. 25). Here we find more evidence of how a commitment to adult education bore on Ohliger's work as a public intellectual. Instead of using "The Madison Review of Books" as his private bully pulpit for talking about the latest books, he encouraged the station's listeners to use the program to develop and share their own reactions to these works. This approach corresponded with Ohliger's continuing off-air insistence that WORT remain a place where everyday members of the public could have access to the airwaves. Ohliger saw public radio as an extension of the community, not as an authoritative voice meant to inform the masses. In many ways, his continuing vision for WORT anticipated the contemporary use of the Internet for grassroots journalism and commentary through blogs and Web sites.

Ohliger's dedication to WORT also reflected his deepening appreciation for the idea of community and for Madison in particular. It is fitting that Ohliger first met Chris Wagner when she stopped by his home to record a review for "The Madison Review of Books." In his memoir, he (1997) wrote that "her strong devotion to the values of a true local community of people working together helped me really take to heart that view which previously I had held only intellectually" (p. 31). That devotion to community was stoked by Ohliger's great affection for Madison, which, except for a three-year stint in Springfield, Illinois, was his home town from the early 1970s onward.

The Ohliger Method

The Ohliger method of being a public intellectual was intensely personal, involving plenty of individual outreach, networking, and intellectual exchange. Ohliger pursued an active intellectual life in the Madison community; produced hundreds of essays and bibliographies; served on editorial boards of scholarly and educational journals; and gave numerous talks at various universities, conferences, and meetings. But perhaps the most distinctive aspect of Ohliger's life as a public intellectual was his voluminous correspondence with dozens of independent scholars, activists, academicians, and lifelong learners across the country, first through the postal service and then by e-mail. Many came to him through word of mouth, while others tracked him down after reading some of his work. Some discovered Ohliger and Basic Choices through listings that he placed in periodicals such as *Factsheet Five,* the legendary review of "zines." More than a few of these exchanges ripened into close friendships, including in-person visits with Ohliger and his wife, Chris.

When the Internet age arrived, e-mail became Ohliger's favored medium for exchanging information and opinion with his wide-ranging network of friends and associates outside the Madison area. During his later years, he sent out a periodic Basic Choices newsletter by e-mail as well. Ohliger did not establish a Web site, which would have further publicized his work and made it more accessible. However, it is only a slight exaggeration to say that he made up for this by functioning as a one-man search engine of his extensive files. When someone would express interest in a certain topic, he often responded with a personal note and a packet of materials drawn from those files. An envelope from Ohliger made it fun to open one's mail, no small accomplishment amid the blizzard of bills and sales pitches that make for modern life.

My own association and eventual friendship with John were forged in exactly the manner described above. In 1982 I first read about Basic Choices in Ron Gross's *The Independent Scholar's Handbook* (Gross, 1982), and several years later I contacted John in response to a Basic Choices listing in *Factsheet Five.* At the time I was a recent law school graduate, pursuing a career in public interest law while harboring an ongoing curiosity about higher education and social change. I introduced myself that way to John in a short letter and soon afterward received a package of materials, which was accompanied by a friendly personal note thanking me for my interest in his work.

Subsequently I entered academe as a law professor, and my interest in adult and higher learning led to more frequent exchanges with John. He and Chris visited me in Boston, and I returned the favor with a visit to Madison. Eventually I became an officer of Basic Choices and worked with John on several projects. Once he started to use e-mail, we communicated frequently through that medium. Although we met in person only twice, John became one of my dearest friends, a steadfast source of support, and a deeply influential intellectual mentor.

Unlike the mainstream public intellectual who maintains a clear distance from his audience, Ohliger brought together the life of the mind and the stuff of human interaction. At times this meant abandoning any sense of separation between ideas and emotions, and in this way he could be quite sharp. I have in my files a 1998 letter that John wrote to Mark Satin, a political writer and one-time 1960s activist and draft resistance counselor, in response to Satin's fundraising letter for his new newsletter that sought to position itself as a voice for the "radical middle." Ohliger's tone was bluntly critical, bitingly sarcastic, and often dismissive, a stark contrast to most of his writings. He criticized Satin's references to certain authors and sources, referring to them as "mealy mouthed" and "bullshit"; at the end of the letter, John remarked that he looked forward to reading Satin's "warm, fuzzy arguments" in the newsletter.

And yet Ohliger could exercise substantial self-restraint, as I learned during the course of our friendship. For example, he was a strong critic of the academy. In an August 20, 1990, article, "Wither the University? Wither the University?" John reflected, "Will or should the universities survive? Certainly not in their present shape, or their current lack of a worthwhile form" (1990b, p. 4). After noting that universities faced lower enrollments due to corporate in-house training programs and sharp declines in the pool of eighteen-year-old prospective students, Ohliger observed that they now "scurry to make up for these catastrophes by recruiting older adults, enticing them with false hopes of flourishing professional careers if the 'non-traditional students'—as they are called—will only get a first, second or third degree" (p. 4).

Despite these pointed barbs, John never once, during our hundreds of e-mail exchanges, attempted to question my pursuit of a career as a (heaven forbid) law professor in a conventional educational setting. Although I would complain about the tenure process and voice misgivings about aspects of legal education, he refrained from using those moments to divert me from my vocational path. John could be stubbornly opinionated, but he could also embrace the andragogical values of dialogue, mutual respect, and nonprescription, even in individual exchanges when the temptation to lecture or pontificate must have been considerable.

During the years to come, it is more likely that John Ohliger will be described as an adult educator, political activist, and writer than as a public intellectual. After all, ABC's *Nightline* never sought to interview him, the *New York Times* never invited him to write an op-ed piece, and typing his name into Google yields only a modest number of hits. But Ohliger's eager interactions with members of the public, in ways that often led to ongoing associations and friendships, made him a truly unique public intellectual. Ohliger carried out his work in a largely andragogical mode, and thus he stood as an important counterpoint to the dominant paradigm of a public intellectual. For much of his life, he was an independent scholar and intellectual activist, working through various media to encourage public dialogue and raise important questions about society, learning, and current events. His approach was personal, interactive, and engaging, not hierarchical, directive, and detached. By his example, he taught us that adult education should be voluntary, life affirming, and even fun.

Opportunities and Trade-Offs

We can only speculate about what would have happened had Ohliger remained a full-time academic. In leaving a tenured position at the flagship campus of a major state university, he gave up the kind of abundant support that is provided to full-time faculty, including staff assistance, office space and equipment, and mailing privileges, not to mention a meaningful credential and calling card. In subsequent years, Ohliger himself appeared to have mixed feelings about his decision. Despite his many criticisms of higher education, he continued to remain close to both academicians and academic institutions.

Nevertheless, Ohliger did not produce his most accessible written work and enjoy his most public exposure until after he left his tenured university position. Much of the delightful, iconoclastic writing that he did under the Basic Choices rubric would not have passed for traditional scholarship at Ohio State or any other research university. In addition, his crusade against mandatory continuing education was not greeted warmly by many university adult education departments. Also, his continuing outreach to, and ongoing exchanges with, a wide variety of people would have been seen as eccentric (and even bizarre) by conventional academic colleagues.

In essence, Ohliger opted to forgo the comparative comforts of academe to occupy "a distinctive niche as gadfly and counterpuncher" (Posner, 2001, p. 388). In leaving the academy, Ohliger became much the kind of independent, bohemian public intellectual whose absence has been lamented by the politically disparate likes of Jacoby and Posner. His work was not constrained by academic disciplines, he read widely among genres and categories, and he embraced, rather than merely tolerated, interaction with the broader public. Living modestly and doing his work through Basic Choices, he was not beholden to any university or corporate entity.

By dint of both his personality and work as an educator, Ohliger also personified the ideal of the lifelong learner. A potential trap of being a traditional public intellectual is that one's success is often predicated on taking and defending a fixed set of positions. This transformation into advocacy and punditry can make it difficult to remain a true scholar. A public reevaluation of one's core positions may invite presidential campaign–like accusations of "flip-flopping," and the practice of churning out opinions for public consumption makes it hard to find time for new learning and reflection.

Ohliger, by comparison, never gave up the practice of learning and reflection. On receiving a book recommendation from a friend, he often responded by putting in for it at the library. Although he claimed to oppose "book worship," Ohliger (1997) conceded in his memoir that during many points in his life, he "exhibited an almost compulsive interest in reading and reviewing" (p. 25). As his bibliographical essays consistently demonstrated, he routinely read materials that offered contrasting conclusions and interpretations, but not for the all-too-common purpose within academic circles of trashing opposing viewpoints. He simply continued to revel in the life of an active mind.

Fame

There were trade-offs for Ohliger by adopting this role. One of the biggest was fame. Aspiring public intellectuals would be well advised that the instructional, pedagogical mode, not the facilitative, andragogical one, is the road to prominence, preferably by addressing topics with strong positions that will be fixed in the public eye. Ohliger himself conceded as much. After receiving national attention for his work opposing mandatory continuing education, he would never again bask in such a public spotlight. "After my 15 minutes of fame," he wrote in his memoir, "it was hard, *and still is*, to reconcile myself to an uneventful and unrenowned life" (1997, p. 26).

Ohliger also sacrificed wider exposure and recognition precisely because the bulk of his work was designed to facilitate discussion and further inquiry rather than to defend a viewpoint. One of the beauties of his bibliographical essays is that we can return to them repeatedly, (re)discovering sources and developing new reactions and ideas over time. However, the very nature of that learning process means that we are less likely to credit Ohliger for our new insights and more likely to see them as part of our "self-made" intellectual development. Accordingly, because many of Ohliger's writings were more by way of an invitation than a directive, he probably has not received the credit he deserves for shaping the worldviews of those who have read and used his work.

Money

Finally, the lack of funds and resources made it difficult for Ohliger to disseminate his writings and publicize his work. From the beginning, Basic Choices was a shoestring operation, and it became even more so as it evolved into Ohliger's personal platform. While Ohliger was not given to obsessing publicly about money, he nevertheless recognized the limitations placed on him by lack of funding.

One of the most misguided forms of nostalgia for the long-lost bohemian intellectual is how we have romanticized other people's financial want. Steven Biel, writing about the radical independent intellectuals of Greenwich Village during the 1910s, observed that "beneath the sustaining myth of the cult of poverty, those who dismissed the idea of a career faced real problems in trying to create a stable economic basis for an independent intellectual life," adding that "cycles of hardship and short-lived security could make the independent intellectual life unstable to the point where claims of autonomy seemed merely wistful" (Biel, 1992, pp. 48–50). For example, Randolph Bourne, one of the leading intellects among that Village cohort, wrote of the "hideous" and "appalling" stress and uncertainty of poverty; he lived "most of his life as a writer on the edge of subsistence" (Biel, 1992, p. 48).

It would be an exaggeration to say that Ohliger lived on the edge of poverty. He and his wife, Chris, shared small but comfortable homes over the years, and Ohliger's final residence included a cozy study that he affectionately called the "international headquarters" of Basic Choices. But it is also probably true that Ohliger's ambitions were limited by the modest bank account of Basic Choices, which generally hovered in the (very) low thousands of dollars. If, at times, Ohliger was more "intellectual" and less "public," money was a major reason.

The Ohliger Legacy: A Work in Progress

John Ohliger's legacy as a public intellectual may be partly in the hands of those who have chosen to analyze, preserve, and build on his body of work. This welcome book will help to ensure an ongoing place for Ohliger in the literature of adult education. In addition, a group of educators and activists, including several contributors to this book, are laying the groundwork for the Ohliger Institute for Social Inquiry. The institute will be a small, nonprofit center—not unlike Basic Choices, but more geographically diffuse and "virtual"—that promotes John's writings and nurtures the work of his many friends and associates. For the first time, many of Ohliger's writings will become available on the Web. The institute also will carry on Ohliger's spirit of independent, socially relevant scholarship and action through the new writings and initiatives of its supporters.

Even if it now appears that Ohliger's work will continue to be available, we should be less sanguine over the prospect that the kind of varied and rich life that he led is reasonably available to people today. Returning to Jacoby's basic thesis, we must recognize that the high cost of living in many urban areas makes it very hard to sustain an independent intellectual life. In addition, higher education costs and burgeoning student loan debt mean that many people face heavy financial pressures at a very young age.

In her final book, the late Jane Jacobs, the redoubtable analyst of urban and contemporary life, expressed her fears that we are entering a new "dark age" marked by a decline in families, higher education, effective science, responsive government, and ethics (Jacobs, 2004). Many of us carry similar, deep apprehensions as we observe and experience contemporary culture and politics. It is symptomatic of these concerns that the role of the reflective, interactive, and independent public intellectual remains neglected by a political, social, and economic system that has turned the life of the mind into a commodity. All of this underscores the importance of ensuring that John Ohliger enjoys greater staying power than mainstream public intellectuals who have opted to pursue more ephemeral and superficial moments in the spotlight. We need his work to inspire and inform our own thoughts and actions during the challenging days to come.

References

Basic Choices. (c. 1977). *Basic Choices prospectus: Basic Choices, Inc.: A Midwest center for clarifying political and social options* (2nd draft). Madison, WI: Basic Choices.

Biel, S. (1992). *Independent intellectuals in the United States, 1910–1945*. New York: New York University Press.

Brookfield, S. D. (1986). *Understanding and facilitating adult learning*. San Francisco: Jossey-Bass.

Cohen, P. (2000, February 8). Cultivating scholars, even in the sun. *New York Times*, p. A16.

DePaul University Media Relations. (n.d.-a). *DePaul op-ed guide: How to write an op-ed and get it published*. Chicago: Author.

DePaul University Media Relations. (n.d.-b). *DePaul media guide: Making the most of the media: A DePaul guide to managing the print and electronic media*. Chicago: Author.

Grace, A. P. (1996). Striking a critical pose: Andragogy—missing links, missing values. *International Journal of Lifelong Education, 15*(5), 382–392.

Gross, R. (1982). *The independent scholar's handbook*. Reading, MA: Addison-Wesley.

Honan, W. H. (1990, January 12). The intellectual issue for the 1990s is why America's intellectuals have faded away. *New York Times*, sec. 4, p. 46.

Jacobs, J. (2004). *Dark age ahead*. New York: Random House.

Jacoby, R. (1987). *The last intellectuals: American culture in the age of academe*. New York: Basic Books.

Knowles, M. S., Holton III, E. F., & Swanson, R. A. (1998). *The adult learner*. Houston: Gulf Publishing.

Krupnick, M. (1987, October 25). Today's radicals want tenure. *New York Times*, sec. 7, p. 44.

Melzer, A. M., Weinberger, J., & Zinman, M. R. (Eds.). (2003). *The public intellectual: Between philosophy and politics*. Lanham, MD: Rowman & Littlefield.

Nation Forum. (2001, February 12). The future of the public intellectual: A forum. *Nation*, 29–30.

Ohliger, J. (1981, July). If "learning never ends," does living ever begin? *Second Thoughts*, 6–7.

Ohliger, J. (c. 1982). *Adult education in a world of excessive riches/excessive poverty*. Madison, WI: Basic Choices.

Ohliger, J. (c. 1990). *Radical ideas in adult education*. Madison, WI: Basic Choices.

Ohliger, J. (1990a, July 30). Billy Joel: The fire, the facts and the story. *Adult and Continuing Education Today*, 5.

Ohliger, J. (1990b, August 20). Wither the university? Wither the university? *Adult and Continuing Education Today*, 4.

Ohliger, J. (c. 1993). *Mystery, crime, and adult education*. Madison, WI: Basic Choices.

Ohliger, J. (1997). [My search for freedom's song: Some notes for a memoir]. Third draft. Unpublished raw data.

Perlstein, R. (2002, January 22). Thinkers in need of publishers. *New York Times*, p. A19.

Posner, R. A. (2001). *Public intellectuals: A study of decline*. Cambridge, MA: Harvard University Press.

Small, H. (Ed.). (2002). *The public intellectual*. Malden, MA: Blackwell.

11

Informing Learning for Today's Professionals

Lessons from the Social Critique of Mandatory Continuing Education

Tonette S. Rocco

John Ohliger earned his doctorate in 1966, and from 1967 to 1973 he was on the faculty of Ohio State University (Hiemstra & Goldstein, 1990). As a student and later as a faculty member in adult education, Ohliger would have read about Houle's (1961) purposes of continuing education and Knowles's (1970) concept of andragogy, which Knowles defined as how adults learn. Both Houle and Knowles produced work that became core field knowledge and had a profound impact on the design and practice of adult education as well as the role of adult educators as emerging professionals.

As a field player in this more formalized adult learning culture, Ohliger could hardly have missed being influenced by increasingly pervasive ideas about adults being self-directed and voluntary learners (Houle, 1961; Knowles, 1970). As adult education acquiesced to governments, professional associations, and other institutions mandating formal continuing education for adults, Ohliger began to speak out about the evident contradiction between the field's claim of adults being voluntary learners and the field's complicity in mandating programs that required adult learners to participate in order to learn content that others deemed important.

This chapter discusses this contradiction between the principle of voluntary learning and mandated forms of education. In doing so, it provides both an overview of mandatory continuing education (MCE) and Ohliger's social critique of the notion as it considers the debate and contradictions that shaped its meaning and value.

Mandatory Continuing Education: The Debate and Contradictions

Some have construed adult education's support of MCE and life-long learning to position the adult learner as permanently inadequate. Ohliger provided particularly strong opposition to any such positioning of learners. Indeed he became the social conscience of the field as he exposed the dangers of mandating continuing education (Griffith, 1991). Very few voices have been raised against formal, structured, mandated education as a necessity for the majority of learners across the life span (see Illich, 1971; Reimer, 1971). Yet these voices have warned us against using education as a vehicle for social control, acculturation often to instrumentality, and workplace assimilation. Used for these purposes, education becomes a millstone and a kind of punishment as it replicates the status quo. However, such radical critique has historically found little space in mainstream forms of education. Those who provided it were often labeled radicals for their perceived foolishness and dismissed by some; others disenchanted with the educational system and limits placed on learner freedom saw them as courageous (Elias & Merriam, 1980).

In a short essay, "Invisible, But Pervasive, Adult Education," John Ohliger (2003) provides this vignette about something he read:

> My favorite local newspaper columnist is George Hesselberg, writing for the Wisconsin State Journal. He wrote an excellent column in the November 13th issue about how a woman was kicked out of an adult educa-

tion class apparently because the teacher didn't like how she had interacted with a child of his. But even he uses the term "continuing education." That term was adopted many years ago so that those in "higher" adult education wouldn't get mixed up with those teaching adults how to read [p. 2].

In this brief essay, Ohliger ends by illustrating the trouble with terms used interchangeably to represent different forms of adult education. Continuing education for adults, as it is linked to voluntary education, is intended to encompass such adult learning as attending night school to earn a GED or for leisure. MCE came "to describe the tendency of [U.S.] states and professional associations to require the members of certain vocations and professions to fulfill educational obligations in order to retain or renew their licenses to practice" (Cross, 1981, p. 40). *Continuing education* (CE) and *continuing professional education* (CPE) are terms currently more broadly construed and often used interchangeably with *training* (Daley & Jeris, 2004), with *workplace learning* construed as professional development (Mott, 2000), and with *noncredit* or *degree-generating education* for leisure or personal or professional development (Quigley, 1989). In this milieu, the word *professional* evokes an image of an educated, middle-class, and midlevel or higher worker and excludes working-class and poor people.

These days, *mandatory continuing education* is a term rarely used, and mandating agencies are frequently ignored in the literature bases of adult education and human resources when discussing CPE (van Loo & Rocco, 2006). Moreover, mandatory education is rarely critiqued in terms of its use as a punishment for rule breakers. In this case, mandated education does not carry the term *professional* with it and evokes the image of a poor, nonwhite participant. A distinction can be made between education for professionals that is mandated by a law or a professional organization and training that is provided by for-profit and nonprofit organizations. This distinction is important because it creates the opportunity to acknowledge the parameters that differentiate these educational forms. Another reason the distinction is important is that using the word *professional* denotes social class and a certain amount of individual power within the organization. For each educational form—CPE, CE, training, and MCE—the following questions are addressed differently: How can adult educators determine who benefits, who deems particular knowledge legitimate, and who has access to the educational endeavor (Apple, 2001)?

The phrase *mandatory continuing education* was coined with a full realization of the power contained in the phrase. In personal correspondence on October 15, 1995, John related to me: "By the way, I have some reason to believe that 'mandatory continuing education' as a topic was coined by me. I preferred 'compulsory adult education' or 'forced' or 'legislated' adult ed, but realized that such terms probably would scare the established folks. I vaguely recall suggesting to Roger DeCrow or Stan Grabowski that they consider 'MCE' because it might not put as many people off, since it's milder." Whether or not Ohliger was the first to use the phrase, the issue of MCE was being debated at least by 1970. In that year, an article appeared in the *Journal of the American Medical Association* with a title Ohliger would support: "Mandatory Continuing Education: Sense or Nonsense?" (Brown & Uhl, 1970). The debate about the status of MCE continues in the journals of professions that mandate continuing education.

For his part as an activist, Ohliger kept the MCE controversy alive by being one of the founders of both the National Alliance for Voluntary Learning (Cross, 1981) and Basic Choices (Brockett, 1992). He stimulated the debate by publishing *Second Thoughts* and by being a prolific writer of editorials published in journals in adult education and other fields. The controversies and debate surrounding MCE can be thematically organized: (1) MCE is against democratic principles (Cross, 1981), (2) MCE violates adult learning principles (Kerka, 1994), (3) MCE lacks evidence to support its effectiveness or that learning occurs (Cross, 1981; Kerka, 1994), (4) MCE raises issues of professional autonomy (Kerka, 1994) and accountability (Cross, 1981), and (5) MCE contributes to the commodification of adult education.

MCE Is Against Democratic Principles

Democratic principles include the practice of individual rights, free choice, participatory citizenship, and an interest in the common good (Touraine, 1997). The contradiction comes when individual rights are juxtaposed to the common good. The common good "requires that individual citizens have the commitment and motivation to promote the welfare of the community . . . for the benefit of all" (Boggs, Rocco, & Spangler, 1995, p. 450). This common good is also in the "public interest [and] . . . measured by the soundness of the decisions reached in light of the needs of the community" (Bachrach, 1980, p. 3). From this perspective, individual rights and free choice are negated when MCE, focusing on the common good, is used to rehabilitate citizens "who have failed to function as productive members of our society" (Brockett, 1992, p. 87). Such citizens can include those involved in the criminal justice, welfare, or immigration systems where individuals are controlled. As Hagstrom (1965, n.p., quoted in Ohliger, 1971) asserts, "A major object[ive] in educating the poor is to control them" through continued schooling and educational programs. With regard to the public good aspect, "the prevalent belief is that if we could only get people, especially poor people, through bribery or compulsion to stay, off and on, in the school system, or analogues of the school system, all their lives, then everything would be hunky-dory" (Ohliger, 1971, p. 3). Here Ohliger would question whether democracy is served by serving the common good. Ohliger's concerns are replicated by Touraine (1997) in this summary:

> Democracy exists when there is a political space that can protect citizens' rights from the omnipotence of the state. . . . Democracy exists when the distance between state and private life is recognized and preserved by political institutions and the law. Democracy is not reducible

> to procedures because it represents a set of mediations be-
> tween a unitary state and a multiplicity of social actors.
> The basic rights of individuals must be guaranteed. What
> is more, individuals must feel that they are citizens and
> must participate in the construction of collective life. The
> two worlds of state and civil society must therefore re-
> main separate, but they must also be bound together by
> the representativity of political leadership [p. 26].

Touraine's words provide a perspective that helps us answer Cross's (1981) question—"To what extent should free American citizens be coerced into education?" (p. 42)—with a resounding "No!" This can be the only answer if we value the individual rights and basic choices of free citizens. Of course, Ohliger and others were not only concerned with free citizens. They also felt it equally an-tidemocratic to coerce those in the prison, welfare, immigration, or other systems designed to control the poor and other disenfran-chised to attend educational programs in an effort to rehabilitate or improve them.

MCE Violates Adult Learning Principles

An adult is an individual who may be variously described as a parent, a worker, and a citizen and who "perform[s] social roles typically assigned by our culture to those it considers adults" (Knowles, 1980, p. 24). An adult "perceives herself or himself to be essentially re-sponsible for her or his own life" (Knowles, 1980, p. 24). Adult learn-ing principles or assumptions are based on this concept of what an adult is. For instance, an adult's self-concept moves toward being self-directed in learning, and experience is a resource for learning. Other assumptions are that adults have a readiness to learn, a problem-centered orientation to learning, and an internal motivation to learn (Smith, 2002). Knowles (1970) cautiously states that "adults are almost always voluntary learners [who] simply disappear from learning experiences that don't satisfy them" (p. 38).

In the first issue of *Second Thoughts*, Ohliger (1978) outlines core beliefs shared by a group of international adult educators. One of these includes "the primacy of voluntary learning" (p. 6). As he wrote in support of this primary belief, Ohliger drew on writing from Illich's (1974) Center for Intercultural Documentation, and he found further inspiration in a 1976 UNESCO statement: "Participation in an adult education programme should be a voluntary matter" (n.p.). Other core beliefs in his outline include "the basic value of free and open discussion" and the importance of a "balance between maximum free learning and minimum instruction, with a significant place for activities not publicly defined as job-related *or* as learning" (Ohliger, 1978, p. 6). These three beliefs set the stage for the contention that MCE is contrary to adult learning principles. Another core belief is that society needs "less hierarchy, bureaucracy, and external authority" (Ohliger, 1978, p. 6). Too often external authorities, and not the adult learner, dictate what content is to be learned and how learning is to be assessed (van Loo & Rocco, 2006). Cervero and Wilson (1994, 1996) took up this issue of power in program planning when they cautioned educators to "pay attention to the people work" (1996, p. 5) and stressed concern for "planning responsibly" in all forms of continuing education.

MCE Lacks Evidence of Its Effectiveness or That Learning Occurs

In education for adults, effectiveness, or producing a desired result, is often used without stating the criteria for evaluating effectiveness. To illustrate, Robertson, Umble, and Cervero (2003) ask, "Is CE effective, and for what outcomes?" and "What kinds of CE are effective?" (p. 146). They found that CE that is based on a needs assessment and is contextually relevant can produce outcomes such as improved knowledge, skills, behavior, and health care. However, these outcomes are context specific, and different studies had different criteria for effectiveness. In this regard, scholars in adult education and the health care professions maintain there is a lack of evidence for effectiveness. Moreover, CPE may hinder learning (Brockett, 1992), and quality or availability of CPE may be inconsistent (Bamball & While, 1996; Perry, 1995). Effectiveness should mean improved client outcomes, and what is learned should be usable, lasting, and transferable to practice. According to Houle (1980), CPE "implies some form of learning that advances from a previously established level of accomplishment to extend and amplify knowledge, sensitiveness, or skill" (cited in Mott, 2000). For learning to occur, providers of continuing education should plan programs that are informed by adult learning theories, and they should evaluate effectiveness based on some measure of learning. However, neither occurs regularly. For example, Furze and Pearcey (1999) lamented the "lack of research showing the impact of CPE on patient care" (p. 355). Since little empirical research exists, Jordan (2000) explored research methods that might help fill the gap between educational input and patient outcomes. Ohliger (1990) observed, "There is no evidence that any of this compulsory adult education is solving these problems" (p. 1).

To ensure accountability, MCE is intended to reach more than a quarter of nursing professionals who would not voluntarily attend continuing education programs (Carpenito, 1991, in Furze & Pearcey, 1999). Accountability is possible only if there is a link between forcing professionals to attend educational programs and actual learning. Cross (1981) illustrates the issue when she asks, "Is compulsory education effective; that is do people who are required to attend continuing education classes necessarily become more competent?" (p. 42). Daley (2001) found that professionals (nurses, adult educators, social workers, and lawyers) constructed knowledge to use in their practice settings from what they had learned through CPE and informally. Other scholars who investigated the learning of nurses found that "a complex set of factors interact to influence the outcomes of CPE, including the nature of the selection process, students' expectations of the programme, the nature of the educational experience, and the receptivity of the practice environment to change" (Ellis & Nolan, 2005, p. 97). Support of colleagues (Jordan,

Coleman, Hardy, & Hughes, 1999) and supervisors' attitudes and actions (Perry, 1995) also play a part in transforming the information delivered during CPE into something learned that is converted into practical knowledge. It would appear that Ohliger's original critique of MCE stands, certainly until more empirical studies are conducted to demonstrate that learning occurs, is transformed into practical knowledge, and has a positive impact on client concerns. To date, there is no evidence of such effectiveness.

MCE Raises Issues of Professional Autonomy and Accountability

A profession is distinguished by initial and sustained education, an association-created set of codes, and accreditation procedures (Queeney, 2000). Professional autonomy is based on three points: "the high degree of control over and influence on" others (Cervero, 1989, p. 518), the fact that professionals "define . . . the problems on which they work" (p. 513), and the criterion that professionals are self-directed learners. The first assumption that professional autonomy is based on control and influence is supported by the notion of professionals as experts. Cervero (1989) presents three viewpoints for the purposes of CPE: functionalist, conflict, and critical. The conflict approach views professionals as competing "for power, status, and money" (p. 518), using their expertise to attain these rewards. In this viewpoint, "The competence of professionals is not the problem. . . . The problem lies in the oppressive system of which professionals are apart" (p. 519). One aspect of this system is commercial support provided by pharmaceutical and other medical vendors for CPE. This support affects the outcomes of CPE (Smith, Cervero, & Valentine, 2006). It leads us to consider a multifaceted question raised by Apple in the Foreword to Cervero and Wilson's book (2001): Whose knowledge is legitimate, and whose knowledge is not?

The second assumption—that professionals define the problems for which they seek solutions—is based on the notion that professionals control their work space. Nurses, teachers, and dental hygienists are among professionals who do not control their work space. They can find themselves ignored when solutions are sought by their superiors (the purported experts), namely, the medical doctors, school principals, and dentists who supervise them. Solutions to problems are found through gathering information informally and formally through attending CPE programs and using both the informal and formal sources to construct knowledge to use in practice (Daley, 2001). As Ohliger (1974, 1978) has pointed out, when formal continuing education program content is mandated by the state or the profession, the learner's choice and autonomy are lessened.

The assumption that professionals are self-directed learners is illustrated by the commonly held belief that "being a professional implies commitment to continuing one's education and the ability to pursue practice-enhancing learning" (Kerka, 1994, p. 1). Accountability or being responsible for using influence wisely, defining problems that are important, and using continuing education to improve practice and outcomes are all concerns for the public, the associations, professionals, and clients. The issues of professional autonomy and accountability hinge on this question: "Who should be charged with developing and enforcing standards for professional accountability?" (Cross, 1981, p. 42). Ohliger (1978) viewed the move toward accountability as a way for society to exert formal control over professionals and decrease individual autonomy. He felt that "some in adult education interpret[ed] [the trend toward accountability] as a demand for MCE" (p. 1). Cervero (1989) provides evidence to support Ohliger's point when he asserts that the passion around MCE is subsiding because as "experience and research" indicate, when continuing education is mandated, about 75 percent of an organization's members are already engaged "at levels exceeding the minimum requirements" (p. 522). However, "CPE participation is no guarantee of learning and improved practice" (Queeney, 2000, p. 376). Other measures used to enhance accountability are credentialing schemes and periodic reexamination. Queeney (2000) observes that "the appearance of accountability" is no longer enough for critics (p. 378). Instead a "demonstrable linkage" between CPE and performance is needed (p. 376).

MCE Contributes to Commodification

As Jonathan Kozol points out, "The hard truth [is] that these credentials and measured areas of expertise and certified ability constitute the irreducible framework of our labor and struggle" (1972, in Elias & Merriam, 1980, p. 168). Most of us want to earn an honest wage for our labor. For some, there is a romanticized notion of learning: "Light comes from learning—just as creation comes everywhere—through integrations, syntheses, not through exclusions" (Lindeman, 1926/1989, p. xxxix). Lindeman goes on to observe that youth are taught that "real life begins" (p. 3) when the learning process ends. However, proponents of deschooling like Illich (1971) saw it differently. Instead "of forcing adults to go back to school on and off all their lives" (Ohliger, 1995, p. 7), it would be better to locate adult learners in "educational *webs* which heighten the opportunity for each one to transform each moment of his [sic] living into one of learning, sharing, and caring" (Illich, 1971, as quoted in Ohliger, 1995, p. 7). Ohliger agreed, since he was a lifelong learner in the way Gross (1977) describes learning across the life span: "Lifelong learning [is] self-directed growth, [which] means understanding yourself and the world . . . and acquiring new skills and powers—the only true wealth which you can never lose" (p. 16). Ohliger (1974) was adamantly opposed to the notion of being forced to go to school on and off because of state or professional mandates. He believed it created a sense of permanent inadequacy in adults.

For Ohliger, adult learning as voluntary learning was contravened when Knowles and the field participated in the commodification of education and, without question, assisted the state by considering how to deliver mandated continuing education. As Kidd (1962) had observed as a field of study and practice emerged, "There is reasonably wide acceptance by the public of the need for *remedial* and *vocational* education" and other forms of continuing education (p. 61). The danger of this popularity, as Kidd perceived it, was that financing of continuing education could be geared toward reproducing the status quo and reducing the value of such endeavors as social education. He felt that steps should be taken so that access was not just for those with a specified educational or employment need. Indeed these issues of access and the purposes of adult education have been debated in field circles for decades. We have continually questioned whether access should be equitable and whether continuing education programs should be market driven (Beder, 1992; Mason, 1992). As this debate goes on, Cervero (2000) provides sobering evidence of the perennial commodification of continuing education: In 1996, "$60 billion dollars was spent" training people, "the majority of whom were professionals and middle and upper management" (p. 5).

There is an irony in faculty with secure middle-class lifestyles ranting against the commodification of education. Rarely when we discuss voluntary learning or mandatory continuing education do we consider the issue of faculty or instructor employment. If all learning is to be voluntary and conducted through learning webs where services are exchanged or bartered, then how are educators to support themselves? The proponents of learning webs and free learning in the 1960s and 1970s were well-educated men who, because of their education and paid positions, could talk about this utopian vision of learning. Although Illich worked in New York City with Puerto Rican parishes, which would not have been wealthy ones (see Chapter Twelve), and even though Ohliger grew up poor, neither educator seemed to make the connection between a structured, credential-earning education and a reasonable standard of living. For Illich and Ohliger, learning ought to be free and voluntary. Interestingly, though, both intellectuals had periods being part of the system they critiqued since both experienced employment in formal educational institutions. Indeed Illich continued to enjoy an upper-middle-class lifestyle throughout his life. Ohliger did not. It can be argued that Ohliger was more the cultural worker in the long run. He sacrificed the stability of an academic career and then spent most of his life creating learning webs in culture and community, first using typewritten letters and the postal service and later moving to the Internet and e-mail.

While I can join Ohliger to warn of the dangers of mandatory continuing education, my income derives from teaching adults in a university where students come to earn another credential. This is the irony of those who speak against the commodification of education. Each day we tread terrain where we guide learning ventures shaped by such factors as privatization and credentialism. However, this does not mean that we should be oblivious to the flaws in mandated education. Rather, we should be even more aware of them as we deal with the tenuous nature of teaching and learning in today's culture, where the instrumental, the technical, and the global are forces that have an impact on what we do.

A Concluding Thought: Do Not Forget How Power and Privilege Permeate Learning

In general, Ohliger, Illich, Houle, and Knowles conceptualized adult learners as being predominantly middle class and having a context for their learning. When Knowles (1970, 1980) described voluntary learners as those who can leave an educational experience that does not meet their needs, he assumed this is natural for all learners. I maintain that in order to be a voluntary learner, the learner enjoys privilege and choice and may be engaged in the learning simply for recreation. A consideration of specific relationships of power adds another dimension. Johnson-Bailey (2002) suggests that there are three perspectives adult educators use regarding race: the color-blind, multicultural, and social-justice perspectives. Here race, class, and access to educational opportunities are intertwined (Sheared, 1999). Knowles and many others involved in an instrumentalized and professionalized practice of adult education possessed viewpoints that can be located in the color-blind perspective. They viewed education as a neutral endeavor in which learners treat peers with respect, and learners are equivalent in abilities and access to education (Johnson-Bailey, 2002). This color-blind perspective is deeply rooted in middle-class values and the invisibility of power and privilege (Rocco & West, 1998).

Social class as a determinant of employment and educational achievement is assumed to be middle or better when discussing CPE. The word *professional,* as it is currently used, implies white-collar work, an initial higher education, and a desire on the part of the learner to enhance knowledge and skills for employability (Thijssen, Van der Heijden, & Rocco, 2008). The perspectives of Knowles, Houle, Ohliger, and Illich toward the issue of continuing education are articulated through the lens of middle-class privilege and the access to education that all four intellectuals enjoyed. Each had educational opportunities that others never know. Although Ohliger grew up in a financially unstable home, he was nevertheless influenced by parents and grandparents who were educated (Ohliger, 1997). Illich grew up with money and privilege and enjoyed an excellent education (Zacharakis, 2003). Along with Knowles and Houle, all four white men obtained doctorates. Each had power and privilege and assumed that education created opportunities for all. Still, Ohliger can be seen as different. After all, he left the financial security of an academic position behind when he could no longer dissociate the nature of emerging professionalized adult education from increasing injustice and a denial of academic freedom. From this perspective, let me leave you with a parting challenge from Ohliger (1971):

> No good purpose is served by saying what bastards we all are. Instead we should devote our energies to seeing clearly the nature of the system we are a willing, or unwilling, part of. Then we need to explore alternatives, hopefully educational alternatives [p. 3].

References

Apple, M. (2001). Foreword. In R. M. Cervero & A. L. Wilson (Eds.), *Power in practice: Adult education and the struggle for knowledge and power in society* (pp. ix-xiii). San Francisco: Jossey-Bass.

Bachrach, P. (1980). *The theory of democratic elitism.* Lanham, MD: University Press of America.

Bamball, K. L., & While, A. E. (1996). Participation in continuing professional education in nursing: Findings of an interview study. *Journal of Advanced Nursing, 23*, 999–1007.

Beder, H. (1992). Adult and continuing education should not be market driven. In M. W. Galbraith & B. R. Sisco (Eds.), *Confronting controversies in challenging times: A call for action* (pp. 69–76). New Directions for Adult and Continuing Education, no. 54. San Francisco: Jossey-Bass.

Boggs, D. L., Rocco, T. S., & Spangler, S. (1995). A framework for understanding older adults' civic behavior. *Educational Gerontology: An International Journal, 21*(5), 449–465.

Brockett, R. (1992). Do we really need mandatory continuing education? In M. W. Galbraith & B. R. Sisco (Eds.), *Confronting controversies in challenging times: A call for action* (pp. 87–93). New Directions for Adult and Continuing Education, no. 54. San Francisco: Jossey-Bass.

Brown Jr., C. R., & Uhl, H. S. (1970). Mandatory continuing education: Sense or nonsense? *Journal of the American Medical Association, 213*, 1660–1668.

Cervero, R. M. (1989). Continuing professional education. In S. B. Merriam & P. M. Cunningham (Eds.), *Handbook of adult and continuing education* (pp. 513–524). San Francisco: Jossey-Bass.

Cervero, R. M. (2000). Trends and issues in continuing professional education. In V. W. Mott & B. J. Daley (Eds.), *Charting a course for continuing professional education: Reframing professional practice* (pp. 3–12). New Directions for Adult and Continuing Education, no. 86. San Francisco: Jossey-Bass.

Cervero, R. M., & Wilson, A. L. (1994). *Planning responsibly for adult education: A guide to negotiating power and interests.* San Francisco: Jossey-Bass.

Cervero, R. M., & Wilson, A. L. (Eds.). (1996). *What really matters in adult education program planning: Lessons in negotiating power and interests.* New Directions for Adult and Continuing Education, no. 69. San Francisco: Jossey-Bass.

Cross, K. P. (1981). *Adults as learners: Increasing participation and facilitating learning.* San Francisco: Jossey-Bass.

Daley, B. J. (2001). Learning and professional practice: A study of four professions. *Adult Education Quarterly, 52*, 39–54.

Daley, B. J., & Jeris, L. (Eds.). (2004). Boundary spanning: Expanding frames of reference for human resource development and continuing professional education. *Advances in Developing Human Resources, 6*(1), 1–115.

Elias, J. L., & Merriam, S. (1980). *Philosophical foundations of adult education.* Malabar, FL: Krieger.

Ellis, L., & Nolan, M. (2005). Illuminating continuing professional education: Unpacking the black box. *International Journal of Nursing Studies, 42*, 97–106.

Furze, G., & Pearcey, P. (1999). Continuing education in nursing: A review of the literature. *Journal of Advanced Nursing, 29*(2), 355–363.

Griffith, W. S. (1991). The impact of intellectual leadership. In J. M. Peters, P. Jarvis, & Associates (Eds.), *Adult education: Evolution and achievements in a developing field of study* (pp. 97–120). San Francisco: Jossey-Bass.

Gross, R. (1977). *The lifelong learner.* New York: Simon & Schuster.

Hagstrom, W. (1965). Poverty and adult education. *Adult Education Quarterly, 15*(3), 145–160.

Hiemstra, R., & Goldstein, A. (1990). *John Ohliger: Personal vita.* Retrieved May 30, 2005, from http://www-distance.syr.edu/pvitajfo.html.

Houle, C. O. (1961). *The inquiring mind: A study of the adult who continues to learn* (2nd ed.). Norman: Oklahoma Research Center for Continuing Professional and Higher Education.

Houle, C. O. (1980). *Continuing learning in the professions.* San Francisco: Jossey-Bass.

Illich, I. (1971). *Deschooling society.* New York: HarperCollins.

Illich, I. (1974, August). *The price of lifelong education.* Cuernavaca, Mexico: Illich Center for Intercultural Documentation.

Johnson-Bailey, J. (2002). Race matters: The unspoken variable in the teaching-learning transaction. In J. M. Ross-Gordon (Ed.), *Contemporary viewpoints on teaching adults effectively* (pp. 39–50). New Directions for Adult and Continuing Education, no. 93. San Francisco: Jossey-Bass.

Jordan, S. (2000). Educational input and patient outcomes: Exploring the gap. *Journal of Advanced Nursing 31*(2), 461–471.

Jordan, S., Coleman, M., Hardy, B., & Hughes, D. (1999). Assessing educational effectiveness: The impact of a specialist course on the delivery of care. *Journal of Advanced Nursing 30*(4), 796–807.

Kerka, S. (1994). *Mandatory continuing education.* ERIC Digest No. 151. Columbus, OH: ERIC Clearing House on Adult Education.

Kidd, J. R. (1962). *Financing continuing education.* New York: Scarecrow Press.

Knowles, M. S. (1970). *The modern practice of adult education: Andragogy vs. pedagogy.* New York: Association Press.

Knowles, M. S. (1980). *The modern practice of adult education: From pedagogy to andragogy* (rev. and updated). Chicago: Association Press.

Lindeman, E. C. (1989). *The meaning of adult education.* Norman: Oklahoma Research Center for Continuing Professional and Higher Education. (Original work published 1926)

Mason, R. C. (1992). Adult and continuing education should be market driven. In M. W. Galbraith & B. R. Sisco (Eds.), *Confronting controversies in chal-*

lenging times: A call for action (pp. 77–86). New Directions for Adult and Continuing Education, no. 54. San Francisco: Jossey-Bass.

Mott, V. W. (2000). The development of professional expertise in the workplace. In V. W. Mott & B. J. Daley (Eds.), *Charting a course for continuing professional practice* (pp. 23–31). New Directions for Adult and Continuing Education, no. 86. San Francisco: Jossey-Bass.

Ohliger, J. (1971, March 24). *Adult education for social action.* Talk presented to Central Ohio Adult Education Association, Columbus, OH.

Ohliger, J. (1974). Is lifelong education a guarantee of permanent inadequacy? *Convergence, 7*(2), 47–58.

Ohliger, J. (1978, May). International group questions mandatory continuing education. *Second Thoughts, 1*(1), 1–3, 5.

Ohliger, J. (1990, September). Straight time and standard brand adult education. *New Horizons in Adult Education, 4,* 1–4.

Ohliger, J. (1995 May/June). Personal reflections: Books to live by. *Adult Learning,* 7.

Ohliger, J. (1997). [My search for freedom's song: Some notes for a memoir]. Third draft. Unpublished raw data.

Ohliger, J. (2003). Invisible, but pervasive, adult education. *Basic Choices Newsletter, Christmas 2003,* p. 2.

Perry, L. (1995). Continuing professional education: Luxury or necessity? *Journal of Advanced Nursing, 21,* 766–771.

Queeney, D. S. (2000). Continuing professional education. In A. L. Wilson & E. R. Hayes (Eds.), *Handbook of adult and continuing education* (pp. 376–377). San Francisco: Jossey-Bass.

Quigley, A. (Ed.). (1989). *Fulfilling the promise of adult and continuing education.* New Directions for Adult and Continuing Education, no. 44. San Francisco: Jossey-Bass.

Reimer, E. (1971). *School is dead: Alternatives in education.* New York: Doubleday.

Robertson, M. K., Umble, K. E., & Cervero, R. M. (2003). Impact studies in continuing education for health professions: Update. *Journal of Continuing Education in the Health Professions, 23,* 146–156.

Rocco, T. S., & West, G. W. (1998). Deconstructing privilege: An examination of privilege in adult education. *Adult Education Quarterly, 48*(3), 171–184.

Sheared, V. (1999). Giving voice: Inclusion of African-American students' polyrhythmic realities in adult basic education. In T. C. Guy (Ed.), *Providing culturally relevant adult education: A challenge for the twenty-first century* (pp. 33–48). New Directions for Adult and Continuing Education, no. 82. San Francisco: Jossey-Bass.

Smith, J. L., Cervero, R. M., & Valentine, T. (2006). Impact of commercial support on continuing pharmacy education. *Journal of Continuing Education in the Health Professions, 26,* 302–312.

Smith, M. K. (2002). Malcolm Knowles, informal adult education, self-direction and andragogy. In *The encyclopedia of informal education.* Retrieved December 28, 2007, from http://www.infed.org/thinkers/et-knowl.htm.

Thijssen, J., Van der Heijden, B., & Rocco, T. S. (2008). Towards the employability-link model: Current employment transition to future employment perspectives. *Human Resource Development Review, 7,* 165–183.

Touraine, A. (1997). *What is democracy?* (David Macey, Trans.). Boulder, CO: Westview Press.

UNESCO. (1976). *UNESCO Recommendation on the Development of Adult Education.* 19th General Conference, Nairobi, Kenya.

van Loo, J., & Rocco, T. S. (2006). Differentiating CPE from training: Reconsidering terms, boundaries, and economic factors. *Human Resource Development Review, 5*(2), 202–227.

Zacharakis, J. (2003). Placing John Ohliger in his proper historical context. *Adult Learning, 14*(3), 24–27.

12

Icons and Pariahs

Mentorship and the Archaeology of Adult Education

Jeff Zacharakis

The research for this chapter began with letters and documents that John sent me beginning in 1986 and with his published articles and essays. After reading some of Ohliger's articles in 1985, I phoned him, asking for advice on where to pursue a doctoral degree. He recommended Northern Illinois University. After this call, I found myself on his mailing list, and we began to exchange occasional letters. We first met shortly after I arrived in DeKalb, Illinois, in 1986. In addition, Chris Wagner, his wife, and Carl Mitcham, an internationally recognized Illich scholar and a professor in the Division of Liberal Arts and International Studies at Colorado School of Mines, sent me relevant letters, documents, and audiotapes from their personal collections, all of which added to the interpretive complexity of this research. Indeed this research would not have been possible without their support.

In the late 1980s, while conducting my historical dissertation research on Highlander Folk School's relationship to the United Packinghouse Workers and their charismatic leaders, Myles Horton and Ralph Helstein, a history professor warned me that nothing is more difficult and more problematic than conducting research on saints and icons. He argued that it is almost impossible to be objective and, regardless of your intellectual integrity, you will be criticized if you do not fully paint your subject in glowing colors. Both Illich and Ohliger are icons among their admirers. Yet this research reveals that they were both human beings with strengths, weaknesses, and idiosyncrasies. Their history is not merely about the intellectual discourse they shared through their writings. It includes a personal relationship within the fluid political milieu of the 1970s and early 1980s. They came from different backgrounds, had different personalities, and grew intellectually and personally along separate paths, all of which had an impact on their relationship and understanding of each other. To understand this relationship, I examined not only their intellectual contributions but also their cultural differences.

Arguably, Ivan Illich was the most influential figure in John Ohliger's career. And arguably, it was John Ohliger who not only introduced Ivan Illich to adult education, but also championed an Illichian philosophy in adult education. Their relationship was generally, but not always, one of close friendship and mutual admiration. However, it was not a relationship between equals. Ohliger looked to Illich for intellectual guidance and support as he developed his thesis against compulsory adult education. He also saw Illich as his mentor during the tumultuous years when he left his faculty position at Ohio State University. During this time, Ohliger emerged as an itinerate philosopher who challenged the perceived cooptation of adult education by his peers who were beginning to abandon the social historical foundations of adult education in favor of professional development and compulsory education. When Illich expanded his intellectual pursuits beyond deschooling, Ohliger felt a tremendous intellectual loss, even though their friendship remained intact. In the end, Ohliger would have to divorce himself from the Illich persona in order to discover and appreciate his own identity.

Elias and Merriam (1995) identify Ohliger as an anarchist within the radical tradition of adult education. While this may be true in terms of John's adherence to Illich's deschooling thesis, it fails to recognize that he was an adherent to the non-elitist ideals of liberal adult education (Meiklejohn, 1948; Liveright, 1959, 1963). Liberal adult education promoted learning about and becoming involved in local, national, and international affairs in order to be a better citizen and create a stronger democracy. Certainly as adult education became more professionalized, Ohliger believed that deschooling was essential if this growing field was to remain true to its historical roots in liberal and progressive education (Elias & Merriam, 1995; Ohliger, 1981). His deschooling thesis was based on theories and concepts developed by Illich and Everett W. Reimer, and it manifested itself as a crusade against mandatory continuing education. This chapter seeks to clarify the Ohliger-Illich relationship, better understand Ohliger's contribution to adult education, and articulate his historical importance to the future of adult education.

Biographical Sketches and Looming Differences

Ohliger and Illich, both born in 1926, came from two different cultures that shaped their worldviews, intellectual beliefs, and relationship with each other. Illich grew up as an intellectual elitist in Eastern and Southern Europe, while Ohliger was a midwestern American populist. Illich exuded confidence, if not arrogance. By contrast, Ohliger was blessed and cursed with modesty and open self-doubt, something I believe was not a source of shame but something he saw as an attribute to his philosophical development.

Illich, Intellectual by Birth

Born in Vienna, Austria, to an aristocratic family, Illich's father was Catholic and a diplomat, and his mother was Jewish. Protected by diplomatic immunity until his father died in 1941, his family fled to Florence, Italy, where he enrolled in the University of Florence and studied chemistry, psychology, and European art history. In 1943 Illich moved to Rome and began his studies at Gregorian University, where French Catholic philosopher Jacques Maritain introduced him to the philosophies and writing of St. Thomas Aquinas. Here Illich studied the relationship between Aristotle's logic and reason and its compatibility with Catholicism's spiritual grounding and scientific reasoning (Inman, 1999). Maritain also introduced Illich to the philosophy of Henri Bergson, who rejected the economics of "expanding needs that has been fueled by the stimulation of industry in response to the development of modern science" (p. 5). Recognized as a gifted scholar at an early age, Illich earned his Ph.D. in history at the age of twenty-four from the University of Salzburg, where he completed his dissertation on the speculative history of Arnold Toynbee (Illich, 1955). These experiences provide the epistemological basis for Illich's thesis on institutional dominance.

Ordained as a Jesuit priest in 1951, Illich rejected an invitation to study canon law in Rome. Instead he moved to New York City for postdoctoral work. There he discovered the Puerto Rican community, and he asked Archbishop Francis Spellman to assign him to a Puerto Rican parish. Illich saw firsthand the cultural differences within Catholicism and how priests trained in North America and Europe were ill equipped to serve the spiritual needs of Latin Americans. Later, at Illich's request, Cardinal Spellman assigned him to be vice rector of the Catholic University of Puerto Rico, where he was asked to train American priests in various aspects of Puerto Rican and Latin American culture in preparation for missionary work. Resentment toward Illich grew among his peers when he argued that mainland priests and clergy were imposing North American Catholicism on Latin American culture. After Illich opposed the formation of a Catholic political party that was against the reforms (including birth control) of Puerto Rican president Luis Muñoz Marín, he was reassigned to New York, where he was appointed to the political science faculty of Fordham University.

In 1961, with the support of Fordham University and the American Bishops' Committee on Latin America, Illich founded the Center for Intercultural Formation, later renamed the Center for Intercultural Documentation (CIDOC). At the same time, Pope John XXIII called on the American church to send 10 percent of its clergy to Latin America to alleviate the critical shortage of priests. The importance of CIDOC—part conference center, free

university, and publishing house—was to train priests for missionary work and keep all but the most progressive priests away from
Latin America (Inman, 1999). CIDOC was located in Cuernavaca,
Mexico, for its climate, proximity to a university and library, and its
progressive bishop, Mendez Arceo.

Illich enjoyed the support of progressive Catholic leaders as well
as mainstream clerics, including Cardinal Spellman, and did not
support political advocacy and activism. CIDOC was a place for
study and reflection that would result in long-term service to the
poor and disenfranchised. When Cardinal Spellman died in 1967,
Rome began to investigate the role of CIDOC, and in 1968 re-
quested Illich to appear before the Congregation for the Doctrine
of the Faith, which monitors faithful Catholic teaching on moral
matters. Illich was asked to answer a series of questions "aimed at
my work and reputation. . . . [This] cast over me the shadow of 'no-
torious churchmen' and this interferes with my ministry, my work
as an educator, and personal decision to live as a Christian" (Illich,
as cited in Moritz, 1969, p. 220). When he refused to sign an oath of
secrecy about the meeting, arguing it was against the natural law of
honesty, the church prohibited its priests and religious from attending CIDOC. This break with the church ultimately led Illich
to dissolve CIDOC in 1976, after which he moved from university
to university, operating within prestigious intellectual circles—for
example, the Pennsylvania State University in the United States
and the University of Bremen in Germany—as a visiting professor
and guest lecturer. Although he continued with his intellectual
analysis and interpretation of social and cultural institutions, by the
early 1980s his role had diminished as a social critic and had risen
as a historical archaeologist (Mitcham, 2002).

Ohliger's Life on the Fringes of Mainstream Adult Education

Ohliger was born to completely different circumstances than Illich,
and the turmoil of his youth reflected a family in crisis. The year before he was born, his father lost a successful insurance business and
was "driving a horse-drawn bakery truck" (Ohliger, 1997, p. 8) at

the time of his birth. These sad circumstances resulted in his maternal grandfather tirelessly working to convince his mother to divorce his father. In his memoirs, Ohliger (1997) recalls that from the time he was little, he was "the glue that kept his family together" (p. 8). He described his youth and early adulthood as a "pattern of seeking other kinds of relationships while fearing them, where I could be the loving and helpful one. Often I would break off the relationship to avoid what I misinterpreted as rejection or out of an unnamable [sic] fear" (p. 8). While his father was unemployed and underemployed between 1925 and World War II, his family moved frequently, just barely scraping by and paying their bills. In high school he began working part time in the Detroit Public Library and with the high school radio station and newspaper. It was during these early years that he developed a love for words, poetry, and music.

Drafted in 1945, Ohliger served in the army of occupation in Austria and Germany. Here he had his first experience as an adult educator, teaching other soldiers Morse code in a military environment where mandatory attendance was not questioned. Following his discharge in the late 1940s, Ohliger entered Wayne State University under the GI Bill, became active in the Democratic party, and worked part time in the education department of the Michigan Congress of Industrial Organizations Council. Through his work in the army and the union, he began to understand racial prejudice and the lack of African American participation in leadership decisions. He grew more disenchanted with the Democratic party when the liberal wing caved in to the conservative wing in their support of Teamster president Jimmy Hoffa. Ohliger declared that this pivotal experience "converted me from a liberal to a radical" (Ohliger, 1997, p. 15). He began participating in antiwar demonstrations and searching for other like-minded comrades among Trotskyites. He recalled the 1950s as the most politically active decade of his life: "The phony war between Americans and the Soviets jockeying for power was the 'cold' one, and the real wars in Korea, and later Vietnam were officially labeled anything but wars. The Truman administration's introduction of the security state in the mid-1940s led to Joe McCarthy's even more demagogic, but less damaging, red baiting in the early 1950s. So many opportunities for political protest" (p. 18). These were the formative years when Ohliger's adult education philosophies were seeded.

Upon graduating from college, Ohliger (1997) worked briefly in a California factory, but "when routine and boring factory work got to be just too much, I applied for and soon received a one year Fund for Adult Education (FAE) leadership grant to attend UCLA [University of California at Los Angeles] to work on a master's degree" (p. 19). This was the beginning of a five-year association with the fund, where one of his responsibilities was facilitating liberal arts discussion groups. Once he earned his master's degree, Ohliger moved to Chicago to work with two more of the FAE's projects: the American Foundation for Political Education and the Great Books Foundation. In the late 1950s, Ohliger did two years of advanced study at the University of Chicago with Cy Houle. In 1960, he moved back to Berkeley, California (and later Los Angeles), and began volunteering with Radio Pacifica Foundation's station KPFA-FM, another FAE-funded project. When he finished his doctoral dissertation at UCLA in 1966, "The Listening Group in Adult Education," he became director of continuing education at Selkirk College, the first regional community college in British Columbia. At the request of Jack London, professor of adult education at the University of California at Berkeley, he kept an audiotape diary of his experience in Canada.

While Ohliger's early career was intertwined with a broad-based deconstructionist movement in American education, he was also uniquely a product of the adult education movement in the late 1950s through the early 1970s. His work with the Ford Foundation brought him into contact with Robert J. Blakely and A. A. (Sandy) Liveright, two adult educators who understood the importance of liberal education for all citizens. In the early 1960s, he edited an audiotape of Myles Horton discussing his experiences at Highlander Folk School in the home of his graduate advisor at UCLA, Paul Sheats. Sheats was known for his work that connected adult education to community programming and development. By the time Ohliger joined the adult education faculty at Ohio State, he was recognized by some of the most prominent adult educators of the day as an important young professor, especially for his work with radio and media.

While at Ohio State University during the late 1960s, Ohliger became acquainted with the writing of Ivan Illich. This led to their first meeting in 1971, which permanently changed Ohliger's career path:

> In my seven years as a professor at Ohio State University I learned that some of the words I had uncritically absorbed in the standard texts I studied at the University of Chicago and at UCLA were just that—words. We had been told again and again that whatever adult education was, it was voluntary. Looking for someone to support this new-found consciousness that more and more adults were being imprisoned by educational requirements I found one author, Ivan Illich, who led me to others. Illich, and his educational mentor Everett Reimer, were the only persons at the time I could find who recognized the oppressive direction in which schooling was moving [Ohliger, 1997, p. 29].

The revolutionary spirit that emboldened Ohliger in the late 1950s was reawakened by the deschooling movement, the anti-Vietnam student movement, and his frustration with mainstream adult education in the early 1970s.

In 1971 Ohliger (1997) made his first trip to Mexico to present a short paper, "Adult Education: 1984" (referring to George Orwell's novel 1984), at CIDOC. He was awarded the Ivan D. Illich Dystopia Award for this paper: "The prize was a case of tequila. I donated all but one bottle of the tequila to the groups meeting with Illich. The rest of the tequila formed the bases of a party to which Illich contributed the services of a local mariachi band. The party—with the band, the dancing, and the drinking—was a joyous occasion for me; the best honor I have ever received" (p. 31). These were heady years for Ohliger, empowered by his new passion for a liberatory philosophy of adult education, his association with Illich, and his academic position.

Although Ohliger never held a permanent faculty position after leaving Ohio State University, he was a prolific writer throughout his last thirty years, developing a large and committed group of followers and admirers. For someone outside academe, he maintained the intellectual respect and honor of many of his university peers. While he had articles published in many of adult education's mainstream journals (for example, *Adult Leadership* and *Lifelong Learning*), his best writing is in the Basic Choices newsletters and in his personal correspondence. It was here that he had total freedom to express his philosophies and commentaries. Most of Ohliger's intellectual scholarship and professional career was on the fringes of mainstream university adult education.

Why Illich and Not Reimer?

In the late 1950s, while Illich was acting rector at the Catholic University at Ponce, Puerto Rico, he and Everett Reimer began collaborating on the international impact of schooling as an institution: "We were led to ask: What is schooling? So we tried to look at the institution in purely formal terms, leaving out people's intentions with regard to education" (Illich in Cayley, 2005, p. 139). This collaboration matured through the 1960s and into the early 1970s when Illich published *Deschooling Society* (1971a) and Reimer published *School Is Dead* (1971a). For Reimer, schooling was the central focus of his analysis. For Illich, schooling became a springboard for analyses and critique of many of those cultures we take for granted but seldom deconstruct, such as technology, law, and medicine. It was the deschooling thesis that attracted Ohliger to both Illich and Reimer.

Both Illich and Ohliger identify Reimer's importance to their intellectual development. In an interview, Illich described meeting Reimer for the first time in 1956:

> Most of my life is really the result of meeting the right person at the right moment and being befriended by him. This was the case with Everett. . . . It was along this kind of circuitous road that I came to understand [what] this educational system of Puerto Rico was doing. First, thanks to years of conversation with Everett, I read my way into the pragmatists and empiricists of the English tradition of thinkers and philosophers. Second, I asked myself, what do schools do when I put into parentheses their claim to educate? . . . Under the influence of Everett Reimer, I began to engage in the phenomenology of schooling [Mercogliano, n.d., para. 28].

In *Xenophile and the Disenchanted Bureaucrat*, Ohliger (n.d.-b) wrote, "[The] two men, whom I believe to be among the greatest living revolutionary humanists, are frequently referred to by their critics as the most prominent proponents of 'anti-institutionalism' in regard to education. They are Ivan Illich, author of *Deschooling Society*, and Everett Reimer, author of *School Is Dead*." Twenty years after *School Is Dead* appeared, Ohliger (1991) described Reimer as the most unforgettable adult educator he ever met.

The connection between Illich and Ohliger begins with Reimer and his understanding of how the institutionalization of schooling perpetuated inequities at all levels within society. In one of his most important books, Reimer (1971b) writes: "School domesticates—socially emasculates—both girls and boys by a process much more pervasive than mere selection by sex. School requires conformity for survival and thus shapes its students—in a crudely Skinnerian manner—to conform to the norms for survival . . . . The actual survival criteria are quite different. In addition to the wealth of influence of parents, they include the ability to beat the game which, according to John Holt and perceptive teachers, is mainly what successful students learn in school" (p. 1/6). Reimer expands this argument when he writes:

> Different schools do different things, of course, but increasingly, schools in all nations, of all kinds, at all levels, combine four distinct social functions: custodial care, social-role selection, indoctrination, and education as usually defined in terms of development of skills and knowledge. It is the combination of these functions which makes schooling so expensive. It is conflict among these functions which makes schools educationally inefficient. It is also the combinations of these functions which tend to make school a total institution, which has made it an international institution and which makes it such an effective instrument of social control [pp. 1/2–3].

Reimer's analysis of schools concluded that they do more to maintain and even accentuate inequities of class, race, and gender than they do to increase opportunity based on merit and hard work. With the institutionalization of education and learning came the institutionalization of social and cultural bias. As a result, the institution of schools is more important than the idea of learning. Learning assumes a subservient position to schooling, and the institution of schools is closely aligned with other institutions such as government, business (in particular, national and multinational corporations), and the dominant culture and its key power brokers.

Illich's thesis is that education has become an institution that creates dependency rather than liberation of the intellectual self, and under the present system of education, "no one completes school" (1970b, p. 23). The heart of this thesis is that schools reproduce the established order, whether this order is called revolutionary, conservative, or evolutionary (Illich, 1970a). Hence we see programs that prepare and certify people for employment rather than educate them in the abstract so they can work with ideas in broad contextual and relational terms. Thus, schooling that is valued by society determines competency and employability. This in and of itself is not necessarily bad. Only the privileged classes can afford schooling without the promise of some economic incentive. Yet as Illich argued, all too often the curriculum is outdated and schooling resources are inequitably distributed so that the dominant culture is able to strengthen its social position, even though public education is readily available to all. As a result, education is measured by how many years of schooling someone accumulates, which is rather easy to measure, rather than by the knowledge or life skills (including employability) that one gains. Schooling in essence has evolved into a stratification process that is accepted as a ritualized passage into adulthood. Throughout the 1970s, Illich transferred this logic to other institutions, including medicine, technology, law, and religion (Illich, 1973a, 1973b, 1974, 1976).

Ohliger's thesis of adult education was equal in angst to Illich's critique of institutions that dominate our lives. In the late 1960s, Ohliger became closely identified with the intellectual activity that challenged the fundamental purpose of compulsory education. In 1968 he wrote, "Are we seeking a society where adult education, for intents and purposes, would be as compulsory as elementary and secondary education?" (Ohliger, 1968, p. 124). Two years later, Ohliger (1970) further articulated why he was so strongly against required schooling for adults: "If adult education becomes compulsory it will negate all the principles of learning established in the field so far. Such principles are based on the idea that learning is a voluntary act" (p. 250). During the same period, Illich began to gain notoriety for his thesis on deschooling. Illich (1968) wrote in the *Saturday Review*, "The program teaching [adults] such as reading and writing skills, of course, must be built around the emotion-loaded key words of their political vocabulary. . . . Unfortunately, 'adult education' now is conceived principally as a device to give the

underprivileged a palliative for the schooling he [sic] lacks" (p. 57).
Illich (1971b) continued his thesis on deschooling when he wrote,
"The public will see that school is a ritual that hides from its participants the contradiction between [voluntary learning and] the
myth of compulsory learning for the sake of equality that provides
the rationale for schools" (p. 12).

In 1981, *Lifelong Learning* published Ohliger's critique of mandatory continuing education, in which he argues the historical importance of learning as a voluntary act in adult education: "The
emphasis on the value of voluntary involvement in organized adult
education for quality's sake permeates our literature. The names of
Benjamin Franklin, Henry David Thoreau, James Truslow Adams,
C. Hartley Grattan, Morse Cartwright, Lyman Bryson, Eduard C.
Lindeman, and J. Roby Kidd—to cite but a very few—come quickly
to mind. . . . We can dangle jobs and training like a carrot to en-
treat participants, but we cannot mandate learning, and all the
aphorisms in the world are not going to change that fact" (pp. 5,
25). Joining Illich and Ohliger in the deconstruction of public
schooling and mandatory education were many other intellectual
thinkers in education. For example, Joel Spring (1971) wrote, "Public education . . . fulfills the needs of the corporate state for specialized training and an education that inculcated the values of
cooperation and identity with the corporate structure" (p. 4/1). And
Martin Carnoy (1971) questioned whether public education was
first and foremost an economic tool of international development
or international imperialism. More than anyone else, Ohliger was
able to translate the lessons of Reimer and Illich into the practice
of adult education, especially in his advocacy for liberal adult education and his warnings about specialization and vocational mandatory adult education within the corporate structure.

Although Reimer clearly influenced the thinking of Illich and
Ohliger, Ohliger, throughout his writings, more strongly identified
with the Illichian constructs of deschooling and deinstitutionaliza-
tion. In almost every issue of the *Basic Choices* newsletter, Ohliger

cites Illich or notes where Illich will be speaking. Illich was Ohliger's intellectual mentor, and Reimer was the catalyst that brought Ohliger and Illich together.

The Beginning of the Break

From the mid-1970s through to the end of his intellectual career, Illich wrote less as an institutional critic and more as a historian who focused on the evolution and archaeology of institutions. This transition began with the closing of CIDOC in 1976, which can be construed as a response to the threat that CIDOC itself was becoming an institution. Illich's changeover was not so much an abandonment of his earlier vocation to train priests to serve in Latin America and critique modern institutions. Rather, it indicated a shift in his critical focus. Illich chose to engage in a deeper epistemological and personal examination of why modern societies had become so dependent on institutional structures. He wanted to analyze how these institutional structures had led to a certain level of hegemony whereby citizens were less likely to question their social conditions, thus becoming more accepting of institutional constructs in their daily lives (Mitcham, 2002; Illich, 1981, 1982, 1985, 1987). Eugene Burkart (2002) recalls:

> I learned that CIDOC had closed in 1976 and Illich was now teaching at a university in Germany. This gave me pause. Here was the world's foremost critic of education and high-speed transportation teaching at a university, flying around in jets. What was I to make of this? Was Illich a hypocrite? Surprisingly, it was through this example of his life that I would get an answer to my dilemma and find an insight into a way of living in the midst of the industrial society. . . . No, Illich was not a hypocrite. Nor was he a purist or a puritan; he was dealing with the realities of life. The sad fact is that there is

no escape from the industrial economy; there is no way
to live entirely outside it. How could one avoid riding in
cars? [p. 159].

This Illichian transition was not well received by his admirers,
who did not understand his rationale for abandoning the fight
against modernity. Even Illich's mentor, Everett Reimer, questioned
Illich's direction in a phone call to Ohliger (n.d.-a) on May 23,
1986: "Ivan says I helped to rescue him from the church in the 50s
and 60s. Now after hearing him speak again, I think I may need to
help rescue him from academia. His approach is very solid, but es-
oteric, and reaches at most two percent of his audience" (p. 1). By
the mid-1980s, Illich began to fade from the public limelight as he
found it more difficult to get his essays published. Consequently,
many of those who were initially attracted to his deschooling thesis lost interest in their former mentor and ideological voice for their
cause.

By the late 1970s, Ohliger had also begun to question Illich's
change in direction. When Ohliger went to Cuernavaca in January
1976, he kept a diary in which he wrote, "Tried to call Ivan at the
'ranch' on the hill. Got Valentina on the phone (his level headed
associate). Ivan came on the line for a moment, and then said, 'A
call for me on the other line from England.' Valentina chuckled and
I did too. It reminded me of those people who act like big-shots riding around in their autos with telephones. They call you and when
you start to talk they say, 'Sorry, my other phone in the car is ring-
ing'" (Ohliger, 1976, Jan. 7). John also observed that there were
fewer people at CIDOC than he noted on previous trips. The next
day, he wrote, "When I was here before I used to also feel guilty
about finding people I had so much in common with—something
like it was unfair to take advantage of the special nature of this
place—that Ivan has attracted so many folks who have common
concerns. But why not simply accept it, build on it, but not get too
excited about the possibilities or too hopeful of what effect it might

have on my life" (1976, Jan. 8). Ohliger seemed much more sober and less enthusiastic in his assessment of CIDOC and Illich as compared to earlier trips. He had hoped to arrive and work closely with Illich on the annotated bibliography project of Illich's writings and related writings by others who had taken up his work. However, Ohliger found Illich preoccupied with other opportunities. He began to question the significance of his work in Cuernavaca. He was not pleased with Illich's transition away from CIDOC to assume the role of a more traditional scholar whom some of the world's most prestigious academics and universities courted (Ohliger, 1978).

Possibly Ohliger's idealism toward deschooling philosophies, coupled with his mistrust of higher education—no doubt affected by his personal experience at Ohio State University—shaped his quixotic response to the career shifts of Freire and Illich. In 1982, Ohliger wrote:

> I first became acquainted with the work and writing of Ivan Illich and Paulo Freire in the late 60s when I was a professor of education. I was most impressed with trenchant critiques of educational institutions. If someone had predicted then that in 1982 both Illich and Freire would be teaching full time in such institutions I would have concluded that person was off his or her rocker.
>
> Now Freire is permanently ensconced as a professor at the University of Sao Paulo. We even hear rumors that he has been offered the university presidency. And this fall Illich will be the Regents Professor at the University of California in Berkeley. As to what it all means, your guess is as good as mine [p. 4].

There is another interpretation that should be considered. Ohliger, ten years after leaving Ohio State University, wished that he too would have an opportunity to move back into the intellectual confines of a university, where he would be recognized for his intellectual contribution, enjoying the intellectual stimulations of students and occasional faculty members. Moreover, there was a certain financial security that came with an academic position. From Ohliger's memoir, it is clear that his leaving Ohio State University was not an indictment of all universities. Rather Ohliger was looking for a place to belong. In his unpublished memoirs, he reminisced: "I remember telling colleagues and students that I realized wherever I went I would not 'fit in,' but that I was dismayed to realize that fitting-in is becoming more and more required in society. Pointing to the truth of what I said about that requirement—a year or so later, I applied for a faculty position in adult education at Northern Illinois University. One of the prominent professors in the department there told a student friend of mine that I didn't have a chance because I wouldn't fit in" (1997, p. 33).

Following his exodus from Ohio State University, Ohliger continued to write journal articles, participate in academic conferences, and interact with graduate students across the country on a regular basis. Except for no longer having a tenured university position, his work mirrored that of employed academic adult educators. His comments regarding the university appointments of Illich and Freire were as much as anything an expression of envy and remorse, as well as anger toward the adult education professoriate for abandoning him. Even though many academic adult educators admired Ohliger for his passion and intellectual contributions, he was never offered another tenure-track faculty position. In his memoirs, he soberly reflects that "it was hard, *and still is,* to reconcile myself to an uneventful and unrenowned life" (1997, p. 37). It appears that his free spirit and unwillingness to abide by bureaucratic rules could find no home in universities as institutions of conformity and obedience. The academy had ostracized him.

By the mid-1980s, the break between Ohliger and Illich seemed complete, and their communication slowly waned. Yet although there are few personal letters or other documents to indicate the level of their communication, Ohliger continued to refer to Illich frequently in his newsletters in relatively positive terms. Much of their personal communication was through mutual friends such as Illich's close confidant Lee Hoinacki (1994). On at least one occasion during the 1990s, Illich sent Ohliger a copy of one of his essays, "Death Undefeated" (n.d.), that he thought would be of interest, and on another occasion Illich made a modest donation to Basic Choices. Ohliger continued to attend conferences, guest-lecture at universities, and write and lecture on topical issues related to mandatory continuing education and social issues of the times. In his 1993 book review of David Cayley's *Ivan Illich in Conversation* (1992), Ohliger wrote so strong an endorsement that he promised to buy the book from anyone who did not like it. Ohliger's only complaint about the book was "the lack of views of those of us who have disagreed with Ivan while loving him. But our views will find their place in the definitive biography of this important figure on the world's stage" (1993). While these two icons went their separate ways as the 1990s passed, their relationship, although strained from the early 1980s on, was never truly broken.

The relationship between Illich and Ohliger, collaborators throughout the 1970s and into early 1980s is indeed complex. While Ohliger was a disciple of Illich, Illich saw Ohliger as a bibliographer and adult education scholar. Ohliger's letters, diaries, and audiotapes suggest that their relationship was unbalanced, positioning Illich as the icon and Ohliger as the student. For much of their careers, they shared the common stigma of pariah in their sharp criticism of education and society. It is clear that they admired each other, especially in some of the audiotapes when it is just the two of them speaking as friends and colleagues.

Archaeology of Adult Education

While Illich retained the cultural capital of his family and the Catholic church, which provided a cushion when he decided to relinquish his priestly duties, Ohliger had neither family nor institutional capital for support once he left academe. Ohliger held stead-fastly to a vision of what adult education should be, a vision shaped by Reimer, Illich, and others associated with the deschooling and deinstitutional movement of the 1970s. While Ohliger sought spir-itual direction from Illich in particular, in fairness, Illich did not ap-pear to want to be the spiritual leader or icon for this movement, much less for Ohliger. Rather, he wanted the freedom to express his ideas in order to stimulate civic dialogue on key issues that might lead to social change. By the late 1970s Illich realized that his role as a provocateur was no longer self-fulfilling. At this time, he began his intellectual journey as an archaeologist seeking to explain how institutions had become the gods of modernity. Claims that Illich was arrogant and hypocritical are ill founded, as there is no evidence to support that Illich was any different in the 1980s than he was in the 1960s. Illich was aristocratic, well educated, self-assured, and outspoken. Ohliger was not frustrated by Illich's traits or his de-meanor. In reality, Ohliger's problem was unresolved feelings of being abandoned not by Illich but by his adult education peers. This frustration resulted in Ohliger's being critical of Illich's transition toward a more mundane academic lifestyle. There may have been some resentment that he had been unable to make the same tran-sition. When Illich renounced his deschooling thesis in the late 1980s (Mercogliano, n.d.) and chose to work with other intellec-tuals in university settings, Ohliger felt even more isolated.

Yet Illich's move to better understand and deconstruct how or-ganizations control lives of individuals as well as cultures and soci-eties illustrates Ohliger's intellectual limits. As an adult educator, Ohliger was first and foremost stuck within the historical confines of liberal adult education. His critique of adult education, and es-pecially mandatory education, allowed others to label him as a rad-ical adult educator or an anarchist, neither of which was really true. Ohliger was a product of the Fund for Adult Education's philoso-phy and practice of liberal adult education. He never argued for the dissolution of adult education as a field of study or a profession.

Instead, he sought to revitalize a pre-postmodern manifestation of adult education's historical values and philosophies aligned with becoming an educated and more engaged citizen within a vibrant democracy. Ohliger was never able to commit fully to the archaeology of adult education, as was Illich to the archaeology of organizations. Illich's success in the 1970s through his publications as an internationally respected philosopher and social critic gained him access to elite universities in his later life as an intellectual archaeologist. In contrast, Ohliger was not able to go beyond his critique of mandatory adult education and his reliance on voicing his opinions on the fringes of academe through personal correspondence and his newsletter, *Basic Choices*. One might speculate that had Ohliger published books and written articles for prestigious journals, as did Illich, the adult education community would have found it difficult to ignore him. As it was, Ohliger evolved into a single-issue crusader, albeit loved and respected by many, against mandatory or compulsory adult education. His crusade, though, is arguably his greatest contribution to adult education, and it would not have been possible without his enduring relationship to Illich and Illichian ideas. The archaeology of adult education remains a topic in need of serious analysis and research.

While it is true that they were not in regular contact during the later years of their lives, Ohliger always kept abreast of Illich's career and writings, and Illich continued to consider Ohliger a friend. Ohliger never directly expressed his feelings about Illich to me. Still, the ways in which he referred to and critiqued Illich, and the fervor with which he suggested what Illich writings I should read, clearly suggest that he saw Illich as his spiritual mentor from the time they first met.

It is difficult to assess Ohliger's tremendous contribution to adult education without considering his relationship with Illich. Ohliger not only introduced Illich to adult education, but he also integrated Illichian ideas and philosophies into his discourse against mandatory adult education. Illich provided Ohliger with the radical language to become the social conscience of adult education. As a result, Ohliger will remain in our field of study and practice for future generations. Yet the complexity of their relationship exemplifies Ohliger's humanness and honesty, which, from my point of view, are the personal attributes that make him an important adult educator.

References

Burkart, E. J. (2002). From the economy to friendship: My years studying Ivan Illich. In L. Hoinacki & C. Mitcham (Eds.), *The challenges of Ivan Illich.* Albany: State University of New York Press.

Carnoy, M. (1971). *The economics of schooling and international development, 63.* Cuernavaca, Mexico: CIDOC Cuaderno.

Cayley, D. (1992). *Ivan Illich in conversation.* Concord, ON: Anansi Press.

Cayley, D. (2005). *The rivers north of the future: The testament of Ivan Illich as told to David Cayley.* Toronto: Anansi Press.

Elias, J. L., & Merriam, S. (1995). *Philosophical foundations of adult education* (2nd ed.). Malabar, FL: Krieger.

Hoinacki, L. (1994, August 20). [Letter to John Ohliger regarding Ivan Illich]. Unpublished raw data.

Illich, I. (1955). *The philosophical foundations of history writing according to Arnold Toynbee.* Unpublished doctoral dissertation, University of Salzburg, Austria.

Illich, I. (1968, April 20). The futility of schooling in Latin America. *Saturday Review, 51*(16), 57–59, 74–75.

Illich, I. (1970a, October 17). The false ideology of schooling. *Saturday Review, 53*(42), 56–58, 68.

Illich, I. (1970b, December 3). Schooling: The ritual of progress. *New York Review of Books, 15*(10), 20–26.

Illich, I. (1971a). *Deschooling society.* New York: HarperCollins.

Illich, I. (1971b, January 9). De-schooling the teaching orders. *America, 124*(1), 12–14.

Illich, I. (1973a). *After deschooling, what?* New York: HarperCollins.

Illich, I. (1973b). *Tools for conviviality.* New York: HarperCollins.

Illich, I. (1974). *Energy and equity.* New York: HarperCollins.

Illich, I. (1976). *Medical nemesis: The expropriation of health.* New York: Pantheon.

Illich, I. (1981). *Shadow works.* London: Marion Boyars.

Illich, I. (1982). *Gender.* New York: Pantheon.

Illich, I. (1985). *H2O and the waters of forgetfulness: Reflections on the historicity of "stuff."* Dallas: Dallas Institute of Humanities and Culture.

Illich, I. (1987, September). A plea for research on lay literacy. *North American Review, 272*(3), 10–17.

Illich, I. (n.d.). [Death undefeated]. Draft sent to John Ohliger between 1992 and 1994. Unpublished raw data.

Inman, P. L. (1999). *An intellectual biography of Ivan Illich.* Unpublished doctoral dissertation, Northern Illinois University.

Liveright, A. A. (1959, March). *Liberal education—Defined and illustrated.* Chicago: Clearinghouse Center for the Study of Liberal Education for Adults.

Liveright, A. A. (1963). New horizons for liberal adult education. *Journal of Higher Education, 34*(8), 437–442.

Meiklejohn, A. (1948). *Free speech and its relation to self-government.* New York: HarperCollins.

Mercogliano, C. (n.d.). An interview with Ivan Illich from the Spring Issue of SKOLE, the *Journal of Alternative Education.* Excerpted from David Cayley's September 1988 interview with Ivan Illich for the CBC Radio Program *Ideas.* Retrieved August 25, 2005, from http://www.spinninglobe.net/illichinterview.htm.

Mitcham, C. (2002). The challenges of this collection. In L. Hoinacki & C. Mitcham (Eds.), *The challenges of Ivan Illich.* Albany: State University of New York Press.

Moritz, C. (Ed.). (1969). Ivan Illich. In *Current biography yearbook.* New York: H. W. Wilson.

Ohliger, J. (1966). The listening group in adult education. *Dissertation Abstracts, 27*(06), 1622. (Published in 1967 as *Listening groups: Mass media in adult education* by the Center for the Study of Liberal Education for Adults, Boston University)

Ohliger, J. (1968, September). Accent on social philosophy: Lifelong learning—voluntary or compulsory. *Adult Leadership, 17*(3), 124.

Ohliger, J. (1970). Accent on social philosophy: Dialogue with myself. *Adult Leadership, 18*(8), 250, 265.

Ohliger, J. (1976, January 7–9). [Ohliger diary of Cuernavaca trip]. Unpublished raw data.

Ohliger, J. (1978, Spring). [Ohliger audio diary of Cuernavaca trip]. Unpublished raw data.

Ohliger, J. (1981). Dialogue on mandatory continuing education. *Lifelong Learning, 10*(10), 5–7, 24–26.

Ohliger, J. (1982, August). Regent's professor Illich. *Second Thoughts, 4*(4), 4.

Ohliger, J. (1991, August 12). The most unforgettable adult educator I ever met. *Adult and Continuing Education Today.*

Ohliger, J. (1993, February 8). Book review: A real money-back guarantee. *Adult and Continuing Education Today*.

Ohliger, J. (1997). [My search for freedom's song: Some notes for a memoir]. Third draft. Unpublished raw data.

Ohliger, J. (n.d.-a). [1967–2000 Illich: Why the breakup of relationships between Ivan Illich and others]. Unpublished raw data.

Ohliger, J. (n.d.-b). *Xenophile and the disenchanted bureaucrat*. Unpublished raw data.

Reimer, E. (1971a). *School is dead: An essay on alternatives in education*. New York: Penguin Press.

Reimer, E. (1971b). *An essay on alternatives in education*. Cuernavaca, Mexico: CIDOC Cuaderno.

Spring, J. H. (1971). Extending the social role of the school. *Education and the rise of the corporate state*, 50, 4/1–38. Cuernavaca, Mexico: CIDOC Cuaderno.

13

Moving Beyond Radical Pessimism
Valuing Critical Perspectives

Michael Collins

Education, in order to keep up the mighty delusion,
encourages a species of ignorance. People are not
taught to be really virtuous, but to behave properly.
—*Kakuzo Okakura (1964)*

The secret in Taoism is to get out of one's own way,
and to learn that this pushing ourselves, instead of
making us more efficient, actually interferes with
everything we set about to do.
—*Alan W. Watts (2000)*

Not long after John Ohliger had recommended that I read the newly published *Tao of Pooh* (Hoff, 1983), his article "The Tao of Adult Education or Learning to Unlearn" appeared in the *Learning Connection* (Ohliger, 1983–84). No doubt like others with whom John shared the gems he uncovered from his voracious reading, I followed his recommendation and read Hoff's joyful and simultaneously instructive version of the English children's classic.

An inclination to view John's seemingly sudden enthusiasm for Taoist insights as merely fanciful might have been understandable— John was given to occasional flights of whimsy—but in error. Far from being capricious, John was in earnest about the need for adult educators committed to political activism and work for social change to lighten up: "Relax folks. The more a heavy, effort-filled duty it is, the less likely the necessary fundamental change will occur. The more you 'hardball' it in the 'struggle,' the more you are, when you come right down to it, playing by the rules of your powerful enemies" (Ohliger, 1983–84, p. 7).

The path that John was "enjoying" in this article meant adopting a practical orientation to activist work and avoiding burnout and debilitating disappointments. An individual could follow this path via Taoist insights and the relaxed watchfulness of Taoist tai chi practice that teaches lightness in movement (*qing*) and the power of knowing when and how to yield without surrendering (*yin*). John felt that walking this path constituted a nicely balanced and optimistic approach—rather than a grimly overdetermined one—to engaging with strategies for social change.

To counter a burgeoning professionalized discourse on self-directed learning and learning how to learn in mainstream adult education, John's vision of a Taoist take on adult education called for learning to unlearn. While many hailed the growing professionalized discourse that privileged the experience of the learner over the role of the teacher as progressive, John saw it differently. Of course, his argument was not with the commonsense awareness that people have the capacity to learn on their own. Rather, he was concerned with and wanted to challenge how we learn through conventional educational methods, particularly in schools. His contention was that formalized learning gets in the way of our innate capacity for autonomous learning. John felt it also gets in the way of the convivial egalitarian intent of adult education as friends learning from friends. Such learning focuses on the creativity, capacity, emotion, hopefulness, helpfulness, and possibility of friends as co-learners. John always attempted to capture this critical social sentiment in his work with students. It finds expression, for example, in this verse from E. E. Cummings, which he quoted in a selection of poems and songs for a graduate seminar syllabus on adult education (Ohliger, 1985, p. 18):

I'd rather learn from
one bird how
to sing
than teach ten thousand
stars how not
to dance

In his critique of formalized adult learning, John wanted to emphasize the harmful effects of professionalization on adult education as a voluntary experience. A preoccupation with the enthronement of a professionalizing practice had virtually prescribed, from the mid-1970s, notions of self-directed learning and learning how to learn as a distinctive pedagogical method under the rubric of andragogy. John, with a deft touch humorously applied, invited us to consider finding a way out of this artificial and professionalized take on self-directed learning as technique by simply invoking *The Tao of Pooh*. Others among us—also concerned with an increasingly professionalized modern practice of adult education—sought with more grim determination to illuminate through critical analysis what we perceived as the negative tendencies to instrumentalize, commodify, and highjack the innate capacities of ordinary men and women for autonomous learning.

We can reasonably infer from John's engagement with the "Tao of Adult Education" a strong suggestion that adult educators themselves have a need for learning to unlearn even, or especially, while extolling the relevance of experience for both the teaching and learning processes in the field of study and practice. This would broadly apply to the determined professionalizers of the field and the equally determined social activists and critical theorists. In John's view of learning, evident in Taoist philosophy and practice, "the intelligent person has learned to be unlearned and has returned to the ways which learned persons have forgotten" (Ohliger, 1983–84, p. 7). These ways require, according to John, the avoidance of information overload. John claimed that even social change adult educators are complicit in a tendency that "sees people drowning in INFOGLUT" (p. 7). (Witness, for example, the emphasis that many adult educators place on the necessity of teaching computer literacy when it turns out that the logic of the technology ensures that users become pertinently proficient, even unavoidably preoccupied, with its vast information-generating capacities once they have access to it.) In his concern about "infoglut," John was particularly prescient in the wake of subsequent communication technologies that have emerged, including e-mail, Web sites, iPods, digital cameras, pagers, and BlackBerries. However, John was by no means a technophobe. Indeed, taking into account his work in the area of media and communications, some of us have viewed him as a technophile. What he really abhorred was the way that "data mania" ties in with the deployment of prescriptive standardized forms of curriculum on adult learners. In contrast, John envisaged the potential of communications technology as providing ways to support the development of emancipatory pedagogies. Rather than being shaped by the overwhelming imperatives of technology, the Tao of Adult Education incorporates their transformative possibilities in a learning process that, for John, "is the way to set people free" (p. 7). John considered learner freedom to be essential to adult education as a truly social endeavor. As he perceived it, professionalization was a thorn in the side of people's freedom to learn.

On Theory and Murky Prose

To a large extent, John Ohliger's objection to critical theory had to do with its adverse effects on the clarity and directness of academic writing in adult education's field of study. Why deploy Frankfurt school critical theory and its critique about the steering effects of technical rationality to describe the obvious about the ways institutionalized, pedagogical practices undermine the learning processes that are nourished by the voluntary, convivial side of adult education? While John otherwise offered very supportive responses to my academic criticisms of competency-based education(CBE)—criticisms that drew on critical theory and phenomenology—he provided me this summary appraisal of my work in a language that certainly left critical theory out: "Prof says CBE sucks." John, purposefully ignoring the theoretical turn, was pretty well on the mark.

On this same theme, an antipathy toward the deployment of theory in favor of readable nonacademicized prose, I recall a visit with John in Madison, Wisconsin. Over a meal with other adult education friends who had some interest in critical theory, he suddenly exclaimed, "I just don't understand Habermas!" I also recall John recanting a previous assessment that he had made of a close mutual friend's use of Jürgen Habermas in a master's project. In a letter to our friend, John wrote, "I feel I owe you an apology and an explanation for the savagery of my criticism of your last chapter and my negative views of Habermas. It is probably closer to the truth that I just don't understand Habermas and writings using his ideas" (Ohliger, personal communication to George Van der Loos, May 14, 1990). Actually, John was more interested in the details of our friend's struggle (as an adult educator) against the administration of Lakeland College in Alberta, which, in our view, had imposed in top-down fashion a dysfunctional competency-based education curriculum model imported to Canada from the United States. It is probably closer to the truth, as I gleaned from subsequent conversations with John, to say that he understood well enough what Habermas was about. However, he objected to the convoluted prose of critical theory and what he perceived as the preoccupation with invoking complex theory as a sledgehammer to crack a nut. John's views on Foucault and the discourses on postmodernity, poststructuralism, and deconstruction were similarly disparaging. In a short commentary exploring various conceptions of nihilism, John wrote, "I did run across references to authors I believe have obfuscated the current literature such as Foucault and Habermas and that old bugaboo of mine 'critical theory' with such murky terms as 'discourse' and 'deconstruction'" (Ohliger, n.d., p. 1). John wrote these observations in the late 1990s. Perhaps willfully ignoring debates that draw sharp differences between the views of Habermas and Foucault, critical theory and postmodernism, Ohliger put them in bed together.

It is not that John Ohliger was uninformed or disinterested in the significance of the Marxian legacy and humanistic socialist thought and activism. Over the years, he put me in touch with the work of notable socialist writers, in particular that of C.L.R. James, whose commitment to the Marxist legacy is in no way diminished by a literary flair and graceful writing. John was intrigued by James's knowledgeable passion for the game of cricket, on which he wrote as a regular correspondent for the English *Manchester Guardian*. For John, here was a Marxist who wrote well and brought a sense of balance to his revolutionary zeal through an inclination for play as well as for radical politics.

In addition to James, John had rubbed shoulders with notable American socialists such as Max Schactman, a Trotskyist who had attempted to develop a new movement within the Marxian legacy that would break with the sectarian tendencies of the past. John was aligned with this kind of progressive political activism. Yet, more in the way of American progressivism, John did not favor—and this is evident in his writings—a development of reasoned arguments that characterizes the Marxian legacy's aim toward a rational society for empowerment through collective solidarity. John placed greater value on what he perceived as the moral imperatives of individual rights and autonomy. Thus, despite his appreciation for dialectical thought and nuanced commentaries over what he viewed as hard-edged dogma, we can discern in John's radical social and political philosophy a tendency to dismantle (reduce) everything to the level of the individual. John had a preoccupation with personal autonomy that entails opposition to any perceived authoritative intrusion into that hemisphere. In part, as I will subsequently take up, we can assess John's preference for the pedagogy of Ivan Illich over that of Paulo Freire in this light.

John described his radicalism as a concern "to get to the root of the issue and work towards fundamental social change for the better"

(Hiemstra & Goldstein, 1990, p. 1). This role for John meant challenging conventional practices and being a rebel within the field of
adult education, especially within the context of academic adult education, which made up a large part of his audience.

Against Mandatory Continuing Education

In an interview for the *Australian Journal of Adult Education* (Brennan, 1987), John conveyed his "rage about mandatory continuing education [MCE]" (p. 55). He had written extensively in his clear-cut
prose against the imposition of MCE on professionals and welfare recipients alike. In particular, John traced the ways that MCE under-
mined aspirations for learning as a voluntary endeavor as well as the
role it played in the cooptation of lifelong education: "The legitimate
understanding of adult education as self-initiated lifelong learning,"
he proclaimed to an academic forum, "is being converted into the
concept of lifelong schooling" (Ohliger, 1980a, p. 50). Elsewhere,
John continuously pushed the issue of MCE and its implications for
lifelong learning with thought-provoking and eminently readable articles, which include "Dialogue on Mandatory Continuing Education" (1981); "Is Lifelong Learning a Guarantee of Permanent
Inadequacy?" (1974; Chapter Four in this book); "Must We All Go
Back to School? The Pitfalls of Compulsory Adult Education" (with
David Lisman, 1978); "Lifelong Learning as Nightmare" (1982;
Chapter Six in this book); and "Reconciling Education with Liberty" (1983). The last article opens in true Ohliger fashion consistent with his penchant for unearthing apt references outside the
professional literature. John begins with a gem of a cutting-edge
quote from Bernard Shaw (Ohliger, 1983, p. 161): "Soon everybody
will be schooled, mentally and physically, from the cradle to the end
of the term of adult compulsory military service, and finally of compulsory civil service lasting until the age of superannuation. Always
more schooling, more compulsion. We are to be cured by an excess
of the dose that has poisoned us. . . . Clearly this will not do. We
must reconcile education with liberty." Drawing on Shaw, John, as

the foremost opponent of MCE, was instructing us on the importance of taking a stand on an issue in which we believed. Moreover, he was coaching us on how to write about it with conviction and clarity.

For a special issue on the topic of MCE in the journal *Setting the Pace,* Paul Ilsley and I, as coeditors, had expected John Ohliger to write a hard-hitting polemic against that prescriptive and reductionistic trend in curriculum design. Instead, he opted for a gentler and more nuanced critical commentary than we had anticipated. He wrote, "First, we must search for a balance between our yearning for order and our desire for liberty. As adult educators we believe that whatever minimal but essential place learning has in everyone's life, it would be better if it were more voluntary than compulsory" (1980b, p. 23). John further cautioned that "above all, we need to preserve our sense of modesty about our own work as adult educators" (p. 25). Paul and I had informed John that we had experienced difficulty finding someone to write wholeheartedly in support of MCE for our special issue. This somewhat surprised us, given that MCE was in vogue and had received a torrent of highly visible support from well-publicized pundits when it emerged as an educational policy initiative. Sounding a restrained yet hopeful note, John responded to this disclosure in his essay: "The fact that it was difficult for the editors of this theme issue to find someone to write unequivocally in favor of mandatory continuing education (MCE), while all around us we are bombarded with demands for more, indicates our longing for a more relaxed view of learning requirements" (p. 23).

Three decades later, the requirements of MCE, or prescriptive variations of it that transgress notions of voluntary learning, draw little in the way of protest or even critical observation. Mandated learning is accepted as a matter of fact by those needing to maintain professional certification, and even by those needing to "earn" official status for receipt of welfare payments by engaging in compulsory job-readiness training schemes. We should not be surprised by this given a critically informed understanding about how institutional power works. Critical analysis reveals that technical rationality imperatives, systems of surveillance and control, and a managerial ethos impose themselves and are widely accepted as par for the course under advanced capitalism. These circumstances, we can readily observe, have intensified during the past two decades. In this light, prescriptive educational policy innovations such as MCE and CBE persist in diminishing natural impulses toward voluntary rather than compulsory learning.

In this moment in civil society, a growing willingness to forgo individual rights in the ideological wake of the "war on terrorism" legitimizes authoritative prescriptions that have further eroded democratic aspirations for self-directed learning. In this ideological climate, it is difficult to counter a pessimistic assessment that critical pedagogy, including the radicalism of John Ohliger, has lost its edge simply because the arena for engaging in dialogue and planning sensible oppositional strategies has shrunk. The balance that Ohliger sought between our yearning for order and our desire for liberty veers perceptibly toward the former. This is all the more reason, in present circumstances, for adult educators in search of a hopeful pedagogy to invoke what John Ohliger referred to as our "Lindeman roots" in a reengagement with "the meaning of adult education" (Lindeman, 1926/1961). In these times, we need to resist the system's powerful cooptation tendencies and uphold the principles of voluntary learning. In this regard, we have to ask: How do we launch a meaningful quest to invent and sustain sensible lifeworld-enhancing initiatives within our institutions, however modest in scope?

Ivan Illich and Paulo Freire

Few would dispute a claim that John Ohliger was instrumental in bringing the ideas of Ivan Illich and Paulo Freire to the attention of adult educators. This is especially true in the case of Illich, given that he and John shared the conviction that institutionalized schooling damaged individuals as free learners. Both educators believed that the pervasive ethos of schooling throughout society serves to frustrate our natural inclinations toward self-directed learning and the realization of our full potential as human beings. In contrast, Freire's pedagogy acknowledges the significance of schools as strategic locations for emancipatory educational practice. Although this stance is oppositional to Ohliger and Illich's strong antischooling stance, John nevertheless characterized Freire and Illich as the two great radical adult educators (Ohliger, 1990a). Indeed in an earlier introductory article on the ideas of Illich, John noted that Illich regarded Freire as his mentor (Ohliger & McCarthy, 1971). Ohliger later wrote, with some regret, on how he perceived the differences that separated Freire and Illich in the 1970s: "Freire opted for rational order and supported the Christian Marxists in Latin America and elsewhere. Illich went for spontaneous freedom based on a kind of sophisticated fundamentalist Catholicism" (1990a, p. 5).

Although he appealed for a balanced view in assessing the work of the two men whom he considered the great radical adult educators, it is apparent that Ohliger recognized a field shift toward Freire and criticalist values: "The dominant strain in the radical adult education literature—so-called critical theory or critical pedagogy—places almost total reliance on rationality. Just look at the recent books by or about Paulo Freire and see if you don't agree" (1990a, p. 5). Ohliger himself placed greater value on Illichian ideas and analysis. In a later personal reflection on his influences, Ohliger (1995a) opted for Illich's *Deschooling Society* (1971) as his first choice when he listed books that had been most meaningful for his development as an adult educator. In John's mind, then, *Deschooling Society* preceded Freire's landmark book, *Pedagogy of the Oppressed* (1981, first published in 1972), which he also admired, in order of importance. Still Ohliger appealed for an approach that would "bring the two disparate perspectives together in a way that would enhance the value of both" (1995b, p. 1). John was critical of the "politically correct" educators whom he perceived as turning "Freire into an icon and Illich into a pariah" (p. 1). In actuality, however, Freire's pedagogy had long been criticized within the radical literature of adult education. For example, Youngman (1986) had provided critique from a Marxian perspective nearly a decade earlier. As well, it can be reasonably argued, without turning Illich into a pariah and Freire into an icon, that the shortcomings as well as the brilliance of Illich's work and its implications for a radical progressive pedagogy should be taken seriously (Collins, 1998).

Illich (1971) provided an instructive polemic against schooling as an institution, deploying it in his critique as a telling metaphor to illuminate the way systems of surveillance and control shape contemporary society. Moreover, his graphic observations on intriguing notions like the erosion of the commons, the displacement of vernacular values, and, as a countermeasure, the development of tools for conviviality are as insightful for us as the theorizing of Jürgen Habermas (1984) on the colonization of the lifeworld. Unlike Illich, and to Ohliger's distaste (as previously noted), Habermas has been concerned in his analytical work to develop a grounded (authoritative) theory of communicative action as the rational basis for a more just society. From Habermas we derive the means to account for the way learning processes are systematically (mis)shaped under conditions of advanced capitalism as well as the means to identify relevant (that is, sensible) counterstrategies within institutional as well as community-based settings. Habermas's work provides us with the reasoning for why we should pursue an emancipatory pedagogy in which we can invoke Illich's progressive ideas as well as Freire's strategies for raising critical consciousness and advancing empowerment of ordinary people. John Ohliger's preference was for the brilliantly metaphoric and anarchistic style of Illich over the measured—ponderous and obscure, in John's view—theoretical work of Habermas intended to prefigure the emergence of a more rational society.

Those of us who have experience with the kind of educational alternatives such as home schooling, free universities, and learning exchanges that Illich and Ohliger favored can confirm that such arrangements are eminently workable. This feasibility is especially so for middle-class people who already have the resources (including cultural capital) to cull the benefits from countercultural initiatives. Still, it can be argued that antischooling sentiments and the proposed abandonment of publicly funded schooling, especially by the middle class, serve to further undermine the quality of schooling for the majority of children, which plays nicely into the hands of neoconservative ideological agendas that favor privatization (services for profit) at the expense of public provision (Collins, 1998). In this view, the antischooling tendency reinforced by the work of Ohliger and Illich is counterproductive of progressive educational aims, and it weakens past gains made for the provision of public education and other services. It is also relevant to note that the foremost opponents of schooling and the entire system of credentialing are themselves typically well-credentialed individuals who benefit from the advantages that accrue from their formal qualifications.

With regard to their strong anti-institutional stance, both Illich and Ohliger looked largely to the academy—and, in the case of Illich, to the church—as the primary sources of informed audiences for the legitimation and appreciation of their work. In their polemics, there is a discernible level of dependency on as well as rebelling against the institutional arrangements they oppose. Paulo Freire, for his part, understood that our schools, conventional workplaces, and other institutions, as well as families and communities, are all vitally strategic locations for engagement with an emancipatory pedagogy. At the same time, and aside from the Marxian critique of Freire (Youngman, 1986), it is apparent that even Freirean pedagogy has been widely invoked within educational circles in a way that takes the political edge off its aspirations for social change through education for critical consciousness. Remembering that John Ohliger, despite his apparent preference for Illich, called for a more balanced assessment of the contributions of Illich and Freire, perhaps it is time for us to make a more measured assessment of their contributions to adult education. As we engage in this assessment, we might well wonder whether John overburdened both of their reputations by enthroning them as *the* two great adult educators.

Beyond Radical Pessimism

Returning to the theme of the opening section of this chapter, John Ohliger warned radical adult educators about the debilitating effects of overburdening ourselves in the earnest pursuit of social justice. Rather than harnessing a cheerful but realistic sense of hope in our emancipatory pedagogical endeavors, this overburdening invites pessimism, cynicism, and, ultimately, burnout. Thus, as we work to make society more just, we should proceed ready to laugh at ourselves and at the circumstances that frustrate our aspirations on a daily basis. Levity is crucial for a hopeful approach so "we can work together toward a new balance . . . [and] cope with the threat of the technoeconomic snowball in a climate of mutual support" (Ohliger, 1980b, p. 25). John understood that we need humor and a light touch to keep us engaged and enthusiastic as we search for opportunities. "You shall know the truth," John (1990b) advises us, "and the truth shall make you laugh" (p. 25). In this vein, we are emboldened to be cheerfully upfront about our moral and political commitments and unafraid to write about them without academicized obfuscation.

When we edited the special issue of the journal *Setting the Pace* that focused entirely on mandatory continuing education, Paul Ilsley and I were initially dismayed at what we perceived as archcritic John Ohliger's whimsical response instead of a hard-hitting polemic against the tendency toward MCE. Looking back at Ohliger's (1980b) essay in that special issue now, I feel the piece, which opens with a poem, still serves as an antidote to the pessimism that can emerge from overly determined expectations of critical pedagogy. John's fired-up writing demonstrated his inclination to place his hopes in the creative capacities of the individual learner as a counterforce to the repressive effects of standardized mass education. It also demonstrated his tendency to privilege feelings over thought (see also Ohliger, 1985). The poem follows below. It aptly expresses John's critically informed sense of hope and his belief that radical commitment, sustained by literary insights rather than theory development, is truly enhanced by a lifelong willingness to celebrate the joy of everyday living, even in hard times. Moreover, it shows that John could capture the critical moment and frame it as an optimistic one that is about "searching for balance, coping with threats, [and] looking for opportunities" (p. 22):

> Our nonperfect god is in her/his egalitarian heaven
> and all's right with the world.
> Everything is good.
> Yet there is much evil awash in the land—
> hubris, greed, topdownism, scientism, envy.
>
> There is a gap
> between the basic goodness (not perfection) of us all
> as ordinary persons with that of god in us, and
> the evil that is an inexplicable part of us all
> as separated specializers in a world of massive
>   institutions.
> This gap
> constitutes the space from pole to pole
> of the existential paradoxical contradictory dialectic
>   dilemma
> that all of us are enmeshed in
> every moment of our lives.
>
> Thus
> a single human life cannot be summed up
> as either good or evil, but
> as a balancing act encompassing these polar
>   moralities.

No society, no tyranny, no concentration camp, or
   torture chamber
can ever totally remove the joy of life;
but certainly
some arrangements get in the way
less than others
and some may even help to make life
a little bit better.

References

Brennan, B. (1987). Conversation with John Ohliger. *Australian Journal of Adult Education, 27*(3), 52–56, 65.

Collins, M. (1998). *Critical crosscurrents in education.* Malabar, FL: Krieger.

Freire, P. (1981). *Pedagogy of the oppressed.* New York: Continuum.

Habermas, J. (1984). *The theory of communicative action.* Boston: Beacon Press.

Hiemstra, R., & Goldstein, A. (1990). *John Ohliger: Personal vita.* Retrieved May 30, 2005, from http://www-distance.syr.edu/pvitajfo.html.

Hoff, B. (1983). *The Tao of Pooh.* New York: Penguin Books.

Illich, I. (1971). *Deschooling society.* New York: HarperCollins.

Lindeman, E. C. (1961). *The meaning of adult education.* Montreal: Harvest House. (Original work published 1926)

Lisman, D., & Ohliger, J. (1978). Must we all go back to school? The pitfalls of compulsory adult education. *Progressive, 42,* 35–37.

Ohliger, J. (1974). Is lifelong education a guarantee of permanent inadequacy? *Convergence, 7*(2), 47–58.

Ohliger, J. (1980a). The social uses of theorizing in adult education. *Adult Education, 31*(1), 48–53.

Ohliger, J. (1980b). Searching for balance, coping with threats, looking for opportunities. *Setting the Pace, 1*(1), 22–26.

Ohliger, J. (1981). Dialogue on mandatory continuing education. *Lifelong Learning: The Adult Years, 4*(10), 5, 7, 24–26.

Ohliger, J. (1982). Lifelong learning as nightmare. In R. Gross (Ed.), *Invitation to lifelong learning* (pp. 273–274). Chicago: Follett.

Ohliger, J. (1983). Reconciling education with liberty. *Prospects, 13*(2), 161–179.

Ohliger, J. (1983–84, December/January). The Tao of adult education or learning to unlearn. *Learning Connection,* 7–8.

Ohliger, J. (1985, March). The fictional adult educator. *Basic Choices Newsletter*, 1–34.

Ohliger, J. (1990a, February 12). What is radical adult education? *Adult and Continuing Education Today*, 5.

Ohliger, J. (1990b). Forum: You shall know the truth and the truth shall make you laugh. *Journal of Adult Education, 19*(1), 25–38.

Ohliger, J. (1995a). Personal reflections: Books to live by. *Adult Learning, 6*(5), 7.

Ohliger, J. (1995b). *Taking Freire and Illich seriously or icons and pariahs.* Retrieved October 2, 2006, from http://www.nl.edu/academics/cas/ace/resources/johnohliger.cfm.

Ohliger, J. (n.d.). Work in progress. *Basic Choices Newsletter*, 1.

Ohliger, J., & McCarthy, C. (1971). *Lifelong learning or lifelong schooling? A tentative view of the ideas of Ivan Illich with a quotational bibliography.* Syracuse, NY: Syracuse University Publications in Continuing Education and ERIC Clearinghouse on Education.

Okakura, K. (1964). *The book of tea.* New York: Dover.

Watts, A. (2000). *What is Tao?* Novato, CA: New World Library.

Youngman, F. (1986). *Adult education and socialist pedagogy.* Beckanham, UK: Croom Helm.

Part Four

Narrations on the Life of a Radical Social Educator

Legacies and Critiques

14

Outside Looking In
Challenges to the Professional Field

Phyllis M. Cunningham

I met John Ohliger when I was a graduate student and he was an associate professor of adult education at Ohio State University. He gave me a bibliography on compulsory adult education, and that introduction was the beginning of a beautiful friendship. John and I taught a course together on radical adult education at Syracuse University. As part of a collective valuing adult education as a voluntary endeavor, we helped found and promote the National Alliance for Voluntary Learning (NAVL). This included publishing the daily conference newsletter *NAVL Gazing*, which emerged at the 1979 national Adult and Continuing Education conference in Boston.

As adult educators in arms for almost thirty years, John and I traveled back and forth between DeKalb, Illinois; Madison, Wisconsin; and Springfield, Illinois, plotting and working for social justice and enjoying our friendship. John taught several adult education classes at my university, Northern Illinois University (NIU). He helped numerous NIU graduate students, some through a few e-mails and others over weeks of internship at his Basic Choices office in Madison. I can think of several students who bonded more strongly with John over a distance of at least one hundred miles than they did with any faculty whom they saw daily on our campus. I was pleased and honored when John asked me to be his "best person" when he married his wife, Chris Wagner. I have admired John as one of the few true intellectuals in the current field of adult education.

I could always inspire graduate students by telling them how John, as a portly tenured academic adult educator, became so convinced about the dangers of mandatory lifelong schooling that he gave up his tenured position and his car to work for social justice and change. To help sustain life as he engaged in this work for cultural transformation, John worked as a part-time library clerk two days a week. Postacademia, John dedicated his life to quality living and intellectual critique. Slimmed down and more focused, he could commit himself to adult education that was voluntary, accessible, and respectful of the learner and living.

The papers I used in researching this chapter are from the endless intellectual material and ephemera that John sent me. They have been accumulating in a file in my office since 1981—innumerable eight-and-a-half-by-eleven-inch sheets of paper with copy on both sides and the banner BASIC CHOICES, INC across the top of most of them. Indeed I have now amassed a file some two and a half linear feet high. This pile of primary sources from my friend and colleague John would light up the eyes of many adult education historians. I also have a box of over forty tapes that I dubbed from the reels of *Songs of Social Significance*, which came from a radio program that John had done in San Francisco at Radio Pacifica Foundation's station KPFA-FM.

My file of bibliographies, annotated lists, speeches, letters, and articles provides a well-documented source of John's views as an outsider looking in on adult education as a field of study and practice. His life as an outsider was not easy. Some mainstream adult educators, perceived as leaders in our field, treated John badly. I contend it was because they resented his criticism and his challenge to their hegemony over the field. I firmly believe that John's story should be told because it is rather difficult to stand on the outside and make a critique once you have been on the inside. Accordingly, my task is to tell John's story, including our odyssey together within what was becoming an increasingly professionalized modern practice. First, though, I look at how John defined and practiced adult education in the community.

Practicing Adult Education as Community Education

John loved adult education, and there are few other people as committed to the field as he was throughout his life: "I am proud of being a part of adult education and have been since I started practicing it in the mid-1940s" (Ohliger, 1982, p. 63). John also had a distinct definition of community: "Individuals don't exist, neither do communities, but together they define the whole human population. . . . I believe the person has within him or her self a community beyond words, which transcends the narrower ones of family, group, city, nation, and international power. . . . In my view, creativity arises not from the individual but from a type of mundane community—the common language, symbols, and past imaginative activity of groups—inspired by the eternal community, the community beyond language" (Ohliger, 1987a, p. 4). It seems to me that John saw all adult education as community education. Even if one were meditating, one would be bringing into operation the language and symbols of the eternal community. However, I will write here only about those activities of which I have direct knowledge and in which John was actually engaged with a physical community.

Since much of his activity in the community centered on engaging books and media, culture was clearly an important part of adult education for John. When he was asked to describe his journey as a community educator, John would begin by talking about the after-school job he had had as a thirteen-year-old working at the Utley Branch of the Detroit Public Library. It was there that he grew to love books and their distribution. He established a portable bookstore for the Michigan State Council of local unions, and in the early 1950s, while working for the Ford Foundation, John established discussion groups to take up opposing views regarding what had been read. This work led naturally into his work with the Great Books Foundation that promoted discussion of the Western classics. Next John moved into radio and spent time developing listening groups that would meet for discussion after a broadcast of a controversial question. In 1966 he wrote his dissertation on listening groups at the

University of California, Los Angeles, and later published it as a book (Ohliger, 1967).

Following graduation, John took a position at Selkirk College in British Columbia. This college was unique in that it was dedicated to the community that it served. John's perennial concern was with the participation of ordinary people in voluntary learning. This is exemplified in his description of Buddy DeVito, a board member of Selkirk College:

> Buddy made his living repairing shoes and had comparatively little schooling. He was probably on the Board because he was an important political figure. Not long after, he was elected Mayor. But as he worked in his father's shoe repair shop he practiced the kind of informal adult education that sets the framework for the best in the field. Buddy did not teach, he did not preach. Mainly he listened and conversed. When people came in to get their shoes fixed, they talked with him about their problems and those of the community. Buddy worked with them very informally to gather the collective strength to do something about those problems. And he learned along with them about how to make things better. Of course, formal study has its place, but it should draw its inspiration from the natural settings in which learning occurs [Ohliger, 1982, p. 70].

Later, when John lived in Madison, he was involved with a group that cofounded WORT (a community radio station), the Community Scholarship Roundtable, and "The Madison Review of Books." These projects were conceptualized as educational activities, embedded in the community, which had the full participation of community members. Each project encouraged ordinary people to be active producers of knowledge. The driving energy for all of these community activities was John's conviction that media, books, radio, and listening groups provided ways to strengthen grassroots participation in civil discourse and, in doing so, to strengthen civil society. John never patronized the unschooled person. His public pedagogy assisted learners in building knowledge as a voluntary acquisition. For example, *Songs of Social Significance* had pertinent historical facts interlaced among the songs to contextualize their messages. This creative program revitalized the songs of feminists, workers, suffragettes, and civil rights movements, documenting their struggles and their histories. The songs became cultural representations and expressions that highlighted social movement issues and proclaimed the people's knowledge.

John shared his interest in media within the profession through his work in the Mass Media section of the Adult Education Association, and through its journal *Media and Adult Learning* (MAL). In his bibliography *Really Creative Conferences*, he wrote, "Stroll with me through the almost 20 years of MAL. You'll discover that, at its root, this journal has been dedicated to questioning the value of the typical and the conventional since we published the first of over 70 issues in the fall of 1967" (Ohliger, 1987b, p. 1). John saw the journal as an extension of his work bent on raising issues within the professions and for the professional. His annotated bibliography, which he submitted to MAL, creatively demonstrates how to use popular media (culture) as a tool in thinking critically about the $10 billion business of conference planning. John challenged adult educators to rely on the larger community for critique rather than relying only on professional technical competence. Unfortunately most program planners in the field probably never read John's bibliography, or if it had been assigned to them, they may not have finished it. The bibliography was challenging because it required readers to think about the futility and lack of meaning in their daily work. For many program planners, this was hard to swallow, even if it was done in a humorous manner.

John was the major speaker at two of the annual three-day residential seminars that the progressive Iowa State Education Department put on for state and university adult educators. Prior to the 1995 seminar, John had written to Miriam Temple, who organized these seminars: "My experience is that Freire is usually treated as some kind of an icon—if you would like me to, I could prepare a brief annotated bibliography of critical comments on Freire" (personal communication, n.d.; see also, Ohliger, n.d.). The resulting annotated bibliography that John used at that seminar is divided into ten sections and is very well done (Ohliger, 1995). As I was reading through it, I must admit that although I claim to know Freire, many of the citations and some of the critique in this bibliography were new to me. I also noted that he had included William S. Griffith's critique of Freire. John had had some battles with Griffith, whom he believed had treated him unfairly. The depth of information in his annotated bibliography and his inclusion of Griffith's critique say a lot about the man to me. John was not spiteful when it came to the integrity of his work; he was very thorough and fair in presenting all sides. John did not get trapped in icon worship. I like the way he was able to move beyond ideas to newer expressions when needed. His comments about Blanco Facundo's critical evaluation of Freire-inspired programs in the United States and Puerto Rico, quoted from a paper included in the course pack we developed for the class we taught at Syracuse University, provide an example of this:

> Now as 1985 dawns it is time to get beyond Freire and Illich and return to the searches (for an honorable and open combination of healthy political radicalism and worthwhile adult education). . . . Getting beyond doesn't imply rejection. It just means that we need to recognize how far we have to go to find effective paths to combining education and politics, persons and groups that don't turn them all into the cruel jokes they are today. . . . Blanco Facundo merits our gratitude for pushing open the gates of healthy exploration about the ideas, action, and person of Paulo Freire. She has done her work in a way that could be an example to us all. Combining the personal and the political as she did in her monograph [see Facundo,

1984], avoiding bureaucratic and ideological jargon to the extent that she did, suggest a way to go for all of us [Cunningham & Ohliger, 1987, pp. 403–404].

The Professions and the Professionals

John's first rupture with the profession was in 1973. Nearly fifteen years later, he provided this account: "In the interest of brevity I'm not going to say much about that [his years at Ohio State University] except that while there I discovered the heretical views of Ivan Illich, author of *Deshooling Society*. Discovering Illich probably led me, in combination with a number of more personal factors, to resign from Ohio State in 1973 and take a temporary position with university extension in Madison, Wisconsin where I've [mostly] lived ever since" (Ohliger, 1987a, p. 11).

John's Illich-inspired critique of mandatory continuing education and his expressed disdain for an increasingly professionalized field of study deeply offended some professors. I soon came to realize this during my first months as a new professor at NIU in 1976. I was privy to a discussion that involved two of our NIU professors and one of the field's "great leaders" who was speaking to our students that evening. When one of the NIU professors told the distinguished visitor that something had to be done to get Ohliger back as a professor in the field, the visitor said something like, "No, Ohliger has made his bed. Let him lie in it. He has said a lot that would have been better left unsaid. Behavior has consequences." The other NIU professor interjected, "Whatever happened to freedom of speech on campuses?" No one responded, and the conversation moved in another direction. It was then that I realized how strongly those with power in the field felt about John's critique and how at least some of them had taken it personally, to the point of wanting him to pay for expressing himself.

John did appear to pay. For example, he seemed to be treated more harshly in the publishing arena by editors who were from the old guard in the field of study. One case in point involves John's

Basic Choices Group, which had started in Madison, Wisconsin, in 1976 as a center for clarifying political and social options. The group was invited to write a chapter by the book editor of one of the multiple books comprising the 1980 *Handbook of Adult Education*. They wrote the chapter, which that editor subsequently accepted. However, when he submitted his book chapters to the series editors, the Basic Choices chapter was dropped, with no written explanation to John or his coauthors. The Basic Choices Group had read all the chapters of the book, and they had spent hours writing a critique. They had also suggested another author to write a critique as a companion piece. The book came out with his chapter but not theirs. Such behavior drove John crazy. He felt, rightly or wrongly, that this exclusion amounted to payback time. It is hard to know whether the decision to omit the chapter was based on honest appraisals. Clearly, the editing and review process can be faulted. I know personally that it took editorial intervention with the chapter author to have John included in the chapter listing influential U.S. adult educators in the twenty-fifth anniversary "black book." This book was entitled *Adult Education: Evolution and Achievements in a Developing Field of Study* (Peters, Jarvis, & Associates, 1991). The chapter in question was "The Impact of Intellectual Leadership," by William S. Griffith.

With his initial exclusion, John found himself in good company. Paulo Freire had been left out as well and needed "rehabilitation" to be included, and Myles Horton never made the list. When John was included, Griffith (1991) eventually added this paragraph:

> *John Ohliger* is the only leading influential scholar in this chapter who voluntarily relinquished a tenured professorship at a university to pursue his independent style of scholarly life. He is probably best known for his leadership in producing the periodical *Basic Choices*, a newsletter dedicated to revealing the contradictions within adult education. As an opponent of mandatory continuing professional education, Ohliger organized the

National Alliance for Voluntary Learning. He is a critic of lifelong education, and he questions whether it is really a means of promoting the notion of permanent inadequacy and the development of lifelong schooling as the antidote. With his dedication to adult learning as a vehicle for improving the quality of life, Ohliger has served as the self-appointed conscience of the field, stimulating serious examinations of the commonly accepted popular notions of the appropriate use of adult education [p. 113].

Interestingly enough, despite the dissident status conferred on him by some academic adult educators, John never quite left academe. During the decades after he departed the professoriate, he taught courses at many universities. I am aware that he taught at Northern Illinois University, Syracuse University, the University of Wisconsin, the University of Iowa, Florida State University, the University of Southern Maine, the Pennsylvania State University, the University of British Columbia, the University of Saskatchewan, Sangamon State University, the University of Wyoming, and Florida International University. In 1987, we cotaught a course, Radical Adult Education, at Syracuse University, coediting and publishing our students' papers. John also spoke at innumerable state, regional, and several national conferences. He served on the editorial boards of three mainstream journals. He gave a paper at the 1989 Adult Education Research Conference, and he published a chapter in the *Handbook of Adult and Continuing Education* (Ohliger, 1989). This wide and ongoing visibility in academic adult education clearly indicates that many in the professional field respected and honored John's scholarly work.

Students Mattering, Students Caring

Graduate students were certainly among those who deeply valued John's work. John had long-term student interns from a Social Work Fachhochschule, a university of applied sciences in Germany, and

from NIU and the University of Wisconsin (Social Work). His long
and productive experience with graduate students largely involved
the latter two universities. The NIU experience started in the late
1970s when students got to know him through his teaching and visits or through reading *Second Thoughts*, which started publication
in 1978. At one point, about ten NIU students worked with John
and me to organize people who were doing progressive adult education. This led to a publication called *Compass*, which identified
interested and involved individuals and groups and attempted to
identify resources that could assist them. There were also individual students who developed strong relationships with John. For example, Mickey Helyer, who completed a doctoral dissertation, "A
Marxist Analysis of the Contributions of Benjamin Franklin and
the Junto to Adult Education: A Dialectical Approach," at NIU,
regularly visited Madison, where he would regale John with his latest data on how Franklin was not all that adult educators made him
out to be. John and Mickey were kindred spirits in many ways. It
did not surprise me that Mickey was John's sidekick on the idea to
develop an adult education almanac. Both were delightful icono-
clasts. In 1985 student involvement with John became more intense. John had stopped publishing *Second Thoughts* in 1984. In a
letter to twenty-five NIU students, Mickey Helyer and I wrote,
"John stopped publishing *Second Thoughts* because the newsletter,
though greatly appreciated by over 1000 subscribers, had become a
one person operation. It seemed incongruous that two campuses
[NIU and the University of Wisconsin] with large adult education
graduate programs are next door to Basic Choices, yet an alternative
voice, *Second Thoughts* was ceasing operation for want of persons
wishing to express their concerns in articles, poems, cartoons, etc."
(Cunningham & Helyer, 1985). The students did respond, and in a
one-day meeting with John in Madison, they decided to do three
things: publish an edition of the newsletter, volunteer some help to
the Basic Choices office, and organize some workdays to help with
the office's work. A University of Wisconsin student volunteered as

an intern, and NIU took on the newsletter. Two Saturday workdays were scheduled.

The newsletter was a beehive of activity, although the committee lacked editorial experience. Indeed, putting the newsletter together by committee may have been more than John had bargained for. However, John was impressed with our technical know-how. Dorothy Jossendal, the secretary who worked with us on the *Adult Education Quarterly* journal, volunteered her services in typing up the final copy. As her fingers flew over the keyboard and perfect copy emerged, he was euphoric. One could imagine what it must have been like for him to put out one of those issues by himself. As he said in a thank-you letter to Dorothy, "Getting all that copy typed in one day seemed an impossible task—when we put out a similar sized *Second Thoughts* it would take us two weeks to type that much copy" (Ohliger to Jossendal, personal communication, October 22, 1985). The newsletter was finished in time for the AAACE meeting in Milwaukee.

Over the next months, there was continuous activity between this group and John. Students helped raise fifteen hundred dollars for Basic Choices, which was profiled in an article in the ERIC newsletter. Though we did our best to promote Basic Choices and *Second Thoughts*, our local enthusiasm fell on deaf ears. In a March 1986 letter to me, John wrote, "What (interest) do we have expressed towards another newsletter? No interest has been expressed by anyone. (It was the same at the Milwaukee AAACE meeting.) . . . Looking over this paragraph I want to make sure you understand that I believe putting out the experimental issue was a good idea and certainly worth all the effort you and others put into it. I just don't see that there is interest in having it as a continuing project, and as I've said before I don't want to do it on a catch as catch can basis. One time with all the excitement and hecticity was fun and fine, but not on a regular basis" (p. 1).

As I reflect on this correspondence, I sense a lot between the lines that I missed when I first received it. Instead, I took John at face value, which ended the revival of *Second Thoughts*. The student group activity dropped back to the previous pattern between Madison and DeKalb. John stopped publishing *Second Thoughts* in 1984, and he downsized Basic Choices to a space in his home in 1986. Finances were always a problem. Nevertheless, our resistance to the profession continued—but in other ways.

Mobilizing Resistance to Mainstream Modern Practice

There are bookend national conferences to highlight our continued resistance to an increasingly professionalized practice: the 1977 Adult Education Association conference in Detroit and the 1990 AAACE Conference in Salt Lake City. During this period, a contingent that included John led a concerted effort to push for more democratic and socially just forms of adult education within the profession. The Detroit conference, the first bookend, was the site of a "rump conference" where alternative-practice adult educators met and developed mobilization strategies. John wrote, "In the fall of 1977 Basic Choices arranged a series of 'rump' meetings at the National Adult Ed. conference in Detroit for those who had 'second thoughts' about the baleful trend towards mandatory continuing education (MCE) and other harmful directions of mainstream education. In May 1978 we began publication of this newsletter, *Second Thoughts*, to serve the growing network begun in Detroit of adult educators and others seeking ways to foster personal freedom and justice" (1984, p. 1).

In 1979 about forty invited North American leaders in the field of adult education came together to meet at Highlander, a residential popular education and research center founded in 1932 and located near Knoxville, Tennessee. The center and Frank Adams, who cowrote *Unearthing Seeds of Fire: The Idea of Highlander* (1975) with center founder Myles Horton, had extended the invitations, responding to the "action suggestion in *Second Thoughts* to hold an organizational meeting of concerned persons, perhaps for two or three days, where extended planning for reflection and action could be carried out without the distraction of a convention" (Highlander invitation, 1979, pp. 1–2). John and Art Lloyd from Basic Choices were part of this diverse group that included many academic adult educators. All were interested in renewing adult education as social education. The Highlander staff encouraged the group to focus on an issue and develop an action project. We pinpointed MCE as an issue and used the historical field notion of voluntary learning to focus positively on the issue. Our action project targeted the upcoming AEA conference in Boston. We began by forming the National Alliance for Voluntary Learning (NAVL). As NAVL members, we developed a one-page mission statement for distribution, got ourselves elected as state delegates so we could be active in the AEA's delegate assembly, found places on the conference agenda to insert our message, and arranged for publication of a daily conference newsletter, *NAVL Gazing*. John's iconoclastic friend John Holt assisted with the newsletter, giving us use of his Boston office facilities as our production site.

I will never forget that AEA conference in Boston. Our newsletter was a great hit. It was humorous and issue oriented, characteristics that the national conference lacked. We asked professors in attendance to provide us with statements declaring whether they supported voluntary learning. Many wrote such statements. This might seem ridiculous today, but it was an act of courage for many professors to produce these statements. Indeed, many professors were nervous when we started printing these statements in our newsletter; they were concerned about being associated with what they perceived as left wingers. When the AEA executive committee had uniformed guards keep anyone who had not paid the conference fee from entering the exhibits area, the *NAVL Gazing* headline read, "Educators Use Force to Keep Adults from Learning." We harassed those mainstreamers, poking fun at their bureaucratic foolishness. By questioning issues, we made our paid staff who received substantial salaries think. In a side conversation, AEA's executive director asked me to explain to her what MCE was. So much for how tuned in our leaders were.

The strategy in the delegate assembly was to present two resolutions. The first, which the United Nations had previously issued, stated that participation in adult education should be a voluntary matter. The AEA had already gone on record as a supporter of this resolution several years earlier, so we perceived that this would be a reaffirmation. The second resolution asked for a presidential task force on voluntary learning as well as a report to the Association on Voluntary Learning at its next annual meeting. We felt this resolution had no chance of passing, but we put it forward as a way to force debate.

Present in the delegate assembly, I was dumbfounded when there was almost a one-hour debate on the first resolution supporting voluntary learning. It was voted down when a professor summed up the opposition's view, stating something like, "I can't say what is wrong with this resolution. Since I don't trust those people pushing it, I vote no." In a groundswell of mistrust, the 1979 AEA delegate assembly rejected the first resolution. However, when our second resolution came up, it was unanimously passed. We were astounded. I think the delegates got tired of the arguing. I cannot think of another explanation. AEA president Violet Malone appointed John, Tom Heaney, and Dave Gueulette to the task force, which made them responsible for preparing the report on voluntary learning. The *Task Force Report on Voluntary Learning* was distributed at the St. Louis conference (Heaney, 1981). We had succeeded with this action project, but mobilization issues remained, and we were left struggling to organize ourselves.

By this time Tom Heaney had organized Basic Choices, Chicago, which subsequently morphed into the Lindeman Center. In January 1982, he held the Algonquin conference where participatory research became a major theme. This conference was important because it helped solidify the alternative adult education movement in North America. The conference provided opportunities to hone important linkages among the North American leadership and to further educate us on participatory research. Budd Hall hoped to bring a stronger popular education voice from North America to the International Council for Adult Education, which was holding its General Assembly in Paris that year. John's difficulty was getting money to go to Paris to the General Assembly. Although the advisory council of Basic Choices tried to raise money for him, we were not successful. John's limited ability to be a stronger presence among popular educators on the international stage is one of the tragedies of his eclectic career.

In 1983 we were back at Highlander again, with more momentum and more grassroots participants. Larry Olds, Linda Yanz, and John Gaventa had laid plans for this further mobilization in Paris. We tried organizing ourselves again, but that process was not complete until a Highlander meeting in 1990. This time we were successful in organizing what became the North American Alliance of Popular Adult Educators (NAAPAE) in 1993. In 1994 in Cairo, the NAAPAE also became the official North American Regional Organization in the International Council for Adult Education. In a Basic Choices reflection, John (1990a) recounted, "The 25 women and men gathered at Highlander for the founding conclave came from all regions of the United States and Canada. Their backgrounds include: Blacks; Spanish and French speakers; community organizers; environment, labor, literacy, and religious educators; professors of adult education; and foundation representatives. . . . [The NAAPAE's] planned activities include a newsletter, regional conferences, and dissident presence in establishment institutions and organizations."

NAAPAE took on a life of its own. John played a major part in one activity that the founding NAAPAE group sponsored. This occurred at the AAACE Conference held at Salt Lake City in 1990, which provides the other bookend to our efforts to revitalize adult education as social education. The theme of the conference, "On Trial: The Education of Adults," was made to order for us. Jack Mezirow wrote the indictment, charging "the AAACE with dereliction in fulfilling its original commitment to provide an adult-education movement for the informal education of citizens to participate in democratic social action" (quoted in Ohliger, 1990a). The debate on this issue had center stage throughout the conference. Although we found the association guilty on all counts and won the debate hands down, the resulting policy paper, "Faded Visions and Fresh Commitments: Adult Education's Social Goals," never saw the light of day except on the Web site of National-Louis University (see Mezirow, 1991).

At the 1990 AAACE conference, John also spoke at the social philosophy luncheon, which brought together key thinkers in the foundations of the U.S. modern practice of adult education. He had started preparations for his presentation early, asking for input to a speech tentatively entitled "On Trial: Social Philosophy." Later, he changed the title to "Take a Social Philosopher to Lunch." This speech became an extensive annotated bibliography that provides us with a history of the social philosophy luncheon and a discussion of its role in the politics of AAACE (Ohliger, 1990b). While the conference debate on educating adults might have simulated the theater of the absurd, John's speech constituted an intellectual moment, providing 150 people with in-depth historical analysis of an association tradition. However, John had to shorten his substantive speech to accommodate an unscheduled, last-minute appearance by First Lady Barbara Bush, which was perhaps a harbinger.

Two years later, the planning committee tried to drop the social philosophy luncheon altogether since they did not think it was important. Still the founders of the social philosophy unit were a dedicated group of social educators, some well known like Eduard Lindeman; some generally known like Robert Blakely and John Walker Powell; and some unsung heroes, namely women, including Eleanor Coit, Isabel Haglin, and Mabel Swanson, whom I doubt anyone could identify. According to John, Coit was the social philosophy unit's first president, and the other two women kept it going for over twenty years (Ohliger, 1990b).

The 1990 AAACE conference marked the last time that our group of alternative adult educators mounted a collective strategy to try to bring about change in the association. Those who had been pushing for change either gave up or broke away into other associations as it became clear that internal change was not possible.

Concluding Thought

There was a successful financial campaign to support Basic Choices in 1992–1993 after John and his wife, Chris, had returned to Madison, Wisconsin, from Springfield, Illinois. My own active political involvement with John became more limited after 1994. However, John marked my life and the lives of many others in innumerable ways. I believe that one of his greatest contributions to the adult education profession is his "Manifesto Bibliography" (Ohliger, 1987c). John developed and used this annotated bibliography for the course we cotaught at Syracuse University in 1987. I have given it to every graduate student in my classes at NIU. It is what I want every reader of this book to see. I reproduce its outline here as an appropriate summary statement of John's beliefs and the way he walked through adult education. The manifesto bibliography can be a guiding philosophy for all of us as we mediate our field of study and practice and the interests that direct it.

John Ohliger's Manifesto Bibliography

I. Ideas about People

   A. All people want to learn.

   B. All people are roughly equal in intelligence.

   C. "Meeting needs" starts with distinguishing minimal essential needs from expressed or manipulated wants.

   D. "Common people" are capable of running their own affairs without the control of experts.

   E. The people with more, or equally difficult, problems are not the so called "disadvantaged," "underprivileged," or "laypersons," but the "advantaged," "privileged," or "professionals."

II. Ideas about Society

    A. The present political-economic reality is that nations are run by very small portions of their populations.

    B. Radical structural change in the economic-political system is necessary.

    C. We can live in a world where no one has lasting or unilateral control over anyone else.

    D. Radical structural change is possible so that all people will be able to foster that part of their being which helps more than hinders, loves more than hates, cooperates more than competes. We can live as integral wholes rather than in alienation from others, from the "tools of production," from nature, or from the supernatural.

    E. Necessary and possible radical change will be oppressive if not endowed with a healthy spiritual dimension—an accompanying cultural revolution.

    F. Trends towards increased technocratic control and economic growth must be reversed.

III. Ideas about "Adult Education"

    A. Education-learning is a fragile, delicate, subtle activity linked to personal and social life.

    B. Knowledge-learning is more the experience itself and less the classification of information, the acquisition of facts, techniques, or skills.

    C. The path to truth-knowledge-learning is more personal exploration or mutual interaction and less scientific experimentation or didactic instruction.

    D. Education is never neutral, politically or otherwise.

    E. Standard brand adult education is generally the most conservative and reactionary of the different levels of institutionalized education.

F. Adult education is best seen, not as a field, discipline or
     profession, but simply as those activities of the chronologically
     mature where learning is involved.

References

Adams, F. T., & Horton, M. (1975). *Unearthing seeds of fire: The idea of High-
     lander*. Winston-Salem, NC: J. F. Blair.

Cunningham, P. M., & Helyer, M. (1985, February 11). *Memo to students*.
     DeKalb: Northern Illinois University.

Cunningham, P. M., & Ohliger, J. (1987). *Radical thinking in adult education,
     part II*. Course pack for a summer class at Syracuse University.

Facundo, B. (1984). *Freire-inspired programs in the United States and Puerto Rico:
     A critical evaluation*. Retrieved October 11, 2006, from http://www.uow
     .edu.au/ arts/sts/bmartin/dissent/documents/Facundo/Facundo.html.

Griffith, W. S. (1991). The impact of intellectual leadership. In J. M. Peters,
     P. Jarvis, & Associates, *Adult education: Evolution and achievements in a
     developing field of study* (pp. 97–120). San Francisco: Jossey-Bass.

Heaney, T. (Ed.). (1981). *AEA USA task force report on voluntary learning*.
     Washington, DC: Adult Education Association.

Highlander invitation. (1979). *Second Thoughts, 1*(2), 1–2.

Mezirow, J. (1991, November 15). *Faded visions and fresh commitments: Adult edu-
     cation's social goals*. Policy paper prepared for the American Association
     for Adult and Continuing Education. Retrieved December 15, 2005, from
     http://www.nl.edu/academics/cas/ace/resources/jackmezirow_insight.cfm.

Ohliger, J. (1967). *Listening groups: Mass media in adult education*. Boston: Center
     for the Study of Liberal Education for Adults.

Ohliger, J. (1982). *Adult education in a world of excessive riches/excessive poverty*.
     Madison, WI: Basic Choices.

Ohliger, J. (1984). Second thoughts "takes a break." *Second Thoughts, 6*(1), 1.
     Retrieved January 27, 2009, from http://johnohliger.org/artman/publish/
     article_50.shtml.

Ohliger, J. (1987a). *Learning in the community*. Madison, WI: Basic Choices.

Ohliger, J. (1987b). Really creative conferences. Submitted for publication in
     Media and Adult Learning. Madison, WI: Basic Choices.

Ohliger, J. (1987c). *Syracuse University seminar on radical thought in adult educa-
     tion*. Madison, WI: Basic Choices.

Ohliger, J. (1989). Alternative images of the future in adult education. In S. B. Merriam & P. M. Cunningham (Eds.), *Handbook of adult and continuing education* (pp. 628–639). San Francisco: Jossey-Bass.

Ohliger, J. (1990a). *Democratic social change*. Madison, WI: Basic Choices.

Ohliger, J. (1990b). *Take a social philosopher to lunch this week*. Madison, WI: Basic Choices.

Ohliger, J. (1995). *Critical views of Paulo Freire's work*. Compiled for the 1995 Iowa Community College Summer Seminar. Madison, WI: Basic Choices.

Ohliger, J. (n.d.). *Taking Freire and Illich seriously or icons or pariahs*. Draft. Madison, WI: Basic Choices.

Peters, J. M., Jarvis, P., & Associates. (1991). *Adult education: Evolution and achievements in a developing field of study*. San Francisco: Jossey-Bass.

Reflection
Critical and Radical Themes Abetting Learning for Life and Work

André P. Grace

Phyllis M. Cunningham and John Ohliger were cultural workers in arms. Phyllis's narrative history of her personal and professional relationship with John indicates this as she provides insights into a man she considered one of adult education's true intellectuals. Phyllis, who began working as a professor of adult education in 1976, has made her own impact on field ethics and practice in critical and radical terms that challenge us all to make caring and justice for students pedagogical centerpieces. John, who left academe in 1973, also devoted his life and work to the political and pedagogical task of making caring and justice realities, albeit in his own way as an outsider in an emerging professional field. He worked in community education and engaged in social and political activism through his radical adult education center, Basic Choices, which was established in 1976.

Whether they were working in university classrooms or community venues, Phyllis and John saw both spaces as active cultural sites where hope and possibility were driving forces. Each social educator viewed culture as an ecology of community learning in which participants interact with one another and the world as they produce knowledge and build communities of practice. In keeping with a politics of caring and justice, each shaped culture as a critical and radical space where participants are invited to take part and make choices to create a better world. In today's global change culture of crisis and challenge, this understanding of culture can guide educators concerned with developing and implementing holistic forms of learning for life and work. Giroux (2004) takes this understanding into the present moment:

> Culture is the public space where common matters, shared solidarities, and public engagements provide the fundamental elements of democracy. Culture is also the pedagogical and political ground on which communities of struggle and a global public sphere can be imagined as a condition of democratic possibilities. Culture offers a common space in which to address the radical demands of a pedagogy that allows critical discourse to confront the inequities of power and promote the possibilities of shared dialogue and democratic transformation. Culture affirms the social as a fundamentally political space just as it attempts within the current historical moment to deny its relevance and its centrality as a political necessity [p. 112].

Phyllis and John were at home in this critical and radical cultural space. Both adult educators wrote and practiced in ways that emphasized critical concerns with democracy, freedom, and social justice; and radical concerns with being visible and present in grassroots social and political activism and cultural work. They also valued liberal concerns with being critical thinkers who have the freedom to learn and become well-rounded citizens through engagement in holistic forms of education.

Were Phyllis and John professional educators? They were not in the sense of subscribing to the sterile and instrumental form of professionalism that emerged in U.S. academic adult education after World War II (Grace, 1999). However, they can be considered organic intellectuals and cultural workers who engaged in an ethical and just practice of adult education that was learner centered and community based. Both Phyllis and John valued voluntary participation and placed tremendous value on adult education as social education.

Taking Ohliger's Work into Education in Neoliberal Times

Phyllis provides a cogent reflection on themes in John's work in her narrative reflection. These critical and radical themes include valuing adult education as community education and a voluntary endeavor; exploring the limitations of mandatory continuing education or imposed lifelong learning; linking learner-centered and accessible adult education to advancing quality living and work; using media to engage learners in critical listening and critique; exploring the synergy possible between theory and practice in adult education; and encouraging community members to be active participants and producers of knowledge within communities of practice. These themes certainly have relevance today and for the future as we critique escalating privatization of higher education, mounting instrumentalism in adult education, and increasing commodification of lifelong learning, which is often considered to be replacing adult education (Grace, 2004).

With respect to higher education, the importance of holistic education, choice, and social theorizing has been diminished as colleges and universities fall prey to economic pressures and a neoliberal culture of cyclical lifelong learning for control (Grace, 2004, 2007). John wrote about this in "A Cautious Welcome to the New Millennium" (1999; reprinted in this book as Chapter Eight). It was first included in a special issue of the *Canadian Journal for the Study of Adult Education* entitled *The New Millennium: Realities, Possibilities, and Issues for Adult Education*. John felt that the definition of higher education had been compromised under neoliberalism. This compromise continues in North American colleges and universities, where there is an ongoing transformation of higher education that threatens its traditional emphases on liberal education and producing well-rounded graduates and upholds neoliberal emphases on economistic goals, privatization, and globalization. The commodification of education and the positioning of students as consumers are ascendant in this transformation:

> [In this milieu we are coping with] an intensifying competition among traditional [nonprofit higher educational] institutions; rapid expansion of the new for-profit [degree-granting] and virtual institutions [and corporate universities]; technology and its influence on the way learning takes place; globalization of colleges and universities; and the shift toward restructuring higher education as a market rather than a regulated public sector [Newman, Couturier, & Scurry, 2004, p. xi].

In the face of these change forces that threaten higher education as a space that has been supported by the public it has benefited, Newman et al. (2004) declare there is an erosion of the critical public purposes of higher education. Of course, John made this kind of critique for decades as he rejected mandatory forms of continuing education and the technocracy affecting the direction of adult and higher learning. In neoliberal times when concerns with civil society and the social aspects of learning and work are sidelined in the rush to carry out economic agendas, there are many insights to be gleaned from John's body of work. Higher education should not be allowed to abrogate its historical social responsibility to benefit the wider public. Indeed this responsibility ought to be expanded "to include such functions as creating a skilled and [broadly] educated workforce, encouraging civic engagement in students, serving as an avenue for social mobility, and establishing links with primary and secondary education" (Newman et al., 2004, p. 6). John was a perennial advocate of this encompassing kind of education.

In his critique of technocracy, John problematized the growing instrumentalism pervading learning and shaping mandatory continuing education. This critique is still relevant. For example, the practice of adult education in its contemporary instrumentalized form, focused on information literacy and skill enhancement, aids and abets neoliberalism and its emphases on process, production, and performance. Feminist adult educators Alfred, Butterwick, Hansman, and Sandlin (2007) argue that this focus largely reduces adult education to training workers for service industries and conditioning "lifelong consumer-citizens" (p. 670). Such instrumental education disposes citizens to lives and work soaked in neoliberal ideology that ties prowess in knowledge production, information technology, and throwaway consumerism to the good life and sociocultural progress. John wholeheartedly rejected this instrumentalism in learning. Through his body of work, he consistently demonstrated concern for the erosion that occurs in learning when instrumental concerns are disconnected from social and cultural concerns. We can learn much from John's writing over the decades as we bring his insights to bear on a critique of neoliberalized adult education that focuses on the already educated and their usually sideways (rather than upward) mobility. John was always concerned with the space and place that the uneducated, the undereducated, the unemployed, the underemployed, the poor, and the otherwise marginalized had in adult education. His social critique of mandatory continuing education has contemporary meaning and value as we consider the plight of disenfranchised citizens and immigrants who lack mobility, frozen in a neoliberal wasteland where limited learning and work opportunities exacerbate their plight. Alfred et al. speak to this plight in a synopsis of the institutional barriers to access and accommodation of citizens as learners and workers in educational settings in the United States:

> In capitalistic societies such as the United States, access to formal education beyond secondary education is essential for adults to facilitate their economic mobility. However, due to a number of governmental and societal

factors, the door to higher education for low-income adults is closing; furthermore, changing policies and practices by higher educational institutions and state and federal governments have increasingly limited learning opportunities for adult learners, particularly low-income adults. Among these policies are the "Work First" policies of the Welfare Reform Act, which have limited educational opportunities for individuals and instead forced welfare recipients into minimum wage service industry jobs, adding to the poverty issues for low-income adult learners. The tuition at higher educational institutions, including community colleges, has reflected double digit elevations due to fewer contributions from the state and federal governments, while at the same time the amount of available financial aid (non-loan) has declined [p. 673].

John understood this politics of exclusion and how issues of class and poverty play out in denying citizens and immigrants opportunities for education and economic mobility. A turn to his body of work can help us understand why the rhetoric of contemporary lifelong learning rings hollow for the disenfranchised. It can provide insights as we reflect on how we ought to mediate learning for life and work for citizens and immigrants who see their learning as a journey along a rocky road with endless financial and cultural roadblocks that create inequities in participation.

A turn to John's body of work can also help us as we deal with the increasing commodification of lifelong learning, which has led to its growing prominence in the Organization for Economic Cooperation and Development and other contexts (Grace, 2004). Focusing on the North American context, Barrow and Keeney (2000) note the increasing prevalence of the term *lifelong learning* in educational rhetoric, to the detriment of terms like *adult education* or *continuing education*. They link the current emphasis on lifelong learning to a decline in holistic education that could address instrumental, social, and cultural needs. They state:

> Despite the normative and soothing overtones which the phrase evokes, it too frequently masks an unacknowledged and less reputable ideology: namely a newly sophisticated industrial utilitarianism in which "practical" and "relevant" skills are emphasized at the expense of broader sorts of understanding typified by a liberal education [p. 191].

John made a similar critique for years. Like Barrow and Keeney, he felt that the instrumentalism inherent in industrial utilitarianism focused on advancing economic productivity by attending to competitive individualism at the expense of social advancement. A turn to John's body of work can help us understand how this affects contemporary colleges and universities expected "to become more practically oriented and 'relevant' to the needs of the economy and students [who demand marketable skills and training]" (Barrow & Keeney, 2000, p. 192). John would see this practical, economistic focus as restrictive and tied to an abrogation of social responsibility by higher educational institutions. He would agree with Barrow and Keeney that students need more than skills training. If they are to be flexible and adaptable, they need an education focused on helping them to understand broadly and deeply as they learn to think critically, compare, analyze, synthesize, and evaluate. Barrow and Keeney replicate John's valuing of liberal education when they speak to what learners need to become flexible and adaptable: "In short, what are most needed in this rapidly evolving economy are precisely intellectual abilities that do not have an obvious or immediate utility; what is required is not so much technical know-how, as those various qualities of mind which we subsume under the label of understanding" (p. 193).

From Neoliberalized Education to
Critical Education for Citizenship

Phyllis ends her chapter with an outline of Ohliger's Manifesto Bibliography, which she tells us she has shared as a guide to practice with all her graduate students at Northern Illinois University. We would do well to follow her lead and use it with graduate students in our own adult and higher education classes. This manifesto continues to have tremendous contemporary significance for those of us engaged in critiques of neoliberal forms of lifelong learning and adult and higher education that presume social advancement is derivative of economic advancement. With quality learning for quality life and quality work in the balance in a world marked by instrumental happenstance, today's social educators and cultural workers can find critical and radical inspiration and guidance in the manifesto's ideas. John wrote the manifesto in 1987 amid neoliberalism's emergence as an increasingly dominant ideology wed to globalization, privatization, and other change forces associated with the demise of the welfare state. Over time, neoliberal ideology has had an impact on national and global governance as well as trends in public (K–12), adult, and higher education. In his manifesto, John spoke to the power of money, technocracy, and neoliberal politics and the pressing contemporary need to politicize and revitalize educational sectors as enterprises collectively focused on holistic learning for life and work. Meeting this urgent need ought to be the primary ambition of social educators and cultural workers today.

As his body of work indicates, John was perpetually occupied with challenging educational institutions to move beyond technocratic and economistic preoccupations to value more encompassing forms of education that nurtured critical citizenship. Through his writing and work, John demonstrated that he was an organic intellectual who, like Freire and other radical/critical educators, believed that the value of theory lay in its symbiosis with practice. John's writing shows his prowess at tilling the works of an array of intellectuals who promoted democratic social action. It also shows that he interacted extensively with a cadre of social and political activists. The message in this for educators today is to focus on the mutuality of theory and practice in educational and cultural work for social transformation. The upshot of this message is that educators must remain hopeful that better lives and communities are possible.

This sense of hope permeated John's writing in "A Cautious Welcome to the New Millennium." In this perspective piece, John presented a thematic synopsis of important ideas in his work that parallels the ideas presented in Phyllis's narration and analysis. This thematic synopsis provides a list of key principles that perhaps have even greater relevance in the face of pervasive neoliberalized forms of governance and education. These principles provide a guide for revitalizing education for citizenship against the grain of neoliberalism. They include that education for adults must be a voluntary rather than state-compelled endeavor; educational and cultural work must never lose sight of ethics and justice as energies are directed toward human solidarity and happiness; technology and instrumental education are not solutions to every problem individuals and communities face; holistic education has to include a focus on healthy social approaches to living that foster individual well-being and promote health literacy; and education is a political process that should always accent self and mutual questioning.

Proactive and performing citizens ought to be guided by these principles as they engage in what Welton (2005) describes as a "deliberative learning process" that is ideally directed by "a communicative logic governed by the norm of universal justice" (p. 151). From this perspective, Welton casts citizenship as a core democratic role for which citizens have to learn the art and science of deliberation as they accept their responsibility to contribute to civic advancement and the public good. John would agree with this understanding of citizenship, remembering with Welton the history of adult education as social education in which an ethic of voluntarism is at work. Education built around this understanding of citizenship is much needed today as a critical counterforce to learning that is primarily driven by market forces and "the instrumental logic of efficiency" (p. 151). Welton's perspective is that education for citizenship needs to be a political process driven by the Habermasian belief that a deliberative form of democracy can mobilize and inform citizens. As Welton notes, this belief is grounded in "the foundational importance of the lifeworld for healthy human existence and civil society as the preeminent learning domain" (p. 167). He adds, "The lifeworld pedagogical processes produce the competences that enable actors to speak and act with confidence, resilience, verve and imagination, placing them in a position to take part in processes of reaching understanding and thereby asserting their own identities" (p. 183).

John's own principles of learning show remarkable consistency with Welton's critical perspective. A turn to his body of work can assist critical educators and learners to engage in education for citizenship aimed at reinvigorating civil society as a political site and counterforce to the workings of the market. It can help us shape learning that helps citizens address issues of safety, security, and self-worth while building communities where difference and deliberation shape connection, collaboration, and relationship. Like Welton, John would want participants in education for citizenship to be actively involved in a deliberative learning process. Welton contends that social educators and cultural workers have to commit to this kind of communicative learning; otherwise "civil society can go [from] bad [to worse]" (p. 174). At its center, this learning "foster[s] an inquiring, skeptical attitude to authority's beliefs and actions (indoctrination is not permitted)" (p. 178). This principle guiding learning was at the heart of John's beliefs. It drove him to speak out in the name of democracy, freedom, and ethics. The inquisitiveness and skepticism infusing John Ohliger's work give it timeless value today and into the future until justice for all is achieved.

References

Alfred, M., Butterwick, S., Hansman, C., & Sandlin, J. (2007). Neoliberal welfare reform, poverty, and adult education: Identifying the problem and engaging in resistance. In *Proceedings of the 48th Annual Adult Education Research Conference jointly held with the 26th Annual Conference of the Canadian Association for the Study of Adult Education, Mount Saint Vincent University, Halifax, NS* (pp. 669–676). Halifax, NS: Mount Saint Vincent University.

Barrow, R., & Keeney, P. (2000). Lifelong learning: A North American perspective. In J. Field & M. Leicester (Eds.), *Lifelong learning: Education across the lifespan* (pp. 191–200). London: RoutledgeFalmer.

Giroux, H. A. (2004). *The terror of neoliberalism*. Boulder, CO: Paradigm Publishers.

Grace, A. P. (1999). Building a knowledge base in U.S. academic adult education (1945–1970). *Studies in the Education of Adults, 31*(2), 220–236.

Grace, A. P. (2004). Lifelong learning as a chameleonic concept and versatile practice: Y2K perspectives and trends. *International Journal of Lifelong Education, 23*(4), 385–405.

Grace, A. P. (2007). Envisioning a critical social pedagogy of learning and work in a contemporary culture of cyclical lifelong learning. *Studies in Continuing Education, 29*(1), 85–103.

Newman, F., Couturier, L., & Scurry, J. (2004). *The future of higher education: Rhetoric, reality, and the risks of the market*. San Francisco: Jossey-Bass.

Ohliger, J. (1999). A cautious welcome to the new millennium. *Canadian Journal for the Study of Adult Education, 13*(2), 7–18.

Welton, M. (2005). *Designing the just learning society*. Leicester, UK: National Institute of Adult Continuing Education.

15

A Mindful Commitment to Connecting Women Toward Intellectual Community

Lee Karlovic

So what can a deceased, German American, bookish, Caucasian, cat-loving, thick-hearty-ale-drinking, World War II veteran, who, in the last century, wrote, "I am not a feminist" (Ohliger, 1990a, p. 4) possibly offer us in the twenty-first century? This became the grounding question during my close reading of several hundred letters and e-mails, and never enough time in Ohliger's extensive personal library. There I focused on his writings and audio creations, especially more informal and recent ones as they pertained to gender. When I understood how much of Ohliger's time and energy postacademia and postcommunity media involvement revolved around his "communicants," and how so many of them were women, it seemed appropriate to explore some of these women's perspectives. Communicants can mutually contribute information and other gifts. How and what did Ohliger contribute to the communicants?

Through my research and my communication with Chris Wagner, Ohliger's wife, I identified and located ten women, ranging in age from their forties to their eighties. Each had communicated with Ohliger occasionally or frequently, in person, by letter, and by e-mail, one as early as 1969. One had never met Ohliger in person. Three had worked or volunteered with Basic Choices, a think tank and "project in values clarification" that Ohliger and some colleagues had started (Untitled article, 1981, p. 8). Some had worked with Ohliger while he was at Ohio State University. Nine are American and of European American ancestry. All are well schooled and privileged: they have completed one or more college degrees. Three, to my knowledge, self-identify as feminist.

John "Connection" Ohliger

These women, in telephone interviews and e-mail, as well as his other women correspondents, repeatedly came up with a single word rarely experienced in a sustained way in this time—*connection*—to best describe Ohliger. It seemed that *connection* could easily have been Ohliger's middle name. He had a creative capacity that did not seem to depend on geographical miles, characteristics such as an age difference, or quantity of interaction or in-person meetings.

Ana Gobledale, currently a chaplain at an Australian university and the author of *The Learning Spirit: Lessons from South Africa* (1994), called him "the perfect connector" (interview, July 24, 2005). Helen Modra wrote, "John was the best connector of ideas, so much so that one of my names for him was 'The Bountiful Bibliographer'" (memorial tribute, n.d.). Ohliger made these connections across many fields and levels, whether the person was famous and known or unknown, according to Nancy Reimer (interview, July 28, 2005), coauthor of *Power for All or for None* (1998).

Ohliger's knack for and commitment to connecting women with whatever resources they needed at the time comes across in dozens of instances, such as providing women with "references I should look up, names of colleagues and friends I needed to contact." When Elizabeth Lindeman Leonard mentioned this, she spoke of his generosity while she was working on her book about her father: *Friendly Rebel: A Personal and Social History of Eduard C. Lindeman* (1991). She continued, "John's most valuable asset was his ability to connect people who needed to get together and share resources, ideas, knowledge" (E. Lindeman Leonard, e-mail to the author, June 29, 2005). And according to Betty Granda, former bookstore owner, he had "a rare ability to share without preaching" (e-mail to the author, July 21, 2005).

At other times, Ohliger aided communicants in their search for a workplace or a graduate school that would not destroy the head or heart. He was willing to change the way he taught his courses when he learned of a better way, according to Anne Fitzgerald, now a philanthropic educator and consultant and formerly one of Ohliger's students at Ohio State University. She shared how Ohliger moved toward Malcolm Knowles's approach after she exposed him to the ideas and techniques that she had experienced while at Boston University (interview, August 13, 2005).

Many of the women reported their correspondence-with-Ohliger files expanded with multiple, quick, full, and, at times, overwhelming responses to a request for a resource or a contact from "Mr. Networking" (Gabriele Strohschen, interview, July 24, 2005). Then there are the creative expressions that Ohliger put into these women's lives, whether it was one of his "flattering" gifts of sticky-noted, marked books from his review of books, or a cartoon or writing created or shared by one of his correspondents. The women repeatedly reported the receipt of the "perfect" book at times when they were at a crossroads in their lives.

Ohliger used this himself: "When you're at 'loose ends,' uncertain what to do next, feeling lost or confused, what do you do? If you're like me, sometimes you look for a passage in an inspirational book to get you out of that 'loose ends' quagmire. . . . Where *Lao Tzu* can be especially helpful is in getting beyond 'loose ends' to help you see that your confusion may lie in 'loose beginnings,' being lost about your origins, about where to start, about what should be the fundamental but first small step in a long and health-giving journey" (Ohliger, n.d., n.p.).

Searching for Freedom in Community

Then there's the co-creation of a freedom in mindfully connecting toward intellectual community, whether it was through discovery

of a lifelong friend or new activity or an idea that nudged communicants to take a direction not yet taken. For example, when
Ohliger, with his background in community radio and his lifelong
interest in the media, learned that Strohschen, one of the women
interviewed for this chapter, conceived of and was planning a national underground media conference, he wholeheartedly promoted
and participated in the event.

This "gentle and unassuming" man, who was also a "guy's guy"
and a "danger" to the powers that be, could be "a bastard" (affectionately labeled) at times. Yet not one woman intimated a hint of
sexism in their communications and interactions. And he did not
play a sexual favor game either. As Kate Hawkes (interview, July 17,
2005), now the proprietor of a coffee café in Springfield, Illinois,
and formerly a worker with Basic Choices, said, "Sexism was not in
his nature." What was in his "nature," though, appeared to be a pattern of "frequent unsolicited encouragement" (Granda, e-mail, July
21, 2005). Ohliger supported women in their moves toward becoming the selves they wanted to be, toward co-creating a society
to which they wanted to belong. Three women reported they knew
that Ohliger's belief in them and in their directions was unwavering and long-standing.

The women often reported that no matter how much time had
gone by and no matter how many unwritten letters or responses to
John's queries for connection there were, they could easily pick up
where they left off. One woman said it reminded her of her best girl-
friend with whom she could freely confide anything. This open,
communicative space of ebb and flow echoed my own interactions
with Ohliger, whom I first met at a Highlander Center gathering in
the 1980s. It was an incredibly freeing experience to be consciously
vulnerable. Ohliger did not impute permanent or temporary cogni-
tive, mental states or labels when my actions veered away from my
words and values. That is not to say that he did not at the same
time challenge me. Often the challenge ended up being about inviting uncertainty as I came up against unacknowledged intellectual

and emotional boundaries and began to shatter the illusions into which I had been socialized.

While another might ask, "What's on your mind?" Ohliger would as often ask—or more frequently ask—"How are you feeling?" It was not a superficial exchange of introductory pleasantries that he might have learned in an adult education workshop for men learning to communicate with women about their feelings. It was more an invitation into "how acutely and fully we can feel. . . . [For] once we know the extent to which we are capable of feeling . . . [a] sense of satisfaction and completion, we can then observe which of our various life endeavors bring us closest to that fullness. . . . Having experienced the fullness of this depth of feeling and recognizing its power, in honor and self-respect we can require no less of ourselves" (Lorde, 2000, p. 570).

Just Talking Ideas

Then there was the "delightful freedom, the joy" of discovering and exercising the intellect, as noted by seven of the women describing their Ohliger connections. One said Ohliger helped her "give herself permission to do what she wanted to do beyond stifling institutional and bureaucratic requirements." Ohliger "freed me up from needing, depending on somebody else's gold stars." In talking about her time with Ohliger, whom she first met in 1978, Gobledale recounted, "[We were] just talking ideas in a couple of good conversations" (interview, July 24, 2005). The opportunity to "just talk ideas" in busy lives was consistently reported to be a big plus by several of these women. Ohliger also noted it, mentioning "sparkling" conversations like these in his notes for his memoir, as well as in his correspondence.

His breadth of "just talking ideas" was rare. Camy Matthay, who first encountered Ohliger at a home schoolers' meeting, speaks of this. Matthay is an unschooling activist and author of "Unschooling as a Political Activity" (2000). She is also an "unsuitor," a reference to the corporate business suit she no longer wore, to the derision of former colleagues, when she chose to be a stay-at-home mother. (Her 2002 writing about her unsuitor experience, "S Is for Shame, F Is for Fury, M Is for Mothering," is both perceptive and witty.) In relating her stories about exchanges with Ohliger, Matthay shared the extensiveness of the topics covered in one of their last intellectual exchanges: "unschooling, socialism, Theodor Adorno and Critical Theory, anarchism, George Orwell, the surrealist novel *The Master and Margarita* [Bulgakov, 1995], Gandi Marg, Bertell Ollman (Marxist professor and creator of the game 'Class Struggle'), Brian Martin (Australian 'demarchist'), the Wobblies . . . [and] Crosby, Stills, Nash and Young" (e-mail, July 29, 2005). She also discussed how they encouraged and deepened each other's writings through feedback and the sharing of resources. Just talking ideas could happen anywhere. Granda said she and Ohliger would at times "swim" together, "which for me and John wasn't so much swimming as floating around in the dirty lakes, [and] having long conversations about all kinds of stuff long after the other beachgoers had gone home for the day" (e-mail, July 21, 2005).

Listening and Having Fun

Ohliger could listen to women. He could understand that words can and do hurt people. Sudie Hoffman, a college teacher and a former volunteer with Basic Choices, offered a story that showed Ohliger's "not macho" open-mindedness around language. Once Ohliger shared what he thought was a compliment from a young man with whom he and Hoffman had spent some time. When Hoffman expressed her anger at the sexism of this supposed compliment, Ohliger could have dismissed her, her anger, and her thinking. Instead, according to Hoffman, a "great discussion" ensued about how this related to members of other groups such as African Americans and disabled people on a daily basis. The conversation was a testament to the power of language. Still, Ohliger could have fun with women, but not at their expense. His sense of humor came through loud and clear. For example, Blanca Facundo, a history teacher and author of the 1984 "Freire-Inspired Programs in the United States and Puerto Rico," said she and Ohliger laughed when they learned that the most adamant feminist participant present at the institute they were attending did the laundry for the male keynote speaker.

Later, Ohliger sent this author a postcard in response to my rants and raves that I and other women workers, especially those working in schooling contexts, were expected to "manage our hearts." I had come across the concept of the managed heart in a book by the same name (Hochschild, 1983). I was disturbed that the concept seemed to resonate so fully with both my experience and that of other women. Briefly, the managed heart is about having to (or perceiving having to) enact occupational roles in narrowly prescribed ways. For example, one might be expected to speak in a positive tone and look as if everything is going well regardless of one's real feelings or the troubling nature of certain situations. The managed heart is also about having to (or perceiving having to) perform certain behaviors such as smiling or taking on the responsibility of emotional labor. A 1984 postcard by Kate Gawf that Ohliger sent to me visualized this phenomenon well. It was a cartoon with a grave site where the headstone memorializes a woman with these words: "She was a devoted laundress." The memorial is countered by an expletive from the deceased woman who had cleaned and cooked for others her whole life.

Here's to the "Uns"

Ohliger was interested in "uns," such as unlearning and unschooling. Regarding "the uns," Ohliger wrote, "What's kept the [radio] station [WORT, Madison, Wisconsin] from either going broke or going mainstream for 19 years? My hunch is it's because of 'the you-ens'—'the uns'. The hundreds of people involved over the years who have been: Unabashed, unafraid, uncensorable, unconventional, uninhibited, unorthodox, unpretentious, unstinting, unsung, untiring, and finally, definitely unique! Here's to 'the uns'" (Ohliger,

2000, p. 2). Ohliger celebrated the "uns" such as Granda, one of his two choices as an unforgettable, unintentional adult educator (Ohliger, 1991, p. 4). The "uns" were predisposed toward arts-based inquiry. In his own work, Ohliger sought out "unlikely" places such as song lyrics, car bumper stickers, and slogans for his creative endeavors. He also widely and broadly delved into disciplines and life contexts other than his own. He turned to films and videos such as Jane Wagner's (1991) *The Search for Signs of Inteligent [sic] Life in the Universe*. He worded sticky notes or political buttons such as, "My karma ran over your dogma." He used zines and small press reviews such as Mike Gunderloy's *Factsheet Five* (n.d.), as well as cartoons by Tuli Kupferberg, Nicole Hollander (*Sylvia*), and Cathy Guswaite. These "unbound" creative expressions matched Ohliger's own experience with his self-reported "1500 pages" of writing (talks, bibliographies, and flyers) that consist of stapled, duplicated pieces of paper. He, like most of his communicants and many women writers and journalists throughout history, never wrote a traditionally published, bound book. Yet Ohliger, like many women, contributed behind the scenes to the books of others. In his case, he gave detailed feedback to some of his communicants or helped get them published, or both.

Other "unbound" Ohliger publications include *Second Thoughts*, the newsletter of Basic Choices, as well as *Adult and Continuing Education Today* (ACET), the Learning Resource Network's (LERN) publication in which Ohliger wrote a monthly column. Also, there was the *Adult Educator's Almanac and Weekly Appointment Calendar*, the "almost . . . two-year project" that LERN published as a "group effort" and for which Ohliger took "all responsibility for goofs" (Ohliger, 1989a). These publications are reminiscent of the immediacy and short-lived, or one-time nature, of American feminist writings. Such ephemera included women's membership group herstories and newsletters, petitions, speeches, and event flyers.

Despite his unorthodox (in an academic sense) approaches to writing and producing materials, Ohliger's "unbound" expressions were often as "scholarly" as, or more so than, the more traditional bound expressions that could be found in journals or books. In part, this was because of his exhaustive inclusion of relevant pieces from newspapers, and periodical and book indexes, especially books from and about the arts.

Seeing the Unseen

"He saw what no one else saw," said Hoffman (interview, July 27, 2005). For example, in his search for daily incidents of interest as part of the *Adult Educator's Almanac and Weekly Appointment Calendar*, Ohliger brought us information typically out of our reach: the 1865 factoid about James Stuart's invention of the "lesson sheet as a method of instructing women by mail, . . . [as it] is considered improper for a man to discuss lessons with a woman in person" (Ohliger, 1989a, April 2). And the 1771 "Advertisement in the *New York Mercury* [that encouraged] participation in a course of public lectures on logic by inviting each gentleman, 'if he chooses, to bring a lady with him'" (Ohliger, 1989a, September 30).

Through it all, Ohliger remained committed to participation and access, two values and practices that he had in common with diverse feminists and their projects. Participation was sought in most of his writing projects at every level, from conception and process to result. He invited people to contribute their thoughts or sources on a topic. This invitation included the "quotational bibliographies" and sometimes his more traditional writings, such as articles for journals. Ohliger would fully and accurately transcribe all—not just some or the "best"—respondent contributions to his query about a current topic. He would rarely include his take on the topic of interest along with the query. One exception was when he asked people to share their favorite personal classics. He shared his choices: George Orwell's *Homage to Catalonia* (1938), Frank Adams and Myles Horton's *Unearthing Seeds of Fire* (1975), H. G. Wells's *Tono-Bungay* (1909), and the film/book *Harold and Maude* (Higgins,

1983), as well as his "potential personal classic" (Ohliger, e-mail communication): Beth Loffreda's book *Losing Matt Shepard: Life and Politics in the Aftermath of Anti-Gay Murder* (2000).

Ohliger's bibliographies, according to his wife, Chris Wagner, who had worked with Basic Choices, were not annotated. This is most likely because he thought his participation in this way would unduly mediate the material. Ohliger's decision problematized both the idea of annotation as a neutral communication mechanism and the idea of the annotator as simply a conduit, a mechanized transmitter of information between the sender (author) and the receiver (reader). Ohliger considered it more important to fill the annotative space with a more direct and interactive connection between the sender and receiver. He desired a transformative bridging of the roles of the sender (author) to the receiver (reader) and the receiver (reader) to the sender (author). This approach honored both the authors who were speaking for themselves, without filtering, and the participating readers. The readers were invited to move their own thinking forward and contribute in an organic, intellectual process where their thoughts counted. In this way, the project could become the readers' project, and perhaps a community could arise.

Besides his commitment to participation, Ohliger was committed to enhancing access to timely, updated, fresh information that is widely and broadly communicated. He followed up with everyone who contributed to apprise them of what happened. Communicating this information required huge expenditures of time, focus, and money. He essentially distributed his work freely, with the exception of postage and duplication (and that was negotiable). In addition, Ohliger worked tirelessly to include often unheard voices in his spaces of creative expression. For example, he was reported to invite children and people off the street as guest book reviewers for his community radio program. He sought out and invited students (I was included) and nonacademic practitioners to write articles for *Second Thoughts*.

Questioning Gender and Sex Roles

Throughout my research for this chapter, I was interested in signs and evidence of Ohliger's interest in gender and sex roles. Only a few sources I located related specifically to these roles. They included an eclectic audiocassette and Ohliger's response to a class assignment for a course he taught, both of which are challenging to categorize. They also included an audiocassette with an unidentified singer and a typed poem on Basic Choices stationery, with one line in bold for emphasis. I found these latter two sources enigmatic.

An audiocassette of thirty-two selections of music, poetry, and readings focused on "moving beyond the cage of the two rigidly prescribed sex roles." One of the selections, "Personal Testimony," was a talk on a 1984 program entitled "Beyond the Cage: Androgyny and Liberation" (see Ohliger, 1985). The program was sponsored by the Madison Prairie Unitarian Universalist Society. In his talk, Ohliger stated, "Getting beyond the cage of conventional sex roles to find a healthy personal path can be a frightening, exhilarating, [and] confusing . . . experience." After his friends shared their experiences and thoughts about the topic, Ohliger concluded, "I still don't think that sexuality is a clear cut issue."

The second source is Ohliger's version of his favorite class assignment for a philosophy of education class that he was teaching (see also Ohliger, 1989c). Students were asked to examine major themes by writing them up as human qualities in the manner of J. Ruth Gendler's *The Book of Qualities* (1984), that is, according to how the students believed Gendler might do so. Ohliger's contribution (1989c), "process orientation," involves Dr. Subject Matter and Ms. Process who, while grateful for the help that the doctor gave her in getting her first working experience as a nurse in his office, "decided to look for a different job because she felt he was often too rigid and conservative. . . . They argue a lot but end up realizing they have much in common, even if they use different words to describe what their mutual understandings are" (p. 4).

The third source is an audiocassette of a song by an unidentified male singing "You've Got to Stand for Something." Here a son shares what his father lived and passed down to his son. It is about being "Your own man/Not a puppet on a string/Never compromise what's right and uphold your family name/You've got to stand for something/Or you'll fall for anything." This song was repeated fifteen times on the audiocassette.

The last source is an undated poem by Robert W. Service, "The Men That Don't Fit In." Here are the men who "don't know how to rest . . . [and are] always tired of the way things are." It ends with "HE'S A MAN WHO WON'T FIT IN."

How much Ohliger personally identified with any or all of these sources is unknown. Clearly, the repetition of the song and the capitalization for emphasis in the poem served a purpose. Perhaps he was sharing the song or the poem with his radio audience, or using them for a talk or a session of a group with which he was involved. Perhaps he found them autobiographical.

Working Toward Nonsexist Language

Although it appeared that Ohliger put little sustained focus on what it means to be a gendered person, he had a long-standing interest in what it means to have to read language that is sexist and to communicate with people who use sexist language. In his personal files was a 1975 column by Doris S. Chertow, the new editor of the "Accent on Social Philosophy" column for *Adult Leadership*. Chertow insisted that submitted articles use gender-neutral language: "I plan to set the red pencil to work on all sexist sentences. Scream, holler, protest. But do write. Use the tools of communication in furtherance of our common dream. Don't abuse them" (p. 320).

In a 1981 issue of *Second Thoughts*, Ohliger published "Sexism in Graduate Programs," an article by Sudie Hoffmann, a graduate student in adult education. Hoffmann shared her dissatisfaction with the commonplace use of the masculine pronoun in class readings and by professors in their lectures. Evidently Ohliger thought that sexist language in an American graduate school setting in the 1980s was an issue worthy of space in his newsletter. Four years later, he wrote to the editor of the *Women's Institute of the Free Press* and expressed his concern about the pervasiveness of sexist language in academe:

> [My concern is] [p]rompted by the October 1981 "Sexism in Graduate Programs" author on page 6 where the author states that "the masculine pronoun as a generic pronoun has almost vanished from current forms of print and non-print media." My strong impression, based on reading many books since 1981, is that though this may have been true then, there has been, sad to say, a general return to the use of the masculine pronoun as a generic term along with the return of "man" and "mankind" to designate all of humanity. I note these trends especially among the major publishers who supposedly had adopted the nonsexist language guidelines. My question is, am I correct in perceiving such a baleful trend? Are there articles or books you could refer me to or send me copies of that indicate whether I am correct or incorrect? Are there any efforts going on among major publishers these days in regard to sexist language [Ohliger, personal communication to D. Allen, December 3, 1985]?

From the vantage point of her role, Allen might have been one of the people most likely knowledgeable about any efforts on the American publishing scene. Yet she responded that while this may be happening, she and her colleagues had not focused on this and that she would let Ohliger know of any information if she learned of any work in this area (personal communication, December 29, 1985).

In 1989, Ohliger brought up sexist language once again, this time in his ACET column (1989b) in relation to a proposed award. He suggested that the people who are at odds because they seek worthwhile ends should be awarded "Odds and Ends" statuettes instead of Oscars, Emmys, or Golden Globes. He wrote, "It's time we honored those who don't fit in because they work for good but unpopular causes. Nominations are in order for 'ODDS & ENDS' statuettes for people who are 'odds' because they seek worthwhile 'ends.' Each figurine will have engraved on its base Sam Donaldson's retort from his recent book *Hold On, Mr. President*, 'The time to really question something strongly is when everyone says it's true.'" For the first Odds and Ends statuette, Ohliger nominated Sheila Mulcahy, coordinator of the *Guide to Nonsexist Language and Visuals*. He continued, "Sexist language is coming back with a vengeance. Major publishers and broadcasters have surrendered again to the use of *man* to designate the human race, when men are a minority of our species oppressing the majority. But since this gadfly [ACET] column started six months ago, eighty-five percent of the over 100 letters we've received have been from women." He then went on to develop a bibliography, "*Man* as a False Generic" (Ohliger, 1989b). Ohliger continued to work to garnish support for the idea that sexist language needs to be interrupted and eradicated in a time of ever increasing sound bites. The work was challenging because language is powerful. Lakoff (2004) explains the dynamics at play: ideas "have to be in place before the sound bite can make any sense" (p. 104). "It is not just about language. The ideas are primary—and the language cries those ideas, evokes those ideas" (p. 4).

Ohliger's efforts to address sexism were not characterized by the humorless earnestness of so many feminists. I think one of his favorite pictures exemplifies this well. It is a photo of me and another woman, a mutual friend, sitting at a conference table with Ohliger and a celebrated adult educator whose "sexist" comment provoked our nonverbal responses. Our friend looks affronted. My arms are folded, and I have a skeptical look. It is as if we are saying: Who is going to take this on? And how? The photo reminds me how Ohliger liked to bring humor to bear on a tense and possibly challenging moment.

Years after these encounters with sexism, Ohliger had evidently not put away the issue of sexism and language. In 2004 he still had a "Sexist Language Materials" file in his main desk file drawer in his library. It was the only one of nineteen files on a sociopolitical, cultural issue. All of the others contained important health, financial, and family information. The fact that material on a political issue like sexist language continued to be part of Ohliger's personal files says something about the way he lived his life as a rich interconnectedness of the personal and the political. Indeed one communicant reported that the dynamic "the personal is political" was a frequent topic in her discussions with Ohliger.

Addressing Power and the Political

For Ohliger, the political was more than a matter of voting, supporting a political candidate, or expressing dissent at a protest—all of which he did. It was also about how we humans encounter power—in ourselves, between one other, and in all our relations. Unequal power dynamics were often implicated in Ohliger's projects. Sometimes it was focused directly on an individual and a setting: for example, a colleague who was mistreated in a workplace. Sometimes it was more general: for example, his long-standing efforts questioning the politics of mandatory continuing education as one of the fastest-growing and most profitable sectors of the American adult education industry.

A communication with a colleague gives us a glimpse of Ohliger's ideas and practice around power and the political. In a script of a talk he was to give to the colleague's students, Ohliger writes about being "angry," in part because "most people who call themselves adult educators are too busy protecting their jobs, their turf, or both to protest the real abuses." One of the examples of real abuse that he mentions is the verbal and physical harassment and abuse that Wanda and Brenda Henson, two doctoral students in adult education at the University of Southern Mississippi, faced when they set up Camp Sister Spirit, an adult education retreat center for women in rural Mississippi, their home. Ohliger declared, "I am dismayed that adult educators have not rushed en masse to their defense" (Ohliger, personal communication to Von Pittman, September 15, 1994). In 1998, the Hensons recounted their experience of exclusion in a symposium at the Thirty-Ninth Annual Adult Education Research Conference in San Antonio, Texas (Edwards et al., 1998). I quote it here at length:

> We were both doctoral students at the University of Southern Mississippi; both of us were awarded Masters Degrees in Education in 1992. We took our classes together and our professors knew us as a very proud Lesbian couple. These same professors also knew of our dreams to one day open a Feminist Adult Education and Retreat Center to continue the charitable and educational work of the non-profit organization we co-founded in 1989, Sister Spirit Incorporated. In 1993 our organization purchased 120 acres in Ovett, Mississippi, just 20 miles from the University Campus. Delighted, we shared the news of our dreams coming true with professors and classmates. Then, a letter stolen from our mailbox, intended for Camp Sister Spirit volunteers, revealed to the community (through a newsletter announcement!) that we were Lesbians. The attacks began.
>
> We were eight courses away from our dissertation. In the ensuing year, over 100 hate crimes were committed against us. . . . Going to campus was horrible: we experienced hate-filled mean stares from people we didn't know, and giggles in the classroom when our names were called during attendance. . . . Silence, not support, was what we received from our instructors. . . . What did our Adult Education professors or classmates do or say publicly at that time? Nothing! . . . When we received a call from Frank Adams, formerly of the Highlander Educa-

tion and Research Center, to join a Folk Cooperative School—Marrowbone La Mazorca—we did. At their first meeting, the first order of business was to draft and send a letter to Janet Reno and President Clinton demanding that their Adult Education colleagues be protected. As the newly formed organization "Mississippi for Family Values" held town meetings and raffled guns to raise money for a nuisance law suit against us, it was Frank Adams, Kathleen Rockhill, Lee Karlovic and finally Robert Hill and Phyllis Cunningham that made us know we were an important part of the struggle for human rights and justice [pp. 322–323].

As their comments indicate, the Hensons eventually received some support, albeit sparse, from the U.S. adult education community. Moreover, few, if any, of Ohliger's colleagues in U.S. feminist academic and professional circles attended to the "real abuses" that the Hensons faced. Indeed the feminist focus on women and sex-and-gender inequality was a far narrower focus than Ohliger, a democratic socialist "for more than fifty years" (Ohliger, 2001), would have preferred. Ohliger questioned why so many feminists placed limits on consciousness raising as a way to connect to broader social and political issues such as those the Hensons engaged. As Ohliger saw it, consciousness raising is a form of adult education, a form that needed renewed emphasis. So it is not surprising that at the age of sixty-four, he wrote: "I am not a feminist. When I turned 60 . . . I became officially a member of an oppressed group, old people, so I don't seek identity anymore through other oppressed groups" (1990a, p. 4).

Ohliger may not have been a feminist, but he was drawn to women working to make a difference in U.S. culture and society. For example, he worked in Madison to support the candidacy of Sonia Johnson, the 1984 feminist candidate on the Citizen's party ticket for U.S. president. At this point, he was still actively working with groups toward political change, so he had attended a talk by this Mormon woman who was excommunicated by her church for supporting the equal rights amendment. After her speech, Ohliger (1984) wrote: "She is a sparkling, humorous speaker who addresses issues forthrightly and does not shirk from taking firm positions. . . . What attracted me most to her candidacy was her firm recognition that the values of our country need basic change. As Johnson concluded in her talk in Madison: 'We must begin to love and respect what has been designated "womanly" in this patriarchy: peacefulness, gentleness, and nurturance'" (p. 6). Ohliger valued these gendered human characteristics. Indeed he aspired to exhibit these qualities in his interactions with women communicants. He knew that peacefulness, gentleness, and nurturance characterize the power with dynamics that mark these interactions.

Integrating the Spiritual, the Personal, and the Political

For Ohliger, an interest in the personal and the political is inextricably linked to an interest in the spiritual. Ohliger's interest in the spiritual can best be thought of as an interest in the human spirit and all the potentialities "the human spirit" implies. The two sources that appear to have influenced Ohliger greatly are the literature on Sophia, the goddess of wisdom, and the literature on Taoism.

Ohliger's study of the literature on Sophia began with Riane Eisler's *The Chalice and the Blade* (1987). Kate Hawkes introduced Ohliger to this book while she was working with him on "A Teacher in Their Own Bosom" (Ohliger & Hawkes, 1992), which became a 1992 ACET column, as well as the evolving bibliography of mostly American women adult educators. Ohliger was involved for a time with the Center for Partnership, which Eisler cofounded. The work on Sophia became a central theme of his invited talk at the 1990 social philosophy luncheon at the American Association for Adult and Continuing Education. In formulating his ideas, Ohliger suggested that in "SEARCHING FOR and hearing SOPHIA," wisdom may lead us closer to "FINDING PATHS OUT OF OUR CURRENT WORLD WIDE MORASS" (script of the talk within communication to Von Pittman, September 15, 1994).

Ohliger's path in his later years continued to be one of devoting time and energy to his communicants. He seemed to be searching for ways to know and to act that nourished a creative life-in-community worth living, perhaps as a sustainable resistance and counterresponse to the morass. With his communicants, Ohliger came to understand and experience knowing as "conversation, listening, silence, physical closeness, intuition, and even compassion," which he saw as positive results of "explorations of women's and third world concerns" (Ohliger, 1990a, p. 4).

Ohliger discovered Taoism as based on the *Lao Tzu* or the *Tao Te Ching*, the "Number Two World Best Seller," through his friend Everett Reimer. Ohliger (1990b) wrote that his study of the fifty translations allowed him to think "in new fresh paths, beyond words, almost every time. . . . It feels like an act of creation" (p. 4). Although he "wasn't interested in becoming a Taoist or a feminist," Ohliger found in Taoism "a good place to start to integrate the spiritual, the political, and the personal" (p. 4). Taoism nurtured Ohliger's interest in bridging the contradiction between the political and the spiritual: "I BELIEVE IT'S ABSOLUTELY NECESSARY TO GET OUT THERE AND ACT POLITICALLY TO IMPROVE LIFE. . . . SECOND, I BELIEVE THAT ALL THE POLITICAL ACTION IN THE WORLD WILL NOT CHANGE THINGS BECAUSE THE PROBLEM IS DEEPER THAN POLITICAL. IT GOES TO OUR VERY SOULS AND TO THE SOUL OF THE WORLD. . . . I'M STILL SEARCHING FOR WAYS TO RESOLVE THAT CONTRADICTION" (script of a talk in a communication to Von Pittman, September 15, 1994).

A Final Thought

For the communicants interviewed for this chapter, Ohliger's ways of understanding and knowing took form in rich connections marked by the provision of emotional support accompanied by intellectual rigor and humor. In dialogic interactions, communicants expressed intriguing ideas using nonsexist language as they attended to egalitarian power relations. Ohliger would have been flattered to know that four of these women felt a sense of loss that they had not taken more time to communicate with him, to "know more of and with him," as one woman put it. There was "a sense that he was so much in the background that he was in the foreground" (Strohschen, interview, July 24, 2005). Ohliger's legacy is his voluminous writing. For those who seek transformation of contemporary practices of adult and lifelong learning, it is a rich legacy filled with informative and challenging ideas. Indeed, for existing and would-be communicants, Ohliger's knowledge and understanding can continue to be relevant and meaningful in the sum of our learning, our sharing, and our continued communication.

References

Adams, F. T., & Horton, M. (1975). *Unearthing seeds of fire: The idea of Highlander*. Winston-Salem, NC: J. F. Blair.

Bulgakov, M. A. (1995). *The master and Margarita* (D. Burgin & K. Tiernan O'Connor, Trans.). Dana Point, CA: Ardis.

Chertow, D. S. (1975, April). A common-gender social philosophy. *Adult Leadership, 320.*

Edwards, K., Grace, A. P., Henson, B., Henson, W., Hill, R. J., & Taylor, E. (1998). Tabooed terrain: Reflections on conducting adult education research in lesbian/gay/queer arenas (Symposium). In *Proceedings of the 39th Annual Adult Education Research Conference, University of the Incarnate Word and Texas A&M, San Antonio, TX* (pp. 317–324). Retrieved October 5, 2006, from http://www.adulterc.org/Proceedings/1998/98edwards.htm.

Eisler, R. T. (1987). *The chalice and the blade: Our history, our future*. New York: HarperCollins.

Facundo, B. (1984). *Freire-inspired programs in the United States and Puerto Rico: A critical evaluation*. Retrieved October 11, 2005, from http://www.uow.edu.au/ arts/sts/bmartin/dissent/documents/Facundo/Facundo.html.

Gendler, J. R. (1984). *The book of qualities*. New York: HarperPerennial.

Gobledale, A. K. (1994). *The learning spirit: Lessons from South Africa*. Atlanta, GA: Chalice Press.

Gunderloy, M. (n.d.). *Factsheet five*. Alhambra, CA: Author. Information on this now defunct zine retrieved October 11, 2006, from http://en.wikipedia .org/wiki/Factsheet_Five.

Higgins, C. (1983). *Harold and Maude: A play in two acts*. New York: S. French.

Hochschild, A. R. (1983). *The managed heart: Commercialization of humans feeling*. Berkeley: University of California Press.

Hoffmann, S. (1981, October). Sexism in graduate programs. *Second Thoughts*, 4(1), 1, 6.

Lakoff, G. (2004). *Don't think of an elephant! Know your values and frame the debate*. White River Junction, VT: Chelsea Green Publishing.

Lindeman Leonard, E. (1991). *Friendly rebel: A personal and social history of Eduard C. Lindeman*. Adamant, VT: Adamant Press.

Loffreda, B. (2000). *Losing Matt Shepard: Life and politics in the aftermath of anti-gay murder*. New York: Columbia University Press.

Lorde, A. (2000). Uses of the erotic: The erotic as power. In D. Cornell (Ed.), *Feminism and pornography* (pp. 569–574). New York: Oxford University Press.

Matthay, C. (2000, Fall). Unschooling as a political activity. *Food and Water*, 16–23.

Matthay, C. (2002). *S is for shame, f is for fury, m is for mothering*. Retrieved July 28, 2005, from http:www.swarj.org/shikshantar/resources_camy.htm.

Ohliger, J. (1984, December). A vote wasted. *Madison Independent*, 4(1), 1, 6.

Ohliger, J. (1985, February 24). *Personal testimony: A talk in the program "Beyond the cage: Androgyny and liberation."* Madison, WI: Madison Prairie Unitarian Universalist Society.

Ohliger, J. (1989a). *Adult educator's almanac and weekly appointment calendar*. Manhattan, KS: Learning Resources Network.

Ohliger, J. (1989b, April 10). Man as a false generic. Excerpts from *Odds and Ends*. *Adult and Continuing Education Today*, 19(8), 4.

Ohliger, J. (1989c, Fall). *Qualities assignment*. Philosophy of Education course at Sangamon State University, Springfield, IL.

Ohliger, J. (1990a, November 19). Take a social philosopher to lunch this week. *Adult and Continuing Education Today*, 4.

Ohliger, J. (1990b, December 2). *It goes without saying: A talk/order of service on Lao Tzu* (pp. 1–7). Springfield, IL: Abraham Lincoln Unitarian Fellowship.

Ohliger, J. (1991, August 12). The unintentional, but unforgettable adult educators. *Adult and Continuing Education Today*, 4.

Ohliger, J. (2000). *The early days at back porch radio. Spread the Wort?* Madison, WI: Basic Choices.

Ohliger, J. (2001, April). *Current issues in adult education.* Online discussion forum board. Retrieved April 22, 2001, from http:discussion-board-forum .pl?k=AHE518-LK.

Ohliger, J. (n.d.). Loose beginnings. *Second Thoughts,* n.p.

Ohliger, J., & Hawkes, K. (1992, March 9). A teacher in their own bosom. *Adult and Continuing Education Today,* 4.

Orwell, G. (1938). *Homage to Catalonia.* London: Secker & Warburg.

Reimer, N. K., & Reimer, E. W. (1998). *Power for all or for none.* Oakland, CA: Inkworks Press.

Untitled article. (1981, February). *Second Thoughts, 3*(2), n.p.

Wagner, J. (Writer), & Bailey, J. (Director). (1991). *The search for signs of inteligent [sic] life in the universe.* [Motion picture]. Orion.

Wells, H. G. (1909). *Tono-Bungay.* London: Macmillan.

Reflection
On Bread, Roses, and Paradox

Elizabeth J. Tisdell

L ee Karlovic's chapter is beautifully written. Often such provocative writing sparks images, metaphors, or famous sayings that seem to seep through from the center of my soul into my more conscious mind. In reading her thoughtful musings on John Ohliger's relationships with feminism and with women as both individual "communicants" and comrades in community, I was struck with two strong images that will serve as themes for this response: one that speaks more to the mystery of life and love that Ohliger lived, the other more to his connection to women and feminism.

The first arose out of my first reading of the chapter a few days ago. I immediately thought of paradox and was reminded of the reflections of Trappist monk and social activist Thomas Merton. Drawing on the Old Testament story of Jonah's sojourn in the belly of a whale, Merton (1953) described his own life journey/spiritual journey as "traveling toward destiny in the belly of a paradox" (p. 11). This seems an apt description, not only of Ohliger and how he lived his life but also about his relationship with feminism.

The second arose yesterday, the Saturday of Labor Day weekend 2007, after reading Karlovic's chapter for the second time to prepare my response. I immediately thought of the words and images evoked by the famous feminist song, "Bread and Roses," that sprang out of the women garment workers' strikes in New York and Massachusetts from 1908 to 1912. No doubt, this image arose not only out of Karlovic's writing, but from my own reflections on labor, women's work, and social justice on this Labor Day weekend and the fact that John Ohliger was also a labor educator, who was deeply concerned about capitalism and power relations, as well as connections and relationships among people and in community. For me, these two images—bread and roses, and living in the belly of a paradox—together speak to the interrelationships of community, spirituality, gender relations, feminism, and social activism.

In the Belly of a Paradox

While Karlovic does not discuss paradox in her chapter, she hints at it throughout. It is most obvious toward the end of her piece, where she discusses Ohliger's communication to Von Pittman on September 15, 1994. Ohliger noted that although political action is important, it will not completely change the world because "the problem is deeper than political; it goes to our very souls and to the soul of the world . . . I'm still searching for ways to resolve that contradiction." Resolving contradiction. There we have it! This is life in the belly of a paradox: searching for a way to resolve those contradictions. Drawing on this same quote of Merton of "traveling toward destiny in the belly of a paradox," Parker Palmer (1980) noted nearly thirty years ago that it is living those tensions and contradictions that pulls us open to the spirit or to creativity. Knowing this intuitively probably led to Ohliger's interest in both Taoism, or Lao Tzu, and in Sophia (often called "Lady Wisdom"). Ohliger knew what Merton knew, and what many spiritual writers and social activists know: spirituality and social action need not be opposite ends of the continuum. Living the tension between reflection and action—and in this case between spiritual reflection and social action—can lead to deeper insights about both of these. In the solitude of meditation in whatever its forms, whether prayer, mindfulness meditation on the present moment, or meditation on the words of Sophia or Lao Tzu, Ohliger likely found greater courage to take action. Such meditative reflection often leads one back to the center of one's soul, which sometimes yields a sense of creativity. Ohliger actually spoke to this point when discussing becoming familiar with the fifty translations of the *Tao Te Ching*. According to Karlovic, he said that he discovered "new fresh paths almost every time" and that "it feels like an act of creation." Attempting to resolve the contradictions of paradox is an act of creation. I agree with Ohliger: all the social action in the world will not save humanity, nor will all the meditations or contemplations with no action. But it is perhaps living the tension between these two poles that results in the creativity and the fresh paths that can lead to positive change. This insight should undergird adult education as social education.

There is also an obvious paradox specifically related to feminism in Karlovic's reflections on Ohliger. According to Karlovic, in 1990 Ohliger wrote, "I am not a feminist." I am a bit unclear about the context in which he made that statement, but based on what Karlovic reports that his many women "communicants" said about him, he was certainly an advocate of women, and their rights, and certainly took pains to make an issue of sexist language. Thus, it seems a bit of a paradox that while Ohliger chose not to define himself as a "feminist," he did feminist work in the sense that he was a supporter of women and an advocate for issues important to feminists.

I am reminded of Juliet's comment to Romeo in *Romeo and Juliet*: "What's in a name? A rose by any other name would smell as sweet." So is one actually a feminist if one appears to do feminist work but does not define himself or herself as a feminist? Of course, the answer depends on how one defines feminism. Ohliger probably meant that he did not define feminism as his primary political agenda, and he did not see some of the methods discussed by feminists of his time, such as consciousness raising, as exclusive to feminism but rather as good for adult education in general, and as good for both women and men. He also appeared to "trouble gender" in the way that feminist writer Judith Butler (1990) describes, though I am not sure Ohliger would necessarily ascribe to the same sort of

poststructuralist leanings or language that Butler does in her theorizing. But rather than defining himself as a feminist, according to
Hiemstra and Goldstein (1990) who compiled his vita, Ohliger saw
himself as a "radical educator" and defined radical educators as those
who "get to the root of the issues and work toward fundamental social change for the better." Clearly, he did that in relation to many
issues, including those related to women. He was most obviously
political about it in relation to the issue of gender-inclusive language, knowing how pervasive language is in affecting how people
think. But based on what Karlovic reports about his interactions
with women "communicants," he appeared to be acting in support
of women and their needs and best interests. Thus, he may not have
defined himself as a feminist, but he clearly did some feminist work
that is potentially important to women as adult learners and social
activists.

Bread and Roses

For a number of reasons, the song "Bread and Roses" struck me in
my second reading of Karlovic's chapter as an apt metaphor for John
Ohliger's work on behalf of women and his relationship with his
women "communicants." On this Labor Day weekend 2007, workers everywhere are on my mind; I am particularly mindful of women
workers in light of having read Karlovic's chapter. The song "Bread
and Roses," which initially arose out of the women garment workers' strikes in the northeastern United States, has been used as a
theme and symbol ever since in many women's groups, labor strikes,
and marches dealing with women's labor (Learmonth, 1999). More
recently, it has been used in the international women's march organized locally in 157 countries through the women's meeting in
Beijing in 1995 and culminating with a women's march to the
United Nations in 2000 (Miles, 2000). But the lyrics to "Bread and
Roses" were actually penned by a male poet, James Oppenheim,
who wrote it in solidarity with the women and girls involved in the

garment workers' strike in 1912 (Berke, 1999). Like James Oppenheim, an ally to the women workers of his time, it seemed that
Ohliger worked in solidarity with and on behalf of women, clearly
as an ally to the feminist movement, even if he did not call himself
a "feminist."

The symbol of bread and roses is also rich in meaning. Bread of
course is a metaphor for the need for food, obviously necessary to
sustain life. Roses are metaphorical for beauty and quality of life.
Ohliger, it appears, was concerned with both of these metaphors,
and then some. He was concerned with social justice and sustainability, as well as with the heart, spirit, and soul, and how all of
these play out for women and men. We see evidence of this where
Karlovic writes, in speaking of his women communicants, "Ohliger
aided communicants in their search for a workplace or a graduate
school that wouldn't destroy the head or heart." Indeed, he wanted
that for himself, and when he feared Ohio State was robbing him
of his heart, he left. It reminded me of this quote by Lebanese inspirational writer Kahlil Gibran (1923): "Work is love made visible. And if you cannot work with love but only with distaste, it is
better that you should leave your work and sit at the gate of the
temple and take alms of those who work with joy" (p. 25). Ohliger
not only endorsed the meaning of this quote with his women communicants, but this is also how he lived out his work ethic for himself. This ethic can be expressed something like this: work for bread
and sustainability, but work for roses too. And do work that brings
some sense of joy, quality of life, and meaningful relationships. Such
an encompassing ethic can guide today's social educators as they
mediate learning amid the uncertainties of life and work today.

I was also struck by the "Bread and Roses" metaphor partly because Karlovic used the word *communicants* throughout to describe
the many women Ohliger communicated with. For me, the word
communicants immediately evoked the image of bread. This is no
doubt a vestige of my Catholic background, as the church refers to
people who take communion to partake of the bread of the Eucharist

as "communicants." Indeed, such a symbol, such a word, is also about living together, and sharing bread, in the context of community. Also, the symbol of the rose is often equated with the many incarnations of Lady Wisdom figures throughout history and in different cultural traditions, from Sophia on (Powell, 2001; Ronan, Taussig, & Cole, 1986). We can live together well in the context of community only if we have bread and share it. We can grow into community only if we have the wisdom of Sophia to be able to nurture relationships and some quality of life, and the beauty of the roses. Ohliger knew this. He lived this, and he celebrated and encouraged his women communicants to do the same.

Conclusion

So what does this mean for women and men adult educators who are advocates for social justice of all types and for those who want to be advocates of feminism and all those who trouble gender relations, whether they define themselves as feminist or not? The message is simple enough. Live the tensions of the paradox that pulls us open to creativity. Take action on behalf of women and children, as well as men. Share bread. Publicly recognize the many manifestations of Sophia, or Lady Wisdom. Meditate on Lao Tzu, or Sophia, or whoever gives you inspiration. Take action again. Make bread, nurture roses, find connection with communicants as Ohliger did. Live the paradox. Indeed, the message is simple. It is living it that is so difficult.

References

Berke, N. (1999). Ethnicity, class, and gender in Lola Ridge's "The Ghetto." *Legacy, 16,* 70–81.

Butler, J. (1990). *Gender trouble.* New York: Routledge.

Gibran, K. (1923). *The prophet.* New York: Knopf.

Hiemstra, R., & Goldstein, A. (1990). John Ohliger: Personal vita compiled by Hiemstra & Goldstein. Retrieved September 1, 2007, from http:// www-distance.syr.edu/pvitajfo.html.

Learmonth, A. (2000). Bread and roses (a)cross the Pacific. *Hecate*, 26, 69–87.

Merton, T. (1953). *The sign of Jonas*. Trappist, KY: Abbey of Our Lady of Gethsemane.

Miles, A. (2000). Local activisms, global feminisms, and the struggle against globalization. *Canadian Women's Studies*, 20, 6–10.

Palmer, P. (1980). *The promise of paradox*. Notre Dame, IN: Ave Maria Press.

Powell, R. (2001). *The Sophia teachings: The emergence of the divine feminine in our time*. Brooklyn, NY: Lantern Books.

Ronan, M., Taussig, H., & Cole, S. (1986). *Sophia: The future of feminist theology*. San Francisco: HarperCollins.

16

Cultural Work in the Trenches
John Ohliger and Paul Robeson

Stephen Brookfield

In 1979 I was attending my first major conference in the United States. I had traveled across the pond from England to Boston for the annual American Association of Adult Education conference. One of my most vivid recollections was of constantly bumping into, tripping over, and generally being unable to avoid a group of (mostly) young members of the field handing out daily leaflets under the by-line *NAVL Gazing*. Being a curious limey, I read these leaflets, which turned out to be a series of daily broadsheets railing against the increasing professionalization of the field and calling practitioners to guard the voluntary tradition that defined its practice. As I recall, NAVL stood for the National Alliance for Voluntary Learning. And who was the moving spirit behind these insurrectionary, nay incendiary, pamphlets? I asked. John Ohliger, I was told.

I have to admit that the name meant nothing to me or, I suspect, to most adult educators in the United Kingdom at the time. Of course, that changed when I moved to Canada in 1980 and then to New York in 1982. I began to bump into John at conferences and to become aware of his writings and activities through colleagues such as Michael Collins, Paul Ilsley, Phyllis Cunningham, and Bill Draves. When I resigned a tenured full professorship at Teachers College, Columbia University in 1991, I did not feel as if I had lost my head or stepped into the void. After all, I told myself, John Ohliger had done the same thing and lived to tell the tale. And as the twentieth century came to a close, I began to think about the decline of the public intellectual, a concept fully explored by David Yamada in Chapter Ten in this volume, and how John was one of the few I still could name. I had done my doctoral work on independent learning and been one of Allen Tough's research team in the 1970s that studied how adults successfully learn and change, especially through informal, self-directed learning (Tough, 1979, 1982, 2002). Thus, the idea of the independent scholar, unaffiliated with an institution, free of the compromises required by tenure, was appealing to me. I lived that life only for five years until I joined the University of St. Thomas (Minneapolis-St. Paul) in 1996, where I remain. To its credit, the university has always fully supported my work outside its boundaries; indeed, working with groups, organizations, and individuals outside the university is the second in my contracted list of responsibilities.

As I settled into my life in Minnesota, I became more and more interested in exploring the idea of the adult educator as public intellectual and the public intellectual as adult educator, and I was pleased to see Gramsci's idea of the organic intellectual become claimed by the field in the work of Mayo (1998), Coben (1998), and Holst (2002). Allied with this was the idea that adult educators could also be cultural workers (Freire, 1998) and that popular culture was an important setting for, and vehicle of, adult education. The idea of the adult educator as cultural worker sat easily on my shoulders given the prominence of the work of adult educator and cultural theorist Raymond Williams (1995) in the United Kingdom. Paul Robeson, who spent much of his adult life resident in, or a visitor to, the U.K., was someone who occupied my mind more and more as I thought about organic intellectuals, public intellectuals, and cultural workers. It was when I started to think about contributing to this book that the connections between Robeson and Ohliger began to crystallize for me.

On the face of it, Paul Robeson seems an unlikely connection to John Ohliger. For many people, Robeson is known mostly as the singer of "Old Man River" from the musical *Showboat* and as the theatrical star of *Othello* and *The Emperor Jones* and films such as *Sanders of the River* and *The Proud Valley*. Less well known perhaps are his tireless efforts at organizing, building mass movements, working within a radical presidential campaign, singing to and supporting labor unions, cultural work within the Hollywood studio system, support of colonial struggles across the globe, and his long-standing involvement in the antinuclear movement. It is in this affinity for grassroots organizing and supporting labor struggles that we can draw parallels between Robeson and Ohliger. Both men were driven by their social ambition to build a better world, a more just world with a place for ordinary people disenfranchised by oppressive dominant forces.

Most people who have heard of Robeson are probably dimly aware that he was caught up in the McCarthyism witch hunt of communists in the 1950s and that he famously refused to buckle when called in front of the House Un-American Activities Committee. To the end of his life, he refused to buckle under pressure to denounce the Soviet Union, which for him represented the best hope of providing support for anti-imperialism. And, of course, Robeson was black, Ohliger white. As such, John did not have to suffer the injuries of daily racism or be held up as evidence that racism no longer existed.

Nevertheless, several parallels seem clear to me. First, there is the turn away from security. Robeson was one of the best-known American entertainers in the world, pulling down an enormous salary in the 1940s. As he became a target of the House Un-American Activities Committee, that rapidly dwindled to six thousand dollars per year (Duberman, 1988). In addition, the State Department's confiscation of his passport denied him the chance to earn a living overseas, where he remained hugely popular. Although the dollar figures are very different, John's turn away from the life of a tenured professor marked a similar turn into a more precarious financial way of life. Ohliger's finances certainly placed limits on his ability to travel and network face to face with colleagues in the field that he loved (Ohliger, 1997). As a result of holding fast to their convictions, neither figure was able to depend on a guaranteed and comfortable source of income.

Second, both figures were skeptical of people with big ideas and big words who did not participate in grassroots organization building. John perennially distanced himself from politicians and educators who extolled the virtues of mandatory continuing education in rhetoric caught up in technical optimism that he felt reduced individuals to permanently inadequate lifelong learners (Ohliger, 1974, 1997). He preferred the radical language of the labor movement, as did Robeson. Although the white establishment tried to separate Robeson from the black community by portraying him as a wealthy dilettante, he built an impressive curriculum vitae of involvement in union organizing. He was particularly active in trying to persuade African Americans to join mainstream labor unions, which he saw as the chief and best hope for advancing black interests. He played a major role in the Progressive Party's campaign to elect Henry Wallace as president in 1948. Like Gramsci, he felt that the interests of the working class needed to be represented by a revolutionary party.

Third, Robeson maintained a strong interest in popular culture throughout his adult life. Like John, he was suspicious of the way it represented mainstream interests and the way it disseminated dominant ideology. Ohliger (1974) felt that knowledge, information, and truth associated with scientific progress and technological advancement had cultural currency to the point of sidelining social and cultural concerns. The technological had an allure. Still, Ohliger saw the technological as something to be contested in popular culture. Robeson also viewed popular culture as a site for struggle (another similarity he shared with Gramsci), and he strove to use the Hollywood studio system against itself by promoting films that he felt could help undermine white supremacy.

Fourth, like John, Robeson's interests and involvements were wide ranging and eclectic. Both men were voracious readers with interests that ranged far and wide. John's wide-ranging concerns and experiences are demonstrated in the other chapters in this book. Robeson became an expert on musicology, studied a number of African and Asian dialects, and explored African cultural values, philosophy, art, music, and spirituality. This eclecticism was evident in his internationalism. He traveled the world constantly, initially as a singer and then as a political activist concerned to connect the disenfranchised and dispossessed of different countries and racial groups. As a socialist, Robeson was used to thinking both politically and internationally and constantly argued that workers and racial minorities always had more that connected them than divided them. This was true linguistically and musically; even more important, it was true politically. Robeson was consistent in his efforts to point out the international dimensions of, for example, the struggle for racial equality.

In this chapter, I explore three learning tasks that were present throughout Robeson's life: his cultural work, particularly his attempt to use the Hollywood studio system to present positive images of black life; his attempts to promote racial pride through educating blacks about the tremendous heritage of African culture; and his work to develop a form of collective leadership for social change that centered on grassroots union organizing. Like John, Robeson deserves full consideration as an important adult educator. He never held a position with the title *adult educator*, but he was one in the sense that John defined that term. For Ohliger (1974), the true adult educator engages in and with communities to counter oppressive political, economic, and educational forces. The true adult educator is a resistance or cultural worker who is comfortable working with people outside the establishment and on the margins. For Ohliger, what is most important is that the true adult educator fights cultural forces like mandatory education that leave individuals feeling inadequate and inferior in a rapidly changing learning-and-work world. It was these feelings that Robeson also contested as he encouraged learners and workers to rise up and demand change.

Positioning Paul Robeson

Paul Robeson was one of the towering American public intellectuals of the twentieth century. His biographer claims that at one point in his life, he was the best-known and most admired black man alive (Duberman, 1988). Philip Finer (1978) notes that Robeson's emphasis on racial pride, racial unity, the connection between civil rights organizing in the United States and anticolonial struggles across the globe, and the importance of mass action and collective unity among African Americans means he must be considered the intellectual catalyst for, and forerunner of, Malcolm X, Stokely Carmichael, Huey Newton, and Eldridge Cleaver. Indeed, Malcolm X's well-known distinction between so-called house Negroes (those willing to cooperate with the white power structure to curry temporary favor and an easier life) and field Negroes (those whose rebelliousness meant they rejected servility to whites) was one repeatedly drawn by Robeson. Foreshadowing the later radical stance of the Black Panthers, Robeson castigated the leadership of the National Association for the Advancement of Colored People as his own radicalism exploded after World War II. "How Sojourner Truth, Harriet Tubman, [and] Fred Douglass must be turning in their graves," he wrote in 1949, "at this spectacle of a craven, fawning, despicable leadership able to be naught but errand boys, and—at the lowest level—stooges and cowardly renegades, a disgrace to the Negro people and to the real and true America of which they so glibly talk" (1978, p. 204).

Robeson was one of those rare examples of a successful, admired, and feted leader who sees through the sham of ideological manipulation and risks everything to move to the left. His growing wealth, fame, and international acclaim did not soften his growing criticism of American imperialism and its hostility to the Soviet Union (which Robeson thought was grounded in the Soviet Union's championing of anticolonial struggles across the globe). The more his fame propelled him into international tours and travel, the more he learned of the growing anticolonial movements across the world and the link these had to fighting white supremacy in the United States (and vice versa). Robeson's influence on U.S. affairs was tempered by his growing public and private commitment to socialism (which grew concurrent with the advent of the Cold War) and his refusal to disavow the Soviet Union, even after Khrushchev's 1956 address publicizing Stalin's repression. When the State Department confiscated his passport as he faced the House Un-American Activities Committee, he was, in effect, an exile in his own country.

My personal interest in Robeson stems from the frequent visits Robeson made to the United Kingdom. Growing up in England, I knew the Robeson of "Old Man River" and *Othello*, but I also knew of Robeson the supporter of the Soviet Union who was the target of the House Un-American Activities Committee, of Robeson the ally of the Welsh miners, and of Robeson the passionate speaker at Campaign for Nuclear Disarmament mass rallies. Robeson had strong ties to the United Kingdom. He was a friend of and frequent fundraiser for the British trade union movement, and when the State Department's confiscation of his passport barred him from leaving the United States, he sang to the Welsh workers' Eisteddfod festival over the transatlantic phone line. He famously declared that it was in England that he became an African, chiefly as a result of his study of languages at the London School of Oriental Languages. He also said that it was in Britain where his true radicalization took place, after his introduction to striking Welsh miners. It was also here that in 1939, he made the film that he always felt best represented his cultural and political vision: *The Proud Valley*, a celebration of the Welsh miners' trade union, with Robeson playing the part of David Goliath, an American sailor who finds himself working in the Welsh coal mines. It was no surprise that in 1957, his friends in the United Kingdom formed the National Paul Robeson Committee to lobby for the return of Robeson's passport by the U.S. State Department. This committee included twenty-seven members of Parliament and artistic luminaries such as composer Benjamin Britten, actress Flora Robson, and novelist Kingsley Amis. Perhaps the pressure from the committee and other lobby groups helped, because Robeson eventually had his passport restored.

As a movement leader, Robeson was a practitioner of critical reflection on experience, so frequently lionized in adult education as the quintessential form of adult learning, before the term was invented. As he developed his own conception of race leadership—in a direction that other black leaders wished him to abandon—he continually examined both his motives and assumptions, changing quite significantly his ideas on tactics and strategy regarding how best to challenge white supremacy. He was constantly drawing insights from his analysis of his experiences, which grew ever wider as he struggled with the Hollywood studio system, with the need to internationalize the U.S. black liberation struggle to become part of the world anticolonial movement, and with his attempts to forge alliances between blacks and whites in the trade union movement. From a career that began with fame on the football field (he was "Robeson of Rutgers" in his college days, a legendary athlete), on the stage (his classic Othello is still admired and debated), on the screen (in a series of films such as Showboat that he made for money and dismissed as inconsequential), and in the concert hall (his recordings of spirituals and appearances made him probably the wealthiest black man in America in the 1930s and 1940s), Robeson moved through experiences with anticolonial movements across the globe, with a presidential campaign (the Progressive candidacy of Henry Wallace), and with picket lines and rallies in countless union halls to become, with W.E.B. Dubois, an outspoken critic of white racism and white capitalism. To move from a life of privilege to a lifelong advocacy of socialism that effectively killed his earning potential shows a willingness to reappraise assumptions born of equal parts intellectual honesty and critical conviction.

Robeson was also increasingly committed to developing collective leadership in the African American community, particularly through Negroes assuming prominent positions within trade unions. He is thus squarely in the tradition of adult educators such as Martin

Luther King Jr., as well as Ella Baker (a colleague of Dr. King and a leading civil rights activist from 1930 until her death in 1986) and Septima Clark (another colleague of Dr. King and a civil rights activist from 1919 who worked with the Voter Education Project in the 1960s to increase black voter registration). These adult educators and grassroots activists were skeptical of the prevalence of charismatic leadership. For Robeson, a strategy for African American advancement based on individual leadership exercised by prominent spokespersons shot itself in the foot. Leadership had to be collective for any true change to occur. This was because in collectivity lay the strength of solidarity and also because radical leadership could hope to survive all the enmity and punishment that was visited on it by the white supremacist power structure only if those involved had a sense that they were representatives of, and supported by, a much wider force. He also sought to learn how to practice democracy, long one of the most espoused purposes of adult education, consistently framing himself as both democrat and socialist. In his view, there was no inherent contradiction between the two. Indeed, for Robeson, socialism *was* democracy—the fullest possible realization of political and economic equality. Like Horton, Robeson viewed representative democracy as a sham. True democracy could be said to exist only if the massive economic disparity between rich and poor, black and white, was redressed.

Like Ohliger, Robeson was consistently open to new ideas, and not only in political theory and strategy. If we look for examples of transformative learning—the development of meaning schemes and perspectives that are ever more comprehensive and discriminating (Mezirow, 1991)—Robeson's life represents transformative learning par excellence. He explored widely and seriously his passion for musicology, languages, and the heritage of African culture, being particularly intrigued by the similarities in musical structures he found between African American spirituals and work songs and Eastern modalities. His growing internationalism meant he was consistently learning about other cultures and about the different facets of anticolonial struggles across the globe. Indeed, it was his internationalism that prompted and nurtured his radicalism, particularly his socialism. Had he not traveled to the Soviet Union and been astounded by the lack of racism he experienced there and had he not been open to listening to striking Welsh miners he bumped into outside the Savoy Hotel in London, it is hard to imagine him developing the views he did and the fortitude he subsequently needed to hold them. Robeson also practiced learning to question throughout his life, turning his critical gaze particularly on the evolution of what he felt was an imperialist American foreign policy, on the unwarranted demonization of the Soviet Union by the white Right, and on the use by the white ruling class of what critical race theorists have subsequently labeled black exceptionalism, that is, the idea that because Robeson had a successful career as athlete, singer, and actor, structural barriers to all African Americans had significantly weakened, if not disappeared altogether.

Perhaps the most striking dimension of leadership exemplified by Robeson, however, is his ability to sustain hope in the face of struggle. Few others so exemplify Paulo Freire's call for a *Pedagogy of Hope* (2004). While Ohliger (1974) found value in Freire's work as a guide for exposing political and economic injustice, he was suspicious of criticality, as Grace notes in Chapter Nine and Collins in Chapter Thirteen. This suspicion gave Ohliger second thoughts and probably altered the parameters he set for a pedagogy of hope. In contrast, Robeson displayed a heroic, steadfast, and hopeful independence of thought, despite the considerable cost to himself and the mounting evidence of hostility heaped on him. Essentially his commercial (though not artistic) career as a singer was completely destroyed by his commitment to socialism and his refusal to abandon his support of the Soviet Union. In contrast to the ideological trajectory of many artists and intellectuals who begin as radicals and then temper their convictions as they mature and enjoy success, Robeson went in the opposite direction. The more success he gained, the more he realized how the white power structure was trying to use that success to demonstrate that true equality of opportunity existed for African Americans in the United States. The more he achieved personal wealth and fame, the more he allied himself with the labor movement, anticolonial struggles, and the Soviet Union's efforts to create a socialist, nonracist state.

Robeson's support of the Soviet Union caused the white press either to delete his presence entirely from the cultural-intellectual landscape of the United States or to portray him as an unpatriotic, un-American, communist subversive. As Duberman (1988) notes, by 1960, "his image [was] converted by a now hostile establishment from public hero to public enemy . . . an outcast, very nearly a non-person" (p. xiii). Popular culture has also framed the early biography of this freedom fighter as a minstrel entertainer, a singer of sanitized show tunes such as "Old Man River" from *Showboat*. Robeson constantly fought against this stereotyping. One small example of this is his changing the lyrics in concert of "Old Man River" from "Tote that barge, lift that bail, you get a little drunk and you land in jail" (which portrayed Negro laborers as human oxen and seeking solace in drink) to "Tote that barge, lift that bail, you show a little grit and you land in jail" (which emphasized the laborer's refusal to buckle under capitalism and the white supremacist power structure).

Typical of Robeson's treatment by the white press was their portrayal of his involvement in the Peekskill "riots" of 1949, which was presented as evidence of his dangerous agitation. In fact, the so-called riots were disturbances that whites caused in attempting to stop Robeson from performing. In England, Asia, Africa, and Eastern Europe, however, he was honored as a courageous educator trying to educate both blacks and whites about racism, socialism, and the deep traditions of African culture. In India, the All India Peace Council called for the U.S. State Department to return his passport, and he frequently sent taped messages to conferences such as the Asian African conference in Indonesia.

Popular Culture

Ohliger (1967) knew the power of popular culture, certainly from
the time of his work with listening groups during his doctoral studies.
He knew the influence of radio as a medium to connect people and
encourage communication. Robeson also knew the power of popular culture; his work with it is probably the area of his life that is
known to the broadest number of people.

Beginning as a singer, Robeson expanded his activities to include
film and theater, starring as Othello at Stratford-upon-Avon in the
United Kingdom once the U.S. State Department had returned his
passport to him. For him, art was always politically charged. He tried
to work in the commercial studio system to develop race pride by
providing historically accurate representations of Africans in films
such as *Sanders of the River*. After disavowing the film as "a piece of
flag-waving, in which I wasn't interested . . . [and a] total loss"
(Robeson, 1978, p. 121), he declared, "The big producers insist on
presenting a caricature image of the black, a ridiculous image, that
amuses the white bourgeoisie, and I am not interested in playing
their game" (p. 126). Still he did not lose confidence in film as a
medium of social change, arguing in Gramscian mode that film "is
the medium through which to express the creative abilities of the
masses" and that "only on the screen can the Negro's real place in
the building of the United States be properly shown" (p. 39).

In 1937 Robeson (1978) complained that "things were twisted
and changed and distorted" whenever he worked with film. In 1942
he reiterated (regarding *Tales of Manhattan*), "I thought I could
change the picture as we went along. . . . But in the end it turned
out to be the same old thing—the Negro solving his problem by
singing his way to glory. This is very offensive to my people. It makes
the Negro child-like and innocent and is in the old plantation tradition" (1978, p. 142). Because of his disillusionment with Hollywood's
white bankrollers, he gradually moved away from commercial films
and ceased to target his appeal to a broad audience. Increasingly, he

aimed his acting at members of labor unions, believing that art could help demonstrate the common economic interests of poor working-class whites and blacks and thus play a part in creating a viable mass working-class movement (*The Proud Valley* is the best example of this). He elevated the singing of spirituals to the status of serious, socially committed art, and hence made it a political act, believing that it was one way to educate African Americans and whites of the rich heritage of African culture. Robeson thus viewed popular culture as a powerful medium through which millions of adults outside formal education could be reached. Ohliger held the same view as he used radio, newsletters, and other media to reach a wider public.

When it was clear that the Hollywood studio systems as currently comprised could not be subverted from within, Robeson reappraised his commitment to film. In 1937 he concluded, "One man can't face the film companies. They represent about the biggest aggregate of finance capital in the world. . . . So no more films for me" (1978, p. 120). Declaring that "what I won't do is work for the big companies, which are headed by individuals who would make me a slave, like my father, if they could" (p. 126), he came up with two strategies. First, he proposed an alternative mode of financing, producing, and distributing films that totally bypassed the major studios. Such films would be financed by unions, cultural associations (such as the Council on African Affairs), or wealthy independent backers and would allow him to make films on such topics as the life of a black commander of the Lincoln Brigade in the Spanish Civil War (a project he was never to realize). Second, he suggested that African Americans, union members, and progressive whites boycott studio-produced films, hoping that such a stand would inspire similar boycotts in international markets. It was his conviction that "the mounting of the right kind of campaign could shake Hollywood to its foundations" (p. 126), seriously affecting its members. Consistent with his internationalism, he argued that if elements of the American public took the lead, "help would be forthcoming from all over the world" (p. 126).

Race Pride

A second leadership task Robeson devoted his life to was developing race pride among African Americans. This project had two
dimensions: educating adults about the richness of the African cultural heritage and educating them about the values and practices
that lay at the heart of authentic Negro culture. Like Dubois, Robeson believed that commitments to pan-Africanism and socialism
were compatible. While in London, he conducted a series of substantial adult learning projects, studying at the School of Oriental
Languages and learning a number of African languages, including
Swahili, Yoruba, Efik, Benin, Ashanti, and Tivi. Indeed, he often
said that it was in the United Kingdom that he became an African,
partly as a result of his language studies and partly through his conversations with African seamen in London, Liverpool, and Cardiff.
Increasingly he became a passionate advocate of African Americans'
learning about the rich heritage of African culture, believing that a
lack of knowledge of their culture meant they were denied a potent
source of race pride. As early as 1934, he declared that "in my music,
my plays, [and] my films I want to carry always this central idea: to
be African" (1978, p. 91). The next year he declared that "for the
rest of my life I am going to think and feel as an African—not as a
white man. . . . To me it seems the most momentous thing in my life"
(1978, p. 91). In common with the contemporary Afrocentric turn
away from Eurocentrism, he maintained, "It is not as imitation
Europeans, but as Africans, that we have a value" (1978, p. 92).

The heritage Robeson sought to educate people about was that
of Africa's "great philosophy and epics of poetry" (1978, p. 352),
which he maintained were comparable to the achievements of
Greek and Chinese poetry. He celebrated what he felt he found in
his studies of Africa: the "great precision and subtlety of intona-
tional structure" to be found in African languages, the "rich oral
folklore . . . [and] distinctive decorative art (especially culture)" of
African culture, and the "highly developed and original musical art

distinguished by an extraordinary wealth of rhythm" (p. 352). Yet, he lamented, none of these were evident in the "savage and cannibalistic" images of half-naked black people presented as examples of Africans "as the newspapers, radio, book and lecture propagandists would make them" (1978, p. 228). In the pursuit of an authentic Afrocentrism, he urged an educational campaign to make American Negroes aware of their African roots. The following statement, made in 1934, is typical of this: "The dances, the songs, and the worship perpetuated by the Negro in America are identical with those of his cousins hundreds of years removed in the depths of Africa, whom he has never seen, of whose very existence he is only dimly aware. His peculiar sense of rhythm alone would stamp him indelibly as African" (1978, p. 90). As Robeson conducted this educational project, he become more and more aware of the political underpinnings of the opposition he faced. As he put it, "There was a logic to this cultural struggle, and the powers-that-be realized it before I did. The British Intelligence came one day to caution me about the political meanings of my activities. For the question loomed of itself: If African culture was what I insisted it was, what happens to the claim that it would take 1,000 years for Africans to be capable of self-rule? Yes, culture and politics were actually inseparable here as always" (1978, p. 352).

So after reflecting critically on his earlier assumptions regarding the significance of education about African culture, Robeson switched his emphasis to advocating cultural adult education as a central political component in the black liberation struggle. What was particularly frustrating for Robeson was the fact that American Negroes shared the white supremacist stereotypes of Africa that viewed Africans as uncultured savages, lacking even language. Hence the major purpose of his studies of African language and folk music was "to dispel this regrettable and abysmal ignorance of the value of its own heritage in the negro race itself" (1978, p. 87). His decision to sing only Negro spirituals in concert, charge low admission prices to his concerts, and make independent films financed outside the studio system were all manifestations of this project. These were political statements, not just cultural choices. As his career evolved, he learned more and more the importance of integrating the cultural and political dimensions of educating people about African culture. This became reframed as an important element in the anticolonial struggle rather than an act of purely aesthetic or anthropological education.

Early in his career, in fact, Robeson spoke of Negro culture as emotional and instinctual, a sort of primal connection to a Jungian race memory or cultural DNA. In 1931, for example, he referred to Negro culture as manifesting "a deep simplicity, a sense of mystery, a capacity for religious feeling, a spontaneous and entirely individual cheerfulness" (1978, p. 84). Again, in 1934 he wrote that "the Negro feels rather than thinks, experiences emotions directly rather than interprets them by roundabout and devious abstractions, and apprehends the outside world by means of intuitive perception instead of through a carefully built up system of logical analysis" (p. 86). Contrast this with his much more politicized comments on Negro culture some twenty years later that emphasized the way white capitalists had robbed Negroes of their economic and cultural due: "Billions, literally billions of dollars, have been earned and are being earned from their creation, and the Negro people have received almost nothing" (p. 299). A couple of years earlier, he framed Negro culture as the response of "this enslaved people, oppressed by the double yoke of cruel exploitation and racial discrimination" that produced "splendid, life-affirming songs" (p. 212). That same year he also castigated the way capitalism distorted and perverted Negro music: "Under capitalist conditions . . . our [contemporary] native Negro music has ruthlessly perverted many splendid models of Negro folk music and has corrupted and debased many talented Negro musicians in order to satisfy the desires of capitalist society" (p. 217).

The change in emphasis outlined above illustrates how Robeson's critical reflection on his experiences with movements for social change (artistic, labor, and presidential) caused him to alter dramatically his understanding of, and role within, movements against white supremacy. One of his earliest lessons in this struggle was his quick realization of how the white supremacist power structure used his cultural success as evidence of the lack of racism in the United States. Robeson professed himself always to be aware of the wider struggle his life represented. Speaking of his college football days, he said, "From the time I played on the football field I felt I was struggling for the Negro people, my people, and I was conscious of that struggle" (1978, p. 18). Gradually his understanding of how his success was being manipulated by whites caused him to speak out against it more and more forcefully: "I got tired of serving as an excuse for these cruelties to my people" (p. 266).

In 1937 at a Spanish Civil War rally, he made one of his earliest, and most renowned, declarations of how he had come to place his art—his cultural work—in the service of struggle: "The artist must take sides. He must elect to fight for freedom or slavery. I have made my choice. I had no alternative" (1978, p. 119). Ten years later, this solidified into an abandoning of his lucrative singing and film career for direct political action: "In 1947, on an NAACP picket line in St. Louis, I decided to retire from the concert stage and enter the day-to-day struggle of the people from whom I spring . . . for my people and the working masses of this country" (1978, pp. 319, 383). Having learned of how his success was being used to justify white supremacy, Robeson turned the ideological tables and learned to use it to fight that same supremacy. In contemporary terms, this would be as if Michael Jordan or Michael Jackson, at the height of their fame and their ability to secure millions of dollars in recording contracts and lucrative sponsorships, had announced that they were devoting their talents and energies to forging a mass movement between blacks and labor unions to fight white capitalism, or to reviving the Black Panther Party.

As his political commitment hardened, Robeson reappraised his strategy of serving as an individual spokesperson for African Americans and focused more and more on reframing his practice within a collective movement. An emphasis on individualism marks his conviction of 1939 that "no Negro can help feeling that he represents more than merely himself. . . . I was always conscious of the fact that I had a direct responsibility as a negro" (1978, p. 128). In contrast, a focus on collectivity was evident by the time of his declaration at the Peace Arch on the Canadian border in 1953 that he would spend his "day-to-day struggle down among the masses of the people, not even as any great artist on top somewhere—but right here in this park, in many other picket lines, wherever I could be to help the struggle of the people. And I will never apologize for that. I shall continue to fight, as I see the truth. . . . There is no force on earth that will make me go backward one-thousandth part of one little inch" (pp. 365–366). Here we have a fiery radicalism voiced even as Senator Joe McCarthy's investigations had caused the State Department to confiscate Robeson's passport, but a radicalism expressed in the service of collective, not individual, struggle. Declaring himself to feel "a part of a tremendous collective strength and power" (p. 272), Robeson moved to advocating the sort of collective leadership later championed by Ella Baker.

Collective Leadership

For Robeson, like Ohliger (1997), collective leadership had several interwoven tasks, all of which involved supporting the growth of others. The first was helping African Americans realize the tremendous collective power they could exercise through mass action. He foreshadowed the approach to community organizing of adult educators Septima Clark and Ella Baker by urging blacks to build on the already tremendous organizing spirit alive in black churches to form mass organizations that could exert political pressure. Writing in his autobiography *Here I Stand*, he declared, "For Negro action to be effective—to be decisive, as I think it can be—it must be mass action. Mass action—in political life and elsewhere—is Negro power in motion; and it is the way to win" (Robeson, 1958, p. 107).

The year before, in an echo of Bell Hooks's *Talking Back* (1989), he addressed a rally with these words: "All of us got some talking back to do. Not on TV, not on radio, not long distance, but face to face with the powers that be. I mean mass action, and mass pressure" (1978, p. 325). Around this time, he stressed repeatedly the strength represented by fifteen million African Americans. And in 1964, he noted approvingly, "The power of Negro action, of which I then wrote, has changed from an idea to a reality that is manifesting itself throughout our land. The concept of mass militancy, or mass action, is no longer deemed 'too radical' in Negro life" (p. 472). Ironically, in the 1960s, Robeson's own tremendous sacrifices in the three decades he spent organizing mass action, challenging lynching, supporting anticolonial struggles, and educating African Americans in race pride—all of which helped map out the terrain for the civil rights movement and the different work of Clark, Baker, King, Malcolm X, Carmichael, Cleaver, and others—were almost completely ignored.

Collective leadership stood the greatest chance, in Robeson's view, if it was exercised in the context of a working-class movement led by racially integrated trade unions. Again and again he urged African Americans to join labor unions and for Negro unions to affiliate with the AFL/CIO. For him, the struggles of African Americans and the struggles of the white workers were one struggle, with far more uniting these two groups than dividing them. This quote from 1952 is typical: "The basic unity of the working masses of this land and the Negro people must be forged there. We have the same oppression. We must stretch out our hands and clasp them in never-ending common struggle until victory be the people's" (1978, p. 314). In the trenches of the Spanish Civil War, in the Welsh coal mines, and on the New Jersey docks, Robeson consistently emphasized the power of the union. In particular, he identified Negro leaders within unions as the vanguard of African Americans' interests. Hence, "in relation to our general struggle for civil rights the Negro and trade unionists occupy a key position . . . the Negro trade union members are a strategic link, a living connection with the great masses of the common people of America who are our natural allies in the struggle for democracy" (1958, p. 97).

As Robeson learned about the dynamics of the black liberation struggle, he reexamined his earlier emphasis on self-contained African American unity and found it wanting. With increasing intensity and frequency, he urged African Americans to combine with progressive white allies to form a broad-based people's movement. Robeson believed that Jews, among the different white ethnicities in the United States, were the most natural allies for blacks. He cited the way Jews had helped blacks challenge Jim Crow segregation, and the genocide they had suffered in the Holocaust, as evidence of "the closeness of the age-long struggle of the Negro and Jewish people . . . direct threads which link the interests of the Negro and Jewish people from the earliest days" (1978, p. 391).

In working to convince white and black workers of their shared interests and the importance of building multiracial alliances in which blacks held leadership roles, Robeson anticipated the work of Angela Davis, another African American activist and adult educator who believed social change could occur only within the context of black-led multiracial alliances. He urged African Americans to join the Congress of Industrial Organizations and stood against separate unions based on race. He characterized blacks who refused to join labor unions as "scab labor Negroes" (1978, p. 135), arguing that "the best way my race can win justice is by sticking together in progressive labor unions" (p. 135). Robeson also used his public profile to work successfully to influence presidents such as Franklin Roosevelt (whom he greatly admired) and Harry Truman (whom he criticized for his refusal to move on enacting antilynching laws) as well as supporting the progressive party movement of Henry Wallace.

Conclusion

Paul Robeson and John Ohliger were public intellectuals and cultural workers in the trenches. They started their careers well within their respective fields' mainstream institutions, and they gradually moved outside them as they refused to compromise. Both Robeson and Ohliger worked tirelessly to support grassroots organizing and practiced hope, even as events seemed to contradict their wishes. They framed their practices as extending true democracy, and they refused to have their interests and commitments bound by conventional boundaries.

What can we learn from Robeson's life that informs our understanding of John's? One is the importance of having a rationale for critique and practice. In Robeson's case, this was his lifelong commitment to socialism; in John's case, his commitment to radical democracy, which manifested itself in a trust in the wisdom of so-called ordinary people to help them make good decisions on matters that affect them. Another is the need always to ground critique in local action and specific situations, which for both meant endless travel to picket lines, union halls, and churches. A third is the belief that a well-lived life is not found wholly within the domain of rationalism, but involves emotion, affect, spirituality, and aesthetics. And a fourth is the conviction that capitalist practicality and efficiency are so dominant that we seem to have forgotten questions of merit and worth, questions that ask what purpose is served by being practical and what larger purpose is served by focusing on efficiency. Both men lived a questioning life, and both deserve proper attention from contemporary adult educators.

References

Coben, D. (1998). *Radical heroes: Gramsci, Freire and the politics of adult education*. New York: Garland.

Duberman, M. B. (1988). *Paul Robeson*. New York: Knopf.

Foner, P. (1978). Introduction. In P. Foner (Ed.), *Paul Robeson speaks: Writings, speeches, interviews, 1918–1974*. Larchmont, NY: Brunner/Mazel.

Freire, P. (1998). *Teachers as cultural workers: Letters to those who dare teach*. Boulder, CO: Westview Press.

Freire, P. (2004). *Pedagogy of hope: Reliving "Pedagogy of the oppressed."* New York: Continuum.

Holst, J. D. (2002). *Social movements, civil society, and radical adult education*. Westport, CT: Bergin & Garvey.

Hooks, B. (1989). *Talking back: Thinking feminist, thinking black*. Boston: South End Press.

Mayo, P. (1998). *Gramsci, Freire and adult education: Possibilities for transformative action*. New York: ZED Books.

Mezirow, J. (1991). *Transformative dimensions of adult learning*. San Francisco: Jossey-Bass.

Ohliger, J. (1967). *Listening groups: Mass media in adult education*. Boston: Center for the Study of Liberal Education for Adults.

Ohliger, J. (1974). Is lifelong education a guarantee of permanent inadequacy? *Convergence, 7*(2), 47–58.

Ohliger, J. (1997). [My search for freedom's song: Some notes for a memoir]. Third draft. Unpublished raw data.

Robeson, P. (1958). *Here I stand*. Boston: Beacon Press.

Robeson, P. (1978). *Paul Robeson speaks: Writings, speeches, interviews 1918–1974* (P. S. Foner, Ed.). New York: Brunner/Mazel.

Tough, A. (1979). *The adult's learning projects: A fresh approach to theory and practice in adult learning*. Toronto: Ontario Institute for Studies in Education.

Tough, A. (1982). *Intentional changes: A fresh approach to helping people change*. Chicago: Follett.

Tough, A. (2002). *The iceberg of informal adult learning*. New Approaches to Lifelong Learning Working Paper, no. 49. Toronto: NALL Research Network.

Williams, R. (1995). *The sociology of culture*. Chicago: University of Chicago.

Reflection
God Damn the Pushers

André P. Grace

As I read Brookfield's chapter, it was apparent that Paul Robeson and John Ohliger had a number of common characteristics. Both can be considered organic or public intellectuals who had reputations as confrontational outsiders, and both can be construed as politically naive as they attempted to mediate dominant U.S. social and cultural forces that had immobilizing effects on each of them. Robeson and Ohliger were social activists and cultural workers who shared an affinity for grassroots organizing. In this regard, each advocated for disenfranchised citizens whom they attempted to mobilize in the fight for social inclusion, cohesion, and justice across life domains, including education and work. Both men were leery of institutions whose structures abetted a dominant status quo with its entrenched binaries and hierarchies of power set up to maintain the subjugation of women, blacks, the poor, and other marginalized citizens. Each valued the power of the collective and situated learning in eclectic terms that highlighted the importance of popular culture.

Nevertheless, it seems to me that Paul Robeson and John Ohliger were still profoundly dissimilar. The ideologies to which each subscribed shaped their opposing politics and their contrasting views on citizenship and nation. John was a self-described radical liberal, which was the kind of social democrat he chose to be. However, the excesses of his personality often overshadowed the reality of his democratic politics. John's overt persona and his verbal tirades cast him as an angry, even acerbic educator and social commentator who was critical of his country, its institutions, and its growing imperialism after World War II. Yet underneath it all, John was a devoted American.

Robeson was not similarly devoted. He was a socialist with an affinity for the former Soviet Union, which he said he experienced as a nonracist state. As Brookfield relates, Robeson conflated the terms *socialist* and *democrat*. Of course, Robeson had only a tourist's view of the Soviet Union. As Brookfield indicates, Robeson saw Sovietism and internationalism as counterforces to the racism that he had experienced in the United States. Brookfield also notes that Robeson refused to see any dark side linking Sovietism to the repression of individuals. One can construe that Robeson's Soviet leanings, coupled with his overwhelming experience of racism in the United States, constituted blinders to the reality of Soviet forms of oppression and imperialism. Thus, Robeson was not concerned with interrogating Soviet politics in ways that might expose Sovietism (or a version like Stalinism) as forms of socialism gone awry. After reading Brookfield's account, I wondered whether Robeson had ever considered the geopolitical and ethnocultural complexities of the republics comprising the Soviet Union, complexities that would have made him aware of repressive forces embedded in Sovietism.

As a dissenter, Ohliger was different from the pro-Soviet Robeson. He was attracted to contemporary rebel educators who worked toward democracy as a political ideal of modernity. Criticalist Paulo Freire and fellow radical liberals Ivan Illich and Everett Reimer were key influences. Ohliger (1989) contrasted such resistance educators with mainstream educators of adults who reduced education and learning to technicism without hope: "Worthwhile alternative or off-center educators are more tentative and eschew bliss about the future for the steady stare at the present. Mainstream protagonists foster the enhancement and extrapolation of present dominant technological trends, for instance, the so-called knowledge explosion, the information revolution, or the specter of human obsolescence" (p. 630).

In his quest to revitalize social democracy and reclaim adult education as social education, John (1972) drew on the theorizing and perspectives on practice found in the books these rebels wrote in the early 1970s: Illich's *Deschooling Society* (1971), Reimer's *School Is Dead* (1971), and Freire's *Pedagogy of the Oppressed* (1972). Ohliger (1972) saw each nonconformist educator as a proponent of resistance pedagogy and a "humanistic revolution" since all opted "for new avenues of political and cultural action which should result in a completely different range of meanings for the very concept of learning" (p. 190). These affiliations help to situate John as a social democrat who valued both radical and liberal ideologies. Indeed Ohliger's life's work was to reinvigorate the social to meet the needs of everyday people as free citizens in a democracy. As his memoirs indicate, ordinary people from his past, notably his father, influenced John in this quest (Ohliger, 1997). Growing up during the Great Depression, Ohliger had witnessed his father's demoralizing struggle with unemployment and the deep impact this had had on his family. He provided this reflection in his memoirs:

> After the war [World War I] my father became a very successful insurance agent, selling a million dollars worth of insurance a year up to 1925, when for some still unknown reason he lost the agency. . . . When I was born in the midst of this turmoil in 1926, my father was driving a horse-drawn bakery truck. He never held a "real" job for the rest of his life, except during the Second World War, when he was a security guard. . . . Since my father was essentially without a job in Detroit from before the "Great Depression" to the beginning of the Second World War, we had to move frequently because we often had no money for the rent [Ohliger, 1997, Part 1, pp. 6–8].

In addition to experiencing the social denial of the Great Depression during his early years, John grew up amid the catastrophic destruction of World War II. He graduated from high school in 1944, was drafted into the U.S. Army in 1945, and spent the next three years in the former West Germany. There he fulfilled roles as an information specialist, a newspaper reporter, a writer, and an adult educator of soldiers. During this time, the global response to compounding social devastation was to restructure nations and international relations among them in ways that protected the capitalist order that had been under siege since the Great Depression (Harvey, 2005). In this milieu, the United States emerged as a liberal democracy with military might and a global reach in influence (Harvey, 2005). More specifically, the nation functioned within a political-economic arrangement usually labeled "embedded liberalism" to indicate that market activity was subject to social and political constraints and state regulation (Harvey, 2005, p. 11). John the liberal could value the welfare state that this arrangement produced to advance the social. John the radical, however, contested any erosion or manipulation of the ideals of liberal democracy, especially any aberration from the ideal of public responsibility for education and other social benefits. While the United States and other advanced capitalist countries thrived economically under embedded liberalism during the 1950s and 1960s, these nations also experienced the uncertainty of the Cold War and internal and social upheaval in diverse forms (Harvey, 2005). The insecurity left in the wake of these phenomena deeply concerned John as he worked to nurture community and ethical practices in learning and work contexts. In this work, Ohliger (1969) viewed action and education as inextricably linked pathways to freedom. From John's perspective, a liberal arts education was integral to the reality and practice of freedom: responsible action required knowledge of civil rights, civil liberties, and the contexts enabling or denying freedom. As well, a liberal arts education was necessary to prepare individuals to know what to do with freedom and to ensure that freedom is for all.

John completed doctoral studies at the University of California in 1966 and spent the next year in Canada before becoming a faculty member in academic adult education at Ohio State University. He left that institution in 1973 after a brief tenure. Ohliger had always been an unwavering proponent of adult education as social education, which he felt should be voluntary in nature. He left academe because he had grown disillusioned with the escalating professionalization and commodification of adult education to the point that he could not remain part of the emerging field of study. In a speech that he gave at the University of Saskatchewan in March 1974, Ohliger focused on the trend toward more pronounced professionalization of adult education. He castigated "life-long education pushers" who took the joy out of learning by making adults permanently dependent on lifelong learning (Carlson, 1977, p. 59). Carlson highlights other points from the speech in which John located professionalization as a way to formalize and thus tame adult education. For example, John emphasized that the increasingly professionalized field had reduced knowledge to approved, official knowledge produced, packaged, and marketed by experts usually serving particular interests. As he linked professionalization to "coordination, efficiency, narrow definitions, [transactional] leadership, compulsion, the extension of schooling, certification, accreditation, and licensing" (Carlson, 1977, p. 60), Ohliger challenged adult educators to think long and hard about the impact of professionalization on the field of study and practice and, concomitantly, on learner freedom, choice, and independence. John's consistent concern with learner freedom tied to what he perceived as the need for humanistic revolution go to the heart of his radical liberal view of democracy. As Carlson (1972) relates elsewhere, Ohliger challenged the use of new technology as method in the field's professional turn, concluding this was just another attempt to control the human spirit and lessen opportunities for freedom and growth that had long been the goal of adult education as social education.

The turn to professionalization in the field of study and practice was perhaps a harbinger of things to come under neoliberalism, which Ohliger also critiqued as an assault on democracy. As Harvey

(2005) relates, by the late 1970s, neoliberalism had emerged as an alternative ideology and practice in various advanced capitalist countries plagued by fiscal crises and seemingly uncontrollable high unemployment and inflation. Harvey describes neoliberalism as "a theory of political economic practices that [sidelines the social and] proposes that human well-being can best be advanced by liberating individual entrepreneurial freedoms and skills within an institutional framework [set up to enhance worker performance and productivity to drive economies]" (Harvey, 2005, p. 2). Ohliger (1980) recognized the emerging and wide impact of neoliberalism when he located adult education as a field of study and practice within "an advanced high technology society characterized externally by the expansion of multinational corporations, and internally by the increasing integration of government, industry, and education" (p. 48). Technological advancement and the forces that enable it continue to mark neoliberalism as both an ideology and a practice that favors the economic and the instrumental over the social and the cultural in shaping citizens as learners, workers, and members of communities. John spoke to the fate of education in this neoliberal milieu that favors a technocratic transformation of society at the expense of the liberal purposes of enlightening and humanizing students:

> If life in modern society is defined in technological terms, and techniques appear to be constantly changing and developing, [then] education will be swept up in the same vortex of change and development. Furthermore, if the government, corporate, and professional institutions created to produce and control these techniques grow apace and if access to the fruits of technology is only gained through these organizations, [then] education becomes [technicized and] almost totally dependent on this process [p. 49].

In the face of this erosion of liberal education and the need to accelerate the quest for "a more humanizing and democratic way of life" (p. 53), Ohliger called on adult educators to help adults respond to and cope with the social and cultural problems that neoliberalism leaves in its wake. He challenged adult educators to engage in a reflexive practice in which they critically question present directions and future possibilities for life, civility, learning, and work. Moreover, he challenged them to be activists who work with learners to solve community problems and change their basic, everyday situations. John stated that this was what he tried to do through his organization, Basic Choices, "in the attempt to help groups to better understand and respond to the social context in which they live" (p. 52). In his critique of neoliberalism, John emphasized social inclusion, cohesion, and justice, and he adamantly resisted lifelong educational pushers who reduced individual freedom to freedom to learn instrumentally. He also deplored the invasion of the market into education, which he linked to the institutionalization of learning. In a real sense, what John deplored is what Harvey (2005) calls the *creative destruction* of the social and the institutional supports that contribute to its integrity:

> The process of neoliberalization has . . . entailed much "creative destruction," not only of prior institutional frameworks and powers (even challenging traditional forms of state sovereignty) but also of divisions of labour, social relations, welfare provisions, technological mixes, ways of life and thought, reproductive activities, attachments to the land and habits of the heart [Harvey, 2005, p. 3].

In this creative destruction of the social, Ohliger (1983) recognized the limited and arbitrary institutional power of education when compared to the overarching power of governments and multinational corporations. In his critique of lifelong education, he reduced its emerging practice to a neoliberal means to achieve economic ends. He spoke to its institutionalization when he stated that lifelong education's "most salient focus is the formalizing education dimension of professionalism" (p. 162). He concluded, "In the zealous pursuit of lifelong education, liberty has been left behind and with it much of the modest but real value of education itself" (p. 161). Speaking to the increasing technicism that accompanied increasing professionalism, Ohliger bemoaned the technocratic liberalism embodied in neoliberalism that suggested technology and information technology free workers to take their place in contemporary national and global capitalist economies. He declared, "The gut-level feeling of freedom in everyday life is lost in a welter of [techno-liberal] claims" (p. 163) that tie liberty to corporatism and economic development. Again, Ohliger laid considerable blame on academic adult educators who had bought into professionalism, succumbed to the hegemony of corporatism in education, and pushed lifelong education as a way out. He asserted, "Those [academics] who live at the crest of institutionalized adult education . . . want to show those with their hands on greater levels of power [in governments and multinational corporations] that they are on their side" (p. 163). John detested such pandering. Over the years, he was unrelenting in his critique of academics who enabled the corporate infiltration of universities. In a reflection on higher education "going corporate" (p. 15) during the 1990s, Ohliger (1999) expounded on the educational and financial harm done to individuals as he linked public dissatisfaction with academe to the corporatism that interfered with a primary academic function: to make society more humane. Indeed the intrusion of corporatism into U.S. higher education has become even more pronounced since John wrote his reflection. Roosevelt (2006) provides testament in this summary:

> One of the most striking phenomena in American higher education today is the proliferation of for-profit colleges and universities. Structured as large corporate entities, many of the new for-profit colleges and universities operate like commercial businesses, issue shares of stock that are traded on the stock exchange, and respond to the same competitive market forces that affect other private companies. And they have been highly successful [p. 1].

These for-profit educational institutions explicitly focus on student preparation for jobs into today's global marketplace. Roosevelt argues that this commercialization of higher education and the concomitant decline in liberal education limit politics to a neoliberal discourse that favors market performance over civic life. Her perspective echoes what John had been saying for several decades.

Throughout his lifetime, John resisted processes like professionalization and corporatization that he felt contributed to making education undemocratic. He consistently affirmed liberal education as a way to empower learners and give them the tools to gain and protect their freedom. John's affinity for liberal education is no doubt tied to the value he placed on it during his formative years as a graduate student, educator, and practitioner, which coincided with the golden age of liberal education in the United States (1955–1970). Roosevelt (2006) describes this period as a time when higher education underwent tremendous growth, liberal curricula enjoyed stability, and the Cold War gave relevance to many tenets and concepts of liberal ideology. It was a time when freedom to learn was a mantra tied to living out democratic ideals.

Today, liberal education is remembered "as having an ethos that contrasted with and in some ways counteracted the ethos of the marketplace" (Roosevelt, 2006, p. 3). Perhaps a contemporary turn to liberal education might help revitalize civic life by involving students in a critically reflexive engagement with corporatism, commercialization, privatization, and other change forces. Indeed with market forces infiltrating higher education to the point that the education provided is limited, exclusionary, and lopsided in favor of technology, information technology, and all things instrumental, Roosevelt (2006) suggests that we may be observing such a turn in the complex U.S. history of liberal education. She relates that the American Association for Colleges and Universities and the Carnegie Foundation for the Advancement of Teaching have affirmed the necessity of liberal education to address the pronounced lack of civic engagement in contemporary U.S. society. This revitalization of liberal education for the present moment would include "a new focus on social responsibility and civic engagement, particularly in the form of diversity studies, global knowledge, and service learning" (p. 5). It would engage students in critical thinking and complex problem solving, the hallmarks of liberal education in action. Ohliger would have welcomed this anticipated return to a revitalized liberal education, which has the potential to bring education and action together to help people solve civic problems in the quest to make a better world.

References

Axton, H. (2004, April 20). The pusher. On *Flashes of fire—Hoyt's very best 1962–1990*. [Audio CD]. East Ivanhoe, Victoria, Australia: Raven Records.

Carlson, R. A. (1972). Accent on social philosophy: Coming of age philosophically. *Adult Leadership, 21*(3), 124.

Carlson, R. A. (1977). Professionalization of adult education: Historical philosophical analysis. *Adult Education, 28*(1), 53–63.

Freire, P. (1972). *Pedagogy of the oppressed*. New York: Herder & Herder. (Translated from the original Portuguese manuscript, 1968)

Harvey, D. (2005). *A brief history of neoliberalism*. New York: Oxford University Press.

Illich, I. (1971). *Deschooling society*. New York: HarperCollins.

Ohliger, J. (1969). Adult basic education programs and the liberal arts approach. *Adult Leadership, 17*(10), 417–419.

Ohliger, J. (1972). The visible dissenters. *Educational Studies, 3*(4), 187–191.

Ohliger, J. (1980). The social uses of theorizing in adult education. *Adult Education, 31*(1), 48–53.

Ohliger, J. (1983). Reconciling education with liberty. *Prospects, 13*(2), 161–179.

Ohliger, J. (1989). Alternative images of the future in adult education. In P. Cunningham & S. Merriam (Eds.), *Handbook of adult and continuing education* (pp. 628–639). San Francisco: Jossey-Bass.

Ohliger, J. (1997). [My search for freedom's song: Some notes for a memoir]. Third draft. Unpublished raw data.

Ohliger, J. (1999). Crises in higher education, 1991–98. *College Daze*, no. 1, 15–27.

Reimer, E. (1971). *School is dead: Alternatives in education*. New York: Doubleday.

Roosevelt, G. (2006). The triumph of the market and the decline of liberal education: Implications for civic life. *Teachers College Record*. Retrieved September 5, 2008, from http://www.tcrecord.org/PrintContent.asp?ContentID.

17

John Ohliger's Legacy to Building Social Democracy
WORTS and All

Christina (Chris) Wagner

Editors' note: Originally we had intended to give John the last word in this book. With his passing during the writing of this book, the human and personal side of this radical liberal scholar, social instigator, and communicator extraordinaire is now portrayed through the eyes of his wife, Chris. Her reminiscences of John bring his life into focus as she shares her stories of the man, the educator, and his everyday life. Chris recounts John's abilities to connect with people in deep and meaningful ways, and she reveals snippets of his relationships with his contemporaries. She also revisits his critique of mandatory continuing education and his outreach to citizens as learners and workers through Basic Choices and WORT radio.

John's Gifts: Memories of My Husband as Friend, Mentor, Colleague, and Activist Educator

One of my earliest, fondest, and most vivid memories of John is the way he spoke of his friends, coworkers, and colleagues. John enunciated each person's name clearly and sung it out, as if announcing the name of a person of great importance. Indeed, I remember thinking that John must only know "important" people such as academics, published authors, and icons of various social movements. It took me a couple of years of getting to know John and his wide circle of friends and colleagues to learn that although many of John's friends did indeed fit my narrow definition of "important person," many more did not. Yet John spoke of each of them with the same respect and appreciation, not to mention love and acceptance.

When John connected with someone, he saw and frequently nurtured a seed of greatness in each of them. He made each person feel special at various times, not because he puffed them up or encouraged vanity of any kind, but because he valued their ideas, opinions, and life quests. John saw beyond the traditional trappings of status, money, and power. Whether his friend was a janitor or a gas station attendant, a housewife or a part-time student, a university professor or a social activist, unemployed or idle rich, John's interest or opinion was not affected. Perhaps that was because he loved discussing and, as others will attest, arguing about philosophies, opinions, theories, and countertheories. John recognized that everyone had ideas worth sharing and discussing, and outer trappings of status and power had very little to do with the profundity and value of anyone's ideas. In fact sometimes those trappings stood in the way of a person's ability to reach into his or her soul and pull out these thoughts.

John was like a magician in his ability to engage someone in the discussion of ideas, and he never tired of it. Indeed he never tired of listening completely, responding thoughtfully, and listening again. His gift was that he could pull other people's gifts from his magician's hat. That is one of the things that made him a truly great educator. This gift called from deep within his soul when he ran the bookmobile in the auto factories for the Michigan Congress of Industrial Organizations, when he traveled from city to city five days a week as a part of the Great Books Program, when he helped to start a radio station (WORT), and when he sat down and had a conversation with a friend.

WORTS and All

When John was toying with possible titles for his autobiography, he thought about calling it "WORTS and All." Since the call letters for the radio station he helped to start were W-O-R-T, it was, of course, a play on words. And he loved words! However, more than just including the name of his beloved radio station, he liked the title because it reflected a strong belief that he held: any biography, auto- or otherwise, must include the ugly warts we all have, the mistakes we have made, the wrong paths we have taken, and the hurt we have caused.

John carried a lot of pain in his heart; it was part of what made him so easily hurt. The hurt came from mistakes he had made. It also came from the hurt he caused as well as the hurt others had caused him. John felt that to leave out the warts because they were embarrassing or regretful was dishonest, because they are an essential part of who we are. For example, I remember John's anger after spending a lot of time helping a student who was writing a paper about Ivan Illich. When the paper came out, John saw that it was clearly a puff piece, totally laudatory, with nothing negative about the person or his journey. John was furious because he had provided what he perceived as the good, the bad, and the ugly about Illich. John loved Illich—loved him as a thinker, a writer, and an instigator. More importantly, he loved him as a soulmate and a friend. John shared many "Illich" stories with me: of a morning when he had been sick, and Ivan made him breakfast in bed; and of the time when Ivan came to Madison and spoke in the crowded hall in Pres House, a building that the Presbyterian church owned on the University of Wisconsin, Madison, campus. He wore a large flowing cape, as if he had just emerged from the Middle Ages. John dreamed about Ivan at least once a year for many years after visiting him several times in Cuernavaca. He knew that one could neither understand Ivan nor claim to know the real Ivan if one heard only the good side. And he felt the same way about himself.

It was ironic and a source of great sadness for John that when Ivan Illich died in 2002, the obituary in the *New York Times* was so mean spirited, so opposite the puff piece that John had been angry about the student writing (Martin, 2002, p. A29). John grieved not only for his dear friend, but also for a life that was misunderstood in the end (or so it seemed from the obituary). Fortunately, the *New York Times* does not have the last word, so perhaps there will someday be a balanced account of the life and work of Illich. I remember many years ago, John said that he secretly wished he would have a life that would merit an obituary in the *New York Times*. After Illich's obituary was published, I think he no longer wanted that anymore.

I think it is also ironic that a big reason that John was so well loved by so many people came not from his good side, but from what he perceived as his bad side, from his understanding of what he perceived to be his own life mistakes. John would readily admit that he had made many mistakes on his life path. Despite the fact that he would sometimes repeat a pattern—some would say make the same mistake again—he also learned from his mistakes, although maybe not in a conventional way. What John learned was not necessarily how to avoid repeating a mistake. Instead he learned to understand the power of certain forces to shape our lives regardless of our desire and hard work to suppress or destroy them. His understanding of the contradictions in each of our lives is a part of what made him a great listener, a good friend, and a wise confidant. He also had the ability to laugh—to see the humor in life's lessons and contradictions.

Education as the Freedom to Explore Ideas

"How One Man Saved the Field of Lifelong Learning" (2004) was an article that praised John greatly with words like "one of the foremost adult educators of the 20th century," "almost single handedly defeated mandatory continuing education (MCE)," "saving the field of lifelong learning," and "we owe John Ohliger a great debt for defending voluntary learning" (p. 20). However, I do not think John felt that he saved adult education from the hungry jaws of MCE at all. In fact, he felt that he had most decidedly lost the battle, although he did not regret having fought it. John did hope that his work would have an impact on other individuals who have gone on to make a difference in the field of adult education and elsewhere. I believe that he was aware of the impact that he had on many such individuals and that he was gently and quietly proud of it.

John had little faith in traditional ways of measuring so-called professional standards. He thought that if a teacher worked hard in her classroom, did her own continuing education through reading and discussion (or whatever method she chose), and was a great teacher, no compulsory class or mandatory test was needed. John believed in a gentleperson's agreement among colleagues in any profession that made these other forms of professional measurement unnecessary. As always, John favored professional integrity over professional development.

After John died, I spent some time looking his name up on the Internet. Two sites—http://users.sisna.com/bskene/world1.htm and www.hesston.edu—posted one of my favorite quotes from John: "When we impose ideas on people, we train them. When we create an atmosphere in which people are free to explore ideas in dialogue and through interactions with other people, we educate them" (originally in Ohliger, 1970, p. 250). This quote sums up John's beliefs about education as succinctly and accurately as a brief statement could. John often joked that an adult educator was someone who knew how to arrange chairs in a circle. Of course, that is symbolic of what he did best: create an environment in which people felt inspired and free to talk about any topic as self-directed and collegial learners. John often told me that he was not a good teacher, which meant that traditional lecturing was not his best skill. He certainly did not like things like grading either. Still, his students really loved him and learned so much, I think, because he encouraged them to question and explore the subject before them. He made learning joyous, individual, and voluntary. By individual, I do not mean solitary. I mean that each person found his or her own path in exploring a topic.

The Life in a Day of John Ohliger

When working with John on the Illich files, I came across a delightful article entitled "The Life in a Day of Ivan Illich," which had appeared in the British journal *Teacher* (Myer, 1971, p. 6). I want to tell you about the life in a day of John Ohliger, about the man who bicycled all over the city of Madison, Wisconsin, oblivious to the weather. Sometimes he traveled around Lake Monona and other times even Lake Mendota—a four-hour tour. John was a man who enjoyed a good dinner and a great beer—the more unusual, the better. He always had a book in his hand—sometimes two or three. Most of all, he enjoyed a good talk with friends about anything and everything—philosophical, political, or personal.

John and I met when I reviewed a book for "The Madison Review of Books," a show that he started and hosted for years on WORT radio. John recorded the review on April 1, 1977, as I sat in a chair in his bedroom, which doubled as his makeshift studio. Joanie, my boss at the Rape Crisis Center and a committed WORT leader, had assured me that John was a really nice man when I expressed some consternation about the location of his recording studio. John was kind, offering me a glass of water and telling me to speak slowly and clearly as we recorded the review. He told me about Basic Choices, a project that he was working on. Later, he sent me a letter telling me about it. I responded to it, and on our first date we went to see the movie *Annie Hall*. On another date, I remember eating Chinese food with him at a restaurant on Park Street and seeing a double rainbow as we left the restaurant. It seemed like a sign. Our friendship took different turns and eventually blossomed into love. John often did little things that brought us closer together. Once I opened my apartment door to find a

Christmas package—a blank book with my name as author engraved on the front. I had wanted to write a book about social work history, and this was his way of encouraging me.

I remember spending many afternoons with John leafleting for a political candidate, preparing the Basic Choices newsletter *Second Thoughts* for mailing, picketing, marching, protesting, and writing letters to the editor—all the usual things that you might expect to do with John. I also remember sitting in a hot, mosquito-filled room trying to save the "The Madison Review of Books" and another offbeat show from being thrown off WORT radio. We lost that battle, but it was neither the last battle we fought together nor lost together. Despite that loss, I feel that one of John's major accomplishments was helping to start and maintain WORT radio as a truly community-run station. John gave one of his best speeches ever, a speech about the early days of WORT, at the twentieth-anniversary celebration of the radio station. On its twenty-fifth anniversary, John received a well-deserved award at the WORT-FM annual station meeting (Ohliger, 1994).

Before I moved to Springfield, Illinois, in 1988 to take a job as a librarian, John left Madison for short periods of time to teach and lecture. Once he went to Australia on a speaking tour. I missed John a lot, although I spoke to him almost every day. After John and I were married on May 6, 1989, he joined me in Springfield. Despite missing Madison, John accomplished much during his years in Springfield. He was involved with the local co-op, local alternative media, and a small bookstore. I had lived in Springfield for eight months before John joined me, and I had made few connections in the community. By contrast, John seemed to connect completely with many groups and dozens of individuals in a matter of a few weeks. He found work at the Southern Illinois University Medical School Library in the interlibrary loan department and taught a philosophy of education course at Sangamon State University (now the University of Illinois at Springfield). Once his students told me they worried about my having a much older husband. However, one day John got up in class and informed the students that I had insisted he iron his shirt before going to class. After that, they told me that they did not worry about me anymore.

While we lived in Springfield, John was active in protests against the Gulf War. He had been firmly and consistently against all military action since his days at Ohio State University, when he was faculty advisor to Veterans Against the (Vietnam) War. I would worry the night before a Gulf War demonstration that something might happen to him, and I would not feel relieved until he would come by the library to let me know the demonstration was over. During this time, John and I were involved in helping Doug Kamholz and others to start the Heartland Peace Center. John helped to arrange several seminars at Lincoln Library, the public library where I worked, about Islam, the war, and the difficulties that the local Muslim community faced as a result of the Gulf War.

John's commitment to social justice made him a target of the Federal Bureau of Investigation (FBI). From 1992 to 1996, John tried many times to get a copy of his FBI records as a Freedom of Information Act request. Finally, with the help of an attorney, he received the file—incomplete and expurgated, of course. We were both amazed about how much information (and misinformation) the FBI had collected about John. At one point, the FBI wrongly perceived that John was living in the KPFK-FM radio studio where he worked in Los Angeles. Another report indicated that John's radio shows included not just news commentaries but poetry! Interestingly, I recently came across a newsletter of KPFA, another radio station where John once worked. In it is a picture of John with the caption: "The man who put the quotes around the Cuban crisis, John Ohliger. He now waxes socially significant at KPFK in Los Angeles" (KPFA Radio Station, 1963, p. 14). I also found this insight from John in the newsletter, which I think explains why he, as an adult educator, was so interested and involved in community radio: "KPFA is only accidentally a radio station. Essentially, it is one embodiment of the idea that education is a process of growth never-ending until at the last minute we either turn to the wall in disgust or ask for more light" (p. 3).

Being in Springfield also gave us an opportunity to meet with people who lived in the area or were traveling through. Being between Chicago and St. Louis, this happened more frequently than one might imagine. When we moved into our apartment—the first story of an old house once owned by a congressman who voted against World War I—John thought maybe we should get a guest book for people to sign when they visited us. One of these visitors, Frank Adams—who wrote *Unearthing Seeds of Fire: The Idea of Highlander* with Myles Horton (1975)—came and talked about the Highlander Research and Education Center, past and present, and, of course, politics. Another visitor, Betty Lindeman Leonard, visited us from Champaign-Urbana. John helped her in the editing and publishing of her wonderful book, *Friendly Rebel* (1991), about her father, influential social educator Eduard Lindeman (1926/1961), who wrote *The Meaning of Adult Education*. Lee Hoinacki (n.d.) who had worked with Ivan Illich at his institute in Cuernavaca, Mexico, and lived in southern Illinois, also came to visit us on occasion. Lee and John would talk about Illich, his current writings, his health issues, and his rocky relationships with supporters.

Since John and I both missed Madison, we decided to leave Springfield, where John had spent three years and I had spent nearly four. Our first seven years back in Madison were spent in an apartment on the far west side. During this time, John worked hard on his writing. As well, these were the years when e-mail and the Internet took off in a major way. They were also the years in which John went to Iowa City several summers in a row to teach a class to adult education workers. He loved those summer classes! He also went to a week-long course at the Iowa Summer Writing Festival in 1997 and began work on his memoir.

In 2000, we finally bought a little house in Bay Creek, a neighborhood in Madison with a view of Monona Bay, the area John loved so much. He felt that he had finally come home. He loved the view of the bay from our front window. During the first two years we lived there, John enjoyed biking and walking in the neighborhood. As his health declined in the last year we lived there, his walks became shorter and fewer, and he stopped biking altogether. During this time, John was informed that he would be inducted into the International Adult and Continuing Education Hall of Fame housed at the University of Oklahoma. John was not feeling well enough for the event in April 2002, which was held in Toronto. The Hall of Fame committee arranged for us to participate by speaker phone. We had our own mini-gala event in Madison, with several dear friends and colleagues surrounding us on this momentous occasion. Despite John's mixed feelings about fame, I know that it was generally a proud and happy event for him.

My memory of the last months of John's life is still cloudy. His rapid decline was apparently obvious to everyone but me. Of course, I knew that he napped more, worked less, and generally was not in the best of health. However, I did not perceive these changes as the warning signs that they were. I thought of his decline as slow and gradual, imagining many years ahead for us. I remember him walking around the house with a book in one hand and his beloved cat, Boo, clinging under one arm. I remember him reading in his favorite chair with Boo on his lap, and a beer or a glass of Vernor's ginger ale and a bag of peanuts by his side. He dressed in his soft green robe and funny blue cap, which he wore because his head was always cold. However, I do not want to concentrate on this time, but on some of the better times.

I remember four times when John was feeling better than usual during the last year of his life. The first time was when Bertell Ollman, author of *How to Take an Exam . . . and Remake the World* (2001), came to Madison and spoke at Rainbow Books in the spring of 2003. John was very involved in arranging his visit and introduced him to the audience, which overflowed the small bookstore. I think John called him an oxymoron—a Marxist with a sense of humor. John seemed to rally a second time when we had a big party at our house to celebrate a colleague's graduation and new job. The third memorable day was the small party for John's seventy-seventh birthday in November 2003. I remember John saying to me in the kitchen, "I'm happy." The fourth good day was when he traveled with two friends a couple hours north of Madison on a cold January night to hear John Taylor Gatto, author of *Dumbing Us Down: The Hidden Curriculum of Compulsory Schooling* (2002) and *A Different Kind of Teacher: Solving the Crisis of American Schooling* (2001). Having been named Teacher of the Year three times in New York City, Gatto left teaching and started to speak and write about the damage the public school system does to children. He greeted John as a trusted old friend. I believe that they were parallel forces for voluntary education, Gatto for youth and Ohliger for adults.

Sometime between Christmas and his death on January 25, 2004, John received a call from a friend who asked him to meet with a man who was coming to Madison to look into the possibility of attending graduate school at the University of Wisconsin. Despite the fact that John was ill, he enthusiastically agreed to do so. He spent a cold January afternoon on campus with this man who, by the way, was in his seventies.

Just a few days before that trek, John received a call from a friend who wanted to stop and visit as he passed through Madison. I happened to be home that day, and much to my surprise, John told me that he would like to entertain his guest in the bedroom. He said he did not feel well enough to get up. I served them tea and cookies, not realizing just how sick John was. I could hear the conversation, largely one-sided, as the visitor poured out his heart to John. As usual, John listened and responded with his trademark warmth and support.

These last two memories capture the generous educator and benevolent man that John was. John had a sincere respect and interest in the ideas and struggles of those he met, and he enhanced people's lives by his quiet but mindful listening and thoughtful responses. This was his greatest gift.

Before concluding, I want to take a moment to talk about John and his relationship with religion. John, a long-time Unitarian, joined Trinity United Methodist Church with me after we moved to the Bay Creek neighborhood. In his heart, though, he was still a Unitarian. He told me a few months before he died that he was not "anything," that the best way to describe his religious philosophy was sententiousness. I never wholly believed that. A conspectus of what he believed is perhaps captured in this quote from Annie Besant (circa 1874, source unknown), which John had pasted on the front of his Internet address book: "Varieties of opinion about God are valuable, not mischievous, because each opinion by itself expresses so small a fragment of the mighty truth, and the totality of opinion gives a fuller presentation than could otherwise be gained."

John once told me that when he was a young man, his maternal grandmother wrote to him, asking if he might want to be a minister. John's maternal grandfather had been a Presbyterian minister. In his reply to her, John wrote that he did not know if he believed in God. She quickly wrote back that it did not matter; he could still do much good as a minister. Her reply astonished him. It also foreshadowed the mark he would leave on the world. John did have a calling, and he responded to it wholeheartedly. It was a spiritual calling, as much as any ministry is. He gave of himself generously to countless individuals. His teaching and writing have left a lasting mark on the field of adult education and will continue to guide educators for many years to come.

Postscript: From Bibliographer to Blogger?

John was well known in adult education circles for his thorough and informative bibliographies, including his signature "quotational bibliographies." Had he lived a few more years, I believe he would have quickly added blogging to his repertoire for communicating with others in the world of adult education. Certainly, he was involved in a pre-Internet form of blogging, which he called a multilogue. It involved a group of people who exchanged letters in regard to a previously agreed-on topic. John and some of his colleagues engaged in an extensive multilogue on some of the writings of Ivan Illich.

John did live long enough to see the potential of the Internet for creating blogs as a new forum for discussing important ideas. One of the last wishes he expressed to me was his desire to have a Web site for Basic Choices. Although we lacked money and expertise to complete this project, it was really the rapid decline in health that prevented this task from happening until after his death.

The Web site I have created for John (www.johnohliger.org) includes his published and unpublished writings dating back to the earliest writings I can find. I have also posted articles about John, as well as the complete text of *Second Thoughts*, the newsletter of Basic Choices. In addition, I have added selected columns from *Adult and Continuing Education Today*, transcripts of John's speeches, links to other Web sites, and more. This Web site is a work in progress, as John was a prolific writer. Suggestions for additions or changes are welcome as the project continues to unfold.

References

Adams, F. T., & Horton, M. (1975). *Unearthing seeds of fire: The idea of Highlander*. Winston-Salem, NC: J. F. Blair.

Gatto, J. T. (2001). *A different kind of teacher: Solving the crisis of American schooling*. Berkeley, CA: Berkeley Hills Books.

Gatto, J. T. (2002). *Dumbing us down: The hidden curriculum of compulsory schooling*. Philadelphia: New Society Publishers.

Hoinacki, L. (n.d.). *Lee Hoinacki*. Retrieved August 11, 2005, from http://www.wtp.org/ bios/ hoinackibio.html.

How one man saved the field of lifelong learning. (2004, August). *LERN Magazine*, p. 20.

KFPA Radio Station. (1963, April 18–23). *KFPA program folio*. Los Angeles: Author.

Lindeman, E. C. (1926/1961). *The meaning of adult education*. Montreal: Harvest House.

Lindeman Leonard, B. (1991). *Friendly rebel: A personal and social history of Eduard C. Lindeman*. Adamant, VT: Adamant Press.

Martin, D. (2002, December 4). Ivan Illich, 76: Philosopher who challenged status quo is dead. *New York Times*, p. A29.

Myer, V. G. (1971, October 29). The life in a day of Ivan Illich. *Teacher*, 110.

Ohliger, J. (1970). Accent on social philosophy: Dialogue with myself. *Adult Leadership*, 18(8), 250, 265.

Ohliger, J. (1994). *The early days at back porch radio*. From a speech delivered at the 1994 WORT-FM annual station meeting. Retrieved May 30, 2005, from http://www.wort-fm.org/station/history1.htm.

Ollman, B. (2001). *How to take an exam . . . and remake the world*. Montreal: Black Rose Books.

Reflection

Honoring People, Valuing Ideas, Honoring John

André P. Grace

During the summer of 1987, John Ohliger conducted a seminar with his colleague and dear friend Phyllis M. Cunningham as part of the Syracuse University Kellogg Project. They titled their seminar Radical Thinking in Adult Education, which inspired a later publication with the same name (Cunningham & Ohliger, 1989). One paper they wrote for the seminar opens with a provocative quote that constitutes C. Wright Mills's conclusion to "Mass Society and Liberal Education," a speech he gave in 1954 under the sponsorship of the Center for the Study of Liberal Education for Adults. Mills concluded:

> For publics that really want to know the realities of their communities and nation and world are, by that determining fact, politically radical. Politics as we know it today often rests upon myths and lies and crackpot notions; and many policies, debated and undebated, assume inadequate and misleading definitions of reality. When such myth and hokum prevail, those who are out to find the truth are bound to be upsetting. . . . The role of education, especially of education for adults, is to build and sustain publics that will "go for," and develop, and live with, and act upon adequate definitions of reality [Cunningham & Ohliger, 1989, p. vi].

Like his kindred spirit Cunningham, Ohliger can be characterized as a radical adult educator who sought the truth and was upsetting. Throughout his lengthy career as an adult educator, social activist, and cultural worker, Ohliger joined "with [socially conscious] others to nondogmatically reassert the personal and social necessity for vigorous and fundamental—certainly radical—transformation" (Cunningham & Ohliger, 1989, p. viii). He did this as an eclectic organic intellectual who was "enchanted with words, melodies, expressions, ideas, thoughts, books, cats, protesting, causes, campaigning, picketing, agitating, snowfalls, and the ineffable, plus the friendly light from the sky and the lakes surrounding Madison, Wisconsin" (Ohliger, 1997, part 1, p. 3).

Ohliger used his sixtieth birthday on November 11, 1986, to reflect on his radical role and its fragility and limits in relation to the politics of his location:

> As long as I can remember I have been an injustice collector. But collecting intimate personal injustices or the gross social ones has never been enough. I also felt I needed to identify with groups that are obviously oppressed—the proletariat, ethnic groups, Blacks, women—to become one with, and of, them. For many years I was a fervent activist in various civil rights organizations. But I was always reminded, "You can leave us anytime you want to, because you are not irrevocably one of us." Since my motive for identifying with them was partly my compulsion to collect injustices, that reminder always spoiled my hidden pleasure [Ohliger, 1997, part 3, p. 1].

Toward the end of his life, John wrote, "I'm in the middle of my 75th year, not in the best of health including memory problems, but still a readaholic opposed to book worship. I now see myself as a sententious meliorist" (e-mail correspondence, Basic Choices' mailing list, March 3, 2002). This self-description, which he had also shared with his wife, Chris, seems apt for this passionate yet prickly adult educator who believed that human effort could make a better world. To this end, Ohliger spent his life challenging adult educators to fight for democracy, freedom, and social justice. He wanted adult educators to be more radical change agents, working against the grain of a field of study and practice that he felt had lost its social heart and its voluntary ethos. Through the ups and the many downs, he remained hopeful, as this comment attests:

> I believe hope for the future lies in the melding of humor (including music and poetry) with the best of the left (politics) and the best of the new age (spirituality). . . . We won't move toward a modest, sustainable society until we somehow find a way of bringing together these three approaches. All three have positive—but only apparently opposed—views of these totem concepts: liberation, transformation, and consciousness. Of the three approaches, humor is the essential glue for the other two, partly because it releases the humble—but overemphasized value—of politics and spirituality [Ohliger, 1997, part 3, p. 6].

With these words, John left us with a basis for a pedagogy of hope and possibility. To be aware, to play with ideas, to enable citizens as learners and workers to be free to make choices, to transform against the odds—these intentions were part of John Ohliger's collective ambition. They provide a guide for radicalizing social educators to work for meaningful and lasting change so citizens can freely choose the life, learning, and work they want.

John, the radical liberal, understood the human needs for self-preservation, hope, justice, affirmation, and love. He was a fervent adult educator. In 1982 he ended his article "Is J. Edgar Hoover a Virgin?" with this excerpt from W. H. Auden's poem "September 1, 1939":

Defenseless under the night
Our world in stupor lies;
Yet, dotted everywhere,
Ironic points of light
Flash out wherever the Just
Exchange their messages:

May I, composed like them
Of Eros and of dust,
Beleaguered by the same
Negation and despair,
Show an affirming flame.

These verses capture the world in which John struggled to make positive change, the hope that inspired him to act, and the passionate desire that made him an extraordinary adult educator. John Ohliger was an ironic point of light. As Chris concluded in her chapter, John was a generous man and a mindful listener, with a calling and a passion for adult education as a voluntary social adventure. He remains an inspiration to those who want a field of study and practice and a world that are better.

The reference to Auden was typical of the arts-based pedagogy that John used to draw people in so he could engage with them. John employed poetry in his graduate education classes and in his writing—academic and everyday correspondence—as an andragogical tool. He often used it as a springboard to reflection and critique as he encouraged those in his circle and beyond to engage in processes of making meaning and sense of people, politics, and ideas in a puzzling and challenging world. In Chapter Thirteen in this book, Michael Collins reminds us that John used literary insights from poetry to help him sustain his commitment to radical education.

I wrote the following poem to remember this commitment as it found expression in the words and phrases of those who honored

John's passing. The poem sits John alongside other, often better-known, adult educators and cultural workers who shared his passion for ordinary people and their social education.

Educator Provocateur:
A Poem Found on Reflection in Community

John Ohliger
Educator provocateur
Latter-day scribe
Defender of the social
Consummate outsider
Who keenly eyed the Professional Pharisees
And offered mandatory continuing critique
John asked field colleagues to have second thoughts
He did not like his panoptic view of modern practice
Of adult education seemingly severing its social
    historical roots
John chose possibility as his response
And he energized it with anger and hope
His anger at too much complacency in the field that
    he loved
And his hope for a better world

Some colleagues shunned him
The academy can be a cold place
Others loved him
Because like Eduard Lindeman
He believed that true adult education is social
    education
Because like Septima Clark
He believed that communities can be empowered
Because like Myles Horton
He made his road by walking

Because like Rosa Parks
He sought justice for un-citizens
Because like Jimmy Tompkins
The community was his People's School
Where he rolled up his sleeves and farmed ideas
Knowing like Freire
That change is difficult, but possible
When our pedagogy is one of just ire or indignation

January 25, 2004
An unsung hero goes to glory
Kindred spirits remember
A social educator
A social activist
A cultural worker
A human being
Always becoming
But never quite belonging

(Bob Holderness-Roddam remembers)

John Ohliger
A man who was not afraid to stand up for his beliefs
A source of thought-provoking missives
I hope your spirit has joined those
Of other leaders in your profession—Cody,
    Lindeman, and Horton

(Budd Hall remembers)

John Ohliger
Independent scholar and public intellectual
The conscience of the US adult-education movement
The latter role he played for a lifetime
Campaigning against compulsory lifelong learning

Creating Basic Choices
John was a prodigious bibliographer
Bringing progressive ideas from all walks of life
Into the world of adult educators
This outsider was a constant voice for democratic and
 values-based learning

(David Williams remembers)

John Ohliger was a just man
A sobering voice
A wise counselor
An ethical radicalist
A comrade on the barricades
A voice in the wilderness
A pursuer of dreams
An exemplar of the kind and the caring
And of those who exude a social conscience
A truly great citizen of our Republic, or what's left of it
He was proud of his accomplishments
And driven to seek and want better
Not for himself, but for others
John wore his heart on his sleeve
He took on the burdens of the world
But never to the level of torpor or lethargy
His anguish was always a stir to renewed action and
 thought

(Chris Wagner, John's wife, remembers)

John believed that learning is too precious to be forced
Learning must be joyous, individual, and voluntary

Yes, learning must be joyous, individual, and
 voluntary

This was John's belief
The belief of a liberal humanist
Who spiced up adult education with radical ideas
Lao Tzu wrote
A leader is best when people barely know that he
    exists
John, you are one of adult education's true leaders
Live on in the actions your words inspire
In the name of social democracy
In the name of democratic education
That lifts up ordinary people and values the everyday
Undaunted by the parameters of the compulsory and
    the professional[1]

Note

1. To compare Ohliger's ideas on social education to those of Eduard
   C. Lindeman, read his classic *The Meaning of Adult Education*
   (1961). See Albin (1996) and Sears Botch (n.d.) for Web sites con-
   taining biographies on, respectively, Septima Clark and Rosa Parks.
   To learn more about Miles Horton and the Highlander Research
   and Education Center, read his poignant text with Paulo Freire, *We
   Make the Road by Walking* (1990). For insights on social educator
   Father Jimmy Tompkins, read my (1996) article, "The Gospel According to Father Jimmy: The Missions of J. J. Tompkins, Pioneer Adult
   Educator in the Antigonish Movement," published in *Convergence*.
   To compare the social philosophy of Ohliger to Paulo Freire, read
   his last book, *Pedagogy of Indignation* (2004). Chris Wagner's verse is
   based on her comments in the eulogy that A. Nathans wrote for the
   Madison newspaper *Capital Times* on January 30, 2004. The quote
   by Lao Tzu can be found at http://en.wikiquote.org/wiki/Laozi.

References

Albin, K. (1996). *Rosa Parks: The woman who changed a nation*. Retrieved Octo-
    ber 15, 2006, from http://www.grandtimes.com/rosa.html.

Cunningham, P., & Ohliger, J. (Eds.). (1989). *Radical thinking in adult education*. New York: Syracuse University Publications and the Kellogg Foundation. (ERIC Document Reproduction Service No. ED305462)

Freire, P. (2004). *Pedagogy of indignation*. Boulder, CO: Paradigm Publishers.

Grace, A. P. (1996). The gospel according to Father Jimmy: The missions of J. J. Tompkins, pioneer adult educator in the Antigonish Movement. *Convergence, 28*(2), 63–78.

Horton, M., & Freire, P. (1990). *We make the road by walking: Conversations on education and social change*. Philadelphia: Temple University.

Lindeman, E. C. (1961). *The meaning of adult education*. Montreal: Harvest House. (Originally published in 1926)

Nathans, A. (2004, January 30). Ohliger dies; guided WORT: educator co-founded station. (Madison, WI) *Capital Times*, p. 3B.

Ohliger, J. (1982). Is J. Edgar Hoover a virgin? *Media/Adult Learning, 4*(1), 46–52.

Ohliger, J. (1997). [My search for freedom's song: Some notes for a memoir]. Third draft. Unpublished raw data.

Sears Botch, C. (n.d.). *Septima Poinsette Clark*. Retrieved October 15, 2006, from http://www.usca.edu/casc/clark.htm.

Name Index

Subject Index

F

Faculty, as public intellectuals, 144–148

Feminism, Ohliger on, 273–274, 281–282

"Forum: You Shall Know the Truth and the Truth Shall Make You Laugh" (Ohliger), 79–96

Freedom to choose: importance of, to adult education, 122–123, 124, 130; Ohliger's championing of, 18–19, 30, 132

Freire, Paulo: bibliography about, 230; as influence on Ohliger, 216–217, 296, 310–311; legacy of, 60, 218; Ohliger's criticism of, 25; rational order championed by, 22, 216

Fund for Adult Education (FAE), 8, 60, 189, 201

Future: "learning society" in, 57–58; Lincoln's prediction about corporate power in, 105; as new "dark age," 161–162; Ohliger's essay on compulsory education in, 43–46, 129–130, 190; Ohliger's vision of, 149, 150

G

GI Bill, 116–117, 128, 188

Great Books Foundation, 3, 189, 227, 320

H

Health professions, mandatory continuing education in, 50, 172–173

Higher education: commodification of, 248, 316–317; "equal opportunity" in, 53–55; faculty of, as public intellectuals, 144–148; financial benefit of adult education to, 52–53; marginalization of adult education in, 128–129

Houle, Cyril O.: on *Learning to Be*, 55–56, 131; Ohliger as student of, 8, 165, 189; Ohliger's criticism of, 127, 131

Humor: importance of, 80, 88–92, 335; Ohliger's use of, 219–221, 262–263, 270

I

Illich, Ivan: on balance of learning, 58–59; biography of, 185–187; change of direction by, 196–198, 201; education as viewed by, 193–195; on Freire's work, 60; as influence on Ohliger, 30, 184, 202, 231, 310–311; multilogue on writings of, 331; Ohliger's agreement with ideas of, 215–216, 217, 218; Ohliger's criticism of, 25; Ohliger's relationship with, 34–35, 190, 196–200, 202–203, 321–322; and Reimer, 192, 197; spontaneous freedom championed by, 22, 216

Information overload, 209–210

Information revolution, 80, 83

International Adult and Continuing Education Hall of Fame, 26–27, 328

International Commission on the Development of Education, 55, 62

International Council for Adult Education, 50, 239

"Is Lifelong Adult Education a Guarantee of Permanent Inadequacy?" (Ohliger), 47–63, 213

Ivan D. Illich Dystopia Award, 9, 129, 190–191

Ivan Illich in Conversation (Cayley), 200

J

Journalists, adult education: Brightman as, 14; Ohliger as, 6–7

K

Knowledge: "banking" or "depositing" chauvinism theory of, 60; vs. being, 85–86; belief in facts as, 81, 82–83; Ohliger's "three little questions"

critique of, 313–315; Ohliger's ideas and, 247–251, 252

North American Alliance of Popular Adult Educators (NAAPAE), 239

O

Ohio State University: Ohliger at, 10–11, 165, 190–191, 326; Ohliger's resignation from, 9, 11–12, 198–199, 231, 313

Ohliger, John Funnell: as community educator, 227–231, 245–247; as critical educator, 25–27; as cultural worker, 176, 245, 246–247, 306–307, 309, 334, 337; differences between Robeson and, 289, 309–310; future envisioned by, 149, 150; humor used by, 219–221, 262–263, 270; Ivan Illich Dystopia Award given to, 9, 129, 190–191; as journalist, 6–7; parallels between Robeson and, 289–291, 298, 299, 306–307, 309; as public intellectual, 144; as radical liberal, 4, 21–23, 309, 312; as social democrat, 309–310, 311

—beliefs/ideas of: about adult education, 18; about education, 323–324; about feminism, 273–274, 281–282; about liberal education, 184–185, 312, 317; about participation, 30, 171, 228, 265–266; about politics, 188–189, 271–274, 333–334; about religion and spirituality, 274–275, 280–281, 330; in agreement with Illich, 215–216, 217, 218; on freedom to choose, 18–19, 30, 122–123, 124, 130, 132; and neoliberalism, 247–251, 252

—biography of: chronology of life of, 8–10, 187–191; education of, 116, 117, 178, 188, 189; last year of, 328–329, 334; left academia, 9, 11–12, 198–199, 231, 313; modest lifestyle of, 150, 160–161, 176, 289–290; at Ohio State University, 10–11, 165, 190–191, 326; post-

academic work of, 144, 148–149, 191, 199, 226, 233; at Selkirk College, 9, 189, 228; wife and marriage of, 154, 324–328; youth, 20–21, 187–188, 227, 311

—criticism by: of adult education, themes in, 28–29; of adult educators, 134–135; of commodification of adult education, 19, 30, 175–176; of compulsory adult education, 18–19, 43–46, 129–130; of critical adult education, 25–27; of critical theory and literature, 22, 35, 134–135, 210–213, 216, 217; of Freire, 25; of GI Bill, 117; of Houle, 127, 131; of Illich, 25; of Knowles, 4–5, 59, 127, 131; of *Learning to Be* (UNESCO), 55–58, 130–131; of lifelong learning, 19, 24–25, 29, 130–133, 251; of mandatory continuing education (MCE), 169, 170, 171, 172, 174, 175, 195, 213–214, 219–221, 323; of neoliberalism, 313–315; professional exclusion as result of, 231–233; of professionalization of adult education, 4–5, 117–118, 122–123, 127–128, 209–210, 313; of Reimer, 25; relevance of, 23–25, 248–250; of sexist language, 268–271

—influences on: books and reading as, 20, 159, 227, 259, 265–266, 274–275; Freire as, 216–217, 296, 310–311; Illich as, 30, 184, 190, 202, 231, 310–311; Ohliger's father as, 20, 187–188, 311; Reimer as, 190, 192, 195–196, 310–311

—legacy of: bibliographies as, 97, 330; inducted into International Adult and Continuing Education Hall of Fame, 26–27, 328; to practice of adult education, 38–39, 201–202, 252–254; Web site on, 331; writings as, 24–25, 31, 161, 276, 331

—recollections about: by Cunningham, 225–226, 245–247; by Collins, 211; by Grace, 12–14; by his wife,